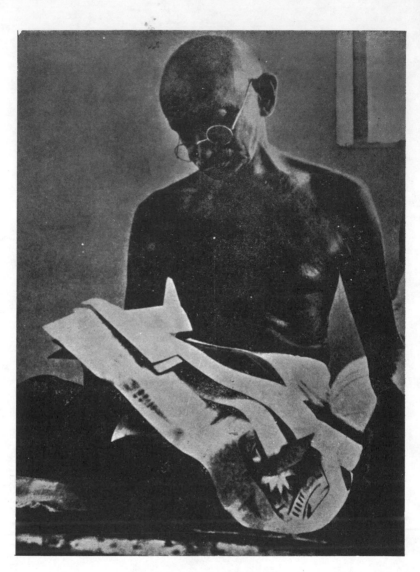

Going Through the Proofs

[*Courtesy:* KANU GANDHI]

Mahatma Gandhi
The Journalist

S. N. BHATTACHARYYA

GREENWOOD PRESS, PUBLISHERS
WESTPORT, CONNECTICUT

Library of Congress Cataloging in Publication Data

Bhattacharyya, S. N. (Sailendra Nath), 1921-
  Mahatma Gandhi, the journalist.

  Reprint. Originally published: Bombay ; New York :
Asia Pub. House, c1965.
  Bibliography: p.
  Includes index.
  1. Gandhi, Mahatma, 1869-1948. 2. Journalists--India--
Biography. 3. Statesmen--India--Biography. I. Title.
DS481.G3B45 1984   070'.92'4 [B]   84-595
ISBN 0-313-24461-8 (lib. bdg.)

Reprinted with the permission of Apt Books, Inc.

Reprinted in 1984 by Greenwood Press
A division of Congressional Information Service, Inc.
88 Post Road West, Westport, Connecticut 06881

Printed in the United States of America

10 9 8 7 6 5 4 3 2 1

To
STHITI
who relieved me of many
onerous tasks so that I could
devote time to this book

The objective of journalism is service.

Mahatma Gandhi

Speak of me as I am ; nothing extenuate
Nor set down aught in malice

Othello, V, **2.**

Introduction

" LORD LINLITHGOW, the Viceroy at New Delhi, said to me, 'Gandhi is the biggest thing in India.' That is correct. Gandhi is a unique phenomenon." Thus wrote Louis Fischer in his book *A Week with Gandhi*.

That he was unique among men, need not be reiterated. He was original in whatever he did. He said something new whenever he spoke. " He thinks aloud and the entire process is for the record." A discussion with him on any subject was a " voyage of discovery ".

His life, whatever activity he was involved in, was an experiment with truth. He could and did take a detached view of everything and so was able to bring out the best.

Whatever work he laid his gentle hands on, he did it with a sincerity of purpose. That always lent strength to the cause. His minute care for details and clear thinking regarding the ultimate objective — good of the people — made all his projects successful. And, his role as a journalist was no exception.

The purpose of this book is to bring his contributions in this sphere to the limelight so that those working in the line could be benefited. To quote Shri Jawaharlal Nehru: " To him life was an integrated whole, a closely woven garment of many colours. A word to a child, a touch of healing to a sufferer, was as important as a resolution of challenge to the British Empire."

Gandhiji once said : " My life is my message." So a journalist ought to be interested in finding out the particular message he preached and practised in the field of journalism. It will be found that his preachings and practices were nothing but selfless service. Like Wickham Steed, he believed that the printing and setting of news or views, were social services.

There are many books on Gandhiji dealing with different aspects of his eventful life. This is an addition to that varied list. In the course of this work, the more the author plunged into the background materials, the more conscious he became of the vastness of the subject and his obvious limitations. During the last seven years that the author was collecting materials on the subject, he met or corresponded with many valued associates of Gandhiji, most of whom gladly helped him. He is grateful to them all and does not want to mention individual names, lest they feel embarrassed.

S. N. BHATTACHARYYA

Acknowledgments

THE author gratefully acknowledges the permission accorded so generously by the Navajivan Trust, Ahmedabad, for using quotations from Mahatma Gandhi's writings, speeches, etc., and also to authors and publishers, for extracts from the following :

My Childhood with Gandhiji by Prabhudas Gandhi ; *Mahatma Gandhi: The Last Phase* by Pyarelal ; *The Nation's Voice* edited by C. Rajagopalachari and J. C. Kumarappa ; *Stray Glimpses of Bapu* by Kaka Kalelkar (all published by Navajivan Publishing House, Ahmedabad) ; *Gujarat and its Literature* by K. M. Munshi, published by Bharatiya Vidya Bhavan, Bombay; *Gandhi : The Master* by K. M. Munshi, published by M/s. Rajkamal Publications, Delhi ; *Mr. Gandhi : The Man* by Millie Graham Polak ; *Incidents of Gandhiji's Life* and *Reminiscences of Gandhiji* edited by Chandrashanker Shukla, published by Vora & Co., Publishers, Bombay ; *A Bunch of Old Letters* by Jawaharlal Nehru ; *A History of the Press in India* by S. Natarajan and *Indian Writing in English* by K. R. Srinivasa Iyengar (all published by Asia Publishing House, Bombay); *All Through the Gandhian Era* by A. S. Iyengar and *At the Feet of Mahatma Gandhi* by Rajendra Prasad, published by Hind Kitabs Ltd., Bombay ; *Gandhi : A Study* by Hiren Mukherjee, published by National Book Agency (Private) Ltd., Calcutta ; *The History of the Indian National Congress*, Vols. I and II by Dr. Pattabhi Sitaramayya, published by Padma Publications Ltd., Bombay; *In the Shadow of the Mahatma* by G. D. Birla, published by Orient Longmans Ltd., Bombay ; *Mahatma — Life of Mohandas Karamchand Gandhi* by D. G. Tendulkar, published by V. K. Jhaveri and D. G. Tendulkar, Bombay ; *Seven Months with Mahatma Gandhi* by Krishnadas, published by S. Ganesan &

ix

Acknowledgments

Co., Madras ; *Mahatma Gandhi* by H. S. L. Polak, H. N. Brails-
ford and Lord Pethick-Lawrence, published by Odhams Press Ltd.,
London ; *The Indian Press* by Margarita Barns and *My Gandhi* by
J. H. Holmes, published by George Allen & Unwin Ltd., London ;
My Early Life by Sir Winston Churchill, published by M/s.
Thornton Butterworth Ltd., London ; *Essays on Education* by
Whitney Griswold, published by the Yale University Press, New
Haven, Conn. (U.S.A.) ; *The Press the Public Wants* by Kingsley
Martin, published by The Hogarth Press, London ; *The Wit and
Wisdom of Gandhi*, edited by Homer A. Jack, published by
M/s. Allyn & Beacon, Boston ; *Principles of Newspaper Manage-
ment* by J. E. Pollard, published by McGraw-Hill Book Co., New
York ; *A Week with Gandhi* by Louis Fischer, published by Inter-
national Book House, Bombay.

Excerpts from *A Free and Responsible Press*, a report of the
Commission on Freedom of the Press, U.S.A., published by the
University of Chicago Press, Chicago, Illinois ; *The Educational
Role of the Press* by Henry De Jourenel & others, published by
the League of Nations, Paris ; *Impressions of Mahatma Gandhi* :
A Portrait by the British Broadcasting Corporation, London, have
also been used.

The author is grateful to the Commonwealth Press Union for
making use of Lord Shawcross' Address ; to the United Nations,
for Mon. S. Lopez, Report on the Freedom of the Press and to
Associated Press of America for quotations from an interview
with Gandhiji conducted by Preston Gover.

Contents

List of Illustrations

1 / *A Free-Lance Journalist*

WHEN on arrival in London in September 1888, to study law, Gandhiji, at the age of nineteen, for the first time read a newspaper, he could scarcely imagine at that time, how actively he would be associated with the newspaper world for the rest of his life.

Gandhiji would spend hours devouring the columns of the *Daily Telegraph*, the *Daily News* and the *Pall Mall Gazette*. Travel stories, with plenty of illustrations, fascinated him particularly. Newspaper reading was a novel experience for him as to quote him " In India I had never had read a newspaper ".[1]

Incidentally, we may mention here that Gandhiji was born in 1869, the same year when the Suez Canal was opened, linking the East with the West. A few years earlier, both the submarine and land telegraph lines were laid between England and India. Reuter's news services were also extended to India. A year before Gandhiji's birth, i.e. 1868, the *Amrita Bazar Patrika* of Calcutta was started. Six years later, *The Statesman* also started its publication.

Newspapers were not only informative and entertaining to him, they made him ambitious as well. Why not write articles for them ? The desire latent in a human being — and he was quite young then — to see his name and article in print was too great a temptation to resist. His friendship with the members of the London Vegetarian Society afforded him an opportunity to write for its organ the *Vegetarian*. He contributed, during his stay of about three years in England, nine articles on diet, customs, festivals, etc., of the Indians. These are his earliest writings on record.

[1] M. K. Gandhi: *An Autobiography or The Story of My Experiments with Truth* (Navajivan Publishing House, Ahmedabad, 1956), p. 47.

The first one was published in the issue of February 7, 1891, under the caption : 'Indian Vegetarian'. Here he dispels the common belief that all Indians are vegetarians and lists the food habits of vegetarians in different parts of his country. In conclusion, he mentions, " *en passant* that the cow is an object of worship among the Hindus, and a movement set on foot — to prevent the cows from being shipped off for the purpose of slaughter, is progressing rapidly ".

In another article in the journal dated March 28, 1891, he describes important Indian religious ceremonies under the caption: 'Some Indian Festivals'. Travel stories which stirred his imagination earlier now enthused him to write these. On reaching India, he sent to the *Vegetarian* the travelogue: ' On my way home again to India '. It was published in two parts — in the issues dated April 9, and April 16, 1892. Three years of writing and staying abroad enlarged not only his scope of writing but made him a better and more accomplished free-lance journalist. Here is a sample. On the return journey, the ship was caught in a storm and in that background he wrote : " If I ventured out on the dock I was splashed with water. There goes a crash ; something broken. In the cabin you cannot sleep quietly. The door is hanging. Your bags begin to dance. You roll in your bed. You sometimes feel as if the ship is sinking. At the dinner table you are no more comfortable. The steamer rolls on your sides. Your forks and spoons are in your lap, even the cruet stand and the soup plate ; your napkin is dyed yellow and so on."[2]

A struggling barrister of Bombay that he was at the time, he had to do something more tangible than indulging in non-remunerative journalism. In April, 1893, he sailed for South Africa, after getting an offer from Dada Abdullah and Co., to defend one of their cases.

South Africa not only shaped many of the ideas and traits of Gandhiji, but made an out-and-out journalist of him as well. If the London Vegetarian Society afforded him a forum to write and speak, the political situation in South Africa chiselled him into a conscientious journalist. He was thrown into the whirlpool of politics. While fighting incessantly against all disabilities imposed on Indians, through representation, petition, memo-

---

[2] *Vegetarian* (London, April 16, 1892).

randum, etc., he did not, for a moment, minimize the important role of newspapers. He would scan through all local papers and reply suitably to any misrepresentation or distortion of facts. Soon he became well known to the newspaper men in South Africa for his zeal in expounding the causes of the Indians.

During the brief spell in India, from the middle of 1896 to November 1896, the year when Marconi invented wireless telegraphy, he was touring the country to enlist the support, among others, of editors for the South African Indian cause. In a letter to the editor of *The Times of India* he wrote : " Publicity is our best and perhaps the only weapon of defence ".[3]

He met Mr. Chesney, editor of *The Pioneer*, Allahabad, who editorially commented on the *Green Pamphlet* — his book describing the condition of Indians in South Africa. Shri G. P. Pillay, editor of *The Madras Standard*, literally placed the paper at Gandhiji's disposal. Gandhiji was not only supplying background material for editorials, but was also improving on those written by others. His mastery of facts and details was instantly recognized and appreciated. The editor of *The Hindu* was equally helpful. Soon he came in touch with editors of *The Amrita Bazar Patrika* and *Bangabasi* of Calcutta. He established good contact with *The Statesman* as well. The following extracts of the interview with *The Statesman* representative will be of interest as it focuses in a nutshell, the main Indian problem in South Africa. Incidentally, Gandhiji was now known in India through his famous *Green Pamphlet* wherein he highlighted the grievances of his countrymen in Africa.

" Will you please tell me, Mr. Gandhi, in a few words," *The Statesman* interviewer asked, " something of the grievances of the Indians in South Africa ? "

" There are Indians," Mr. Gandhi replied, " in many parts of South Africa — in the Colonies of Natal, the Cape of Good Hope, and elsewhere — in all of which, more or less, they are denied the ordinary rights of citizenship. But I more particularly represent the Indians in Natal, who number about fifty thousand in a total population of some five hundred thousand. The first Indians were, of course, the coolies who were taken over under indentures from Madras and Bengal for the purpose of labouring

[3] *The Times of India* (Bombay, October 20, 1896).

in the various plantations. They were mostly Hindus, but a few of them were Mohamedans. They served their contract time, and on obtaining their freedom they elected to stay in the country, because they found that, as market gardeners or hawkers of vegetables, they could earn from three to four pounds sterling per month. In this way, there are, at present, about thirty thousand free Indians settled in the Colony, while some sixteen thousand others are serving their indentures. There is, however, another class of Indians, numbering about 5,000 Mohamedans from the Bombay side who have been attracted to the country by the prospects of trade. Some of the latter are doing well. Many are landowners in a large way, while two own ships. The Indians have been settled in the country for 20 years or more, and being prosperous were contented and happy."

" What then, was the cause of all the present trouble, Mr. Gandhi ? "

" Simply trade jealousy. The Colony was desirous of securing all possible benefit from the Indians as labourers, because the natives of the country will not work in the fields, and the Europeans cannot. But the moment the Indian entered into competition with the European as a trader, he found himself thwarted, obstructed and insulted by a system of organized persecution. And gradually, this feeling of hatred and oppression has been imported into the laws of the Colony. The Indians had been quietly enjoying the franchise for years, subject to certain property qualifications, and in 1894, there were 251 Indian voters on the register against 9,309 European voters. But the Government suddenly thought, or pretended to think, that there was danger of the Asiatic vote swamping the European, and they introduced into the Legislative Assembly a Bill disfranchising all Asiatics, ..."[4]

Gandhiji writes in his autobiography : " Mr. Saunders, editor of the *Englishman*, claimed me as his own. He placed his office and paper at my disposal. He even allowed me the liberty of making whatever changes I liked in the leading article he had written on the situation, the proof of which he sent me in advance."[5]

Gandhiji kept a full account of the expenditure for promoting

[4] *The Statesman* (New Delhi, November 12, 1896).

[5] M. K. Gandhi : *An Autobiography or The Story of My Experiments with Truth* (Navajivan Publishing House, Ahmedabad, 1956), pp. 181–182.

the cause of Indians in South Africa. In the detailed note submitted to the Natal Indian Congress, there is the following entry.[6]

5th July (1896)

Rs. As. P.

Carriage from morning to afternoon and previous evening at Allahabad — visiting editors, etc.　　　　　　　　　　　　　　6　0　0

Acquaintance with editors and working closely with the editorial staff of the newspapers helped Gandhiji in acquiring some inside knowledge of the working of these papers. This emboldened him to start one journal in South Africa. The following interview on board the 'Courland' off Durban, with the representative of the *Natal Advertiser* on January 13, 1897, i.e. immediately on return from India, will throw more light on the subject.

Q. "Have the Indian Congress no intention of starting a newspaper in Natal ?"

A. "There was an intention, not by the Indian Congress, but by a body of workers who sympathize with the Congress, of starting a paper, but that idea had to be given up, simply because I could not see my way to devote my time to that and other work. I had instructions to bring material and Indian type, but as I found it would be impossible for me to work it, I did not bring anything. Had I been able to persuade the gentlemen with whom I was negotiating to come over here, I might have brought the material, but as that fell through, I did not do so."

While a student in London, Gandhiji got acquainted with Mr. Dadabhai Naoroji, leader of the Indian community in England, who in 1890 started the journal *India*, dealing mainly with topics of Indian interest. Gandhiji became the journal's 'Durban, Johannesburg and South African correspondent'. It is not certain whether he was a self-appointed correspondent or one maintained by *India* on an honorarium basis. In any case, Gandhiji's purpose was served. He was ventilating the grievances of Indians in South Africa. Here is a telegram sent by him, and which was published in *India* on 9 September, 1896.

" The court has decided that the Government has power to remove Indians in the Transvaal to locations for both trade and residence. Judge Jorrisen dissented from the decision. Great consternation prevails. It is feared that the removal to locations may paralyse trade. Large interests are at stake. We are

[6] *The Collected Works of Mahatma Gandhi* (The Publications Division, Delhi, 1959), Vol. II, p. 139.

relying upon Mr. Chamberlain's promise to make representations to the Transvaal Government after the trial of a test case, which, he said, was necessary to secure a definite issue."[7]

The famine that broke out in India in 1897, worried Gandhiji very much. The Central Famine Committee, Calcutta, appealed to the British Colonies for contributions. Gandhiji took up the cause for the service of humanity and wrote among others the following letter, dated February 2, 1897, to the editor, *The Natal Mercury.*

SIR,

I venture to offer a few remarks on the Indian famine, regarding which appeal for funds has been made to the British Colonies. It is not perhaps generally known that India is the poorest country in the world, in spite of the fabulous accounts of the riches of her Rajahas and Maharajahas. The highest Indian authorities state that " the remaining fifth (i.e., of the population of British India), or 40,000,000, go through life on insufficient food." This is the normal condition of British India. Famines, as a rule, recur in India every four years. It must not be difficult to imagine what the condition of the people would be at such a time in that poverty stricken country. Children are snatched from their mothers, wives from their husbands. Whole tracts are devastated, and this in spite of the precautions taken by a most benevolent Government....

The present famine bids fair to beat the record in point of severity. The distress has already become acute. The worst time has yet to come, when summer sets in. This is the first time, I believe, that the British Colonies have been appealed to from India, and it is to be hoped the response will be generous....

October 1899 was a landmark in the free-lance.journalism of Gandhiji. The Boer War broke out and Gandhiji, with Indian volunteers, offered his services for tending the sick and the wounded in the battle-field. Once in the job, he gained first hand experience of the battle-field. He recorded these experiences for publication in the *Times of India* of Bombay. Gandhiji thus joined the band of early war correspondents. Incidentally, the Boer War also saw another famous man as a war correspondent. This was Mr. Winston Churchill. While Mr. Churchill, five years younger and a soldier, startled the reading public of England by his interpretative war despatches and military exposures, Gandhiji was, by contrast, a detailed chronicler, mostly confined to the activities of the Indian Ambulance Corps. It helped him in discovering in himself a journalist of no mean talent. At times he was poetic, even in the grim surrounding. Speaking later in Calcutta, he

[7] Ibid. (1960), Vol. III, p. 17.

compared the perfect order at the front and holy stillness to those of a Trappist monastery. He said :

" Tommy was then altogether lovable. Like Arjun, they went to the battle-field because it was their duty. And how many proud, rude, savage spirits has it not broken into gentle creatures of God ? "

In his despatch to the *Times of India* Weekly, published on June 16, 1900, Gandhiji gives a detailed account of the Ambulance Corps, quoting copiously eulogies from local papers. In these despatches he introduced what we now call the human interest story in order to break the monotony of the narrative. He tells how " An Indian woman who lives on the daily sale of her fruits is reported, on the soldiers landing at the Durban Wharf, to have emptied the whole contents of her basket into Tommy's huck saying that was all she could give that day."[8]

A student of journalism would like to compare such material with the vigour of language, knowledge of military science and purposiveness of Mr. Churchill, when he was sending despatches to his paper, the *Morning Post.*

" We must face facts. The individual Boer, mounted in a suitable country, is worth from three to five regular soldiers. The power of modern rifles is so tremendous that frontal attacks must often be repulsed. The extraordinary mobility of the enemy protects his flanks. The only way of treating the problem is either to get men equal in character and intelligence as riflemen, or, failing the individual, huge masses of troops."

Then, in the same despatch, a passionate appeal :

" Are the gentlemen of England all fox-hunting ? Why not an English Light Horse ? For the sake of our manhood, our devoted colonists and our soldiers, we must persevere with the war."[9]

---

[8] Ibid. (1960), Vol. III, p. 141.

[9] Winston Churchill : *My Early Life* (Thornton Butterworth Ltd., London, 1930), pp. 316–317.

2 / *Sponsor Or Editor*

A. INDIAN OPINION

LAUNCHING of the weekly the *Indian Opinion* was no accident. Circumstances were leading to the establishment of a journal in South Africa which could voice effectively the feelings of Indians living under the worst form of apartheid.

The primary activities of the Natal Indian Congress, founded in 1893 by Gandhiji's initiative, were to safeguard Indian interests and acquaint the Englishmen in S. Africa and England and the people of India with the conditions in Natal.

Publicity, as will be seen, was in Gandhiji's blood and he had a knack for it. Even before this direct plunge into the field of journalism, he cultivated, as we have seen earlier, friendship with the editors of influential journals. That was not the age of microphone or radio. His feeble voice could not reach thousands of Indians scattered all over South Africa. Nor could he inform the world outside about the state of affairs in Africa. The Congress had no newspaper of its own. Exposition of the Indian cause could not be expected from the existing ones, mostly in the hands of vested interests. Those who controlled the press, he realised soon, could create a public opinion. He recorded later :

"I believe that a struggle which chiefly relies upon internal strength cannot be wholly carried on without a newspaper — it is also my experience that we could not perhaps have educated the local Indian community, nor kept Indians all over the world in touch with the course of events in South Africa in any other way, with the same ease and success as through the *Indian Opinion*, which therefore was certainly a most useful and potent weapon in our struggle."[1]

[1] M. K. Gandhi : *Satyagraha in South Africa* (Navajivan Publishing House, Ahmedabad, 1950), p. 142.

Shri Madanjit Vyavaharik was an ex-schoolmaster of Bombay and a political co-worker of Gandhiji in South Africa. He established a press — The International Printing Press — at 113 Grey Street, Durban, in 1898. Many of the pamphlets and brochures of the Natal Congress inspired, if not actually written, by Gandhiji, were printed in that press. Gandhiji was also able to inspire Madanjit with the idea to start a weekly. Thus the *Indian Opinion* started its publication and the first issue was out on June 4, 1903, though Gandhiji, in his autobiography, gives the date as 1904.

Mr. George Hendrick, in the article ' Gandhi, Indian Opinion and Freedom ' wrote :

"Even the date *Indian Opinion* began publication is almost always given incorrectly (Gandhi remembered it 1904) and biographers and bibliographers have continued to give 1904 date instead of 4th June 1903."[2]

The first editorial — ' Ourselves ' — an unsigned one, was written by Gandhiji. This is quoted below for the simplicity of language and direct appeal of the content :

We need offer no apology for making an appearance. The Indian community in South Africa is a recognised factor in the body politic, and a newspaper, voicing its feelings, and specially devoted to its cause, would hardly be considered out of place : indeed, we think, it would supply a longfelt want.

The Indians, resident in British South Africa, loyal subjects though they are of the King-Emperor, labour under a number of legal disabilities which, it is contended on their behalf, are undeserved and unjust. The reason of this state of affairs is to be found in the prejudice in the minds of the Colonists, arising out of misunderstanding the actual status of the Indian as a British subject, the close relations that render him kin to Colonists, as the dual title of the Crowned Head so significantly pronounces, and the unhappy forgetfulness of the great services India has always rendered to the Mother Country ever since Providence brought loyal Hind under the flag of Britannia. It will be our endeavour, therefore, to remove the misunderstanding by placing facts in their true light before the public.

We are far from assuming that the Indians here are free from all the faults that are ascribed to them. Wherever we find them to be at fault, we will unhesitatingly point it out and suggest means for its removal. Our country-men in South Africa are without the guiding influence of the institutions that exist in India and that impart the necessary moral tone when it is wanting. Those that have immigrated as children, or are born in the Colony, have no opportunity of studying the past history of the nation to which they belong, or of knowing its greatness. It will be our duty, so far as it may be in our

[2] *Gandhi Marg* (Gandhi Smarak Nidhi, Rajghat, New Delhi, 1958), Vol. II, No. 2, p. 155.

power, to supply these wants by inviting contributions from competent writers in England, in India, and in this sub-continent.

Time alone will prove our desire to do what is right. But we can do very little unaided. We rely on generous support from our countrymen, may we hope for it from the great Anglo-Saxon race that hails His Majesty Edward VII as King-Emperor ? For, there is nothing in our programme but a desire to promote harmony and good-will between the different sections of the one mighty Empire."

In the same issue, the second leading article ' The British Indians in South Africa', as also short notes like ' Is it fair ', ' Virtuous Inconsistency ', ' Better late than never ', ' Words and deeds ', ' Minute by the Mayor ', were written by Gandhiji. Most of the articles by him, unlike those of *Young India* or *Harijan*, were unsigned.

Shri Madanjit, as proprietor of the *Indian Opinion*, gave the following information, as printed on the first page of the first issue, for the consumption of all readers. The underlying spirit is in tune with the main editorial quoted earlier and Gandhiji's influence is unmistakably manifest.

" This weekly newspaper is published in four languages namely English, Gujarati, Tamil and Hindi in the interests of the British Indians residing in South Africa.

The policy of the paper would be to advocate the cause of the British Indians in the sub-continent. But while it would insist upon the rights of the community, it would not be slow to point out to it its responsibilities also as members of a mighty Empire. It would persistently endeavour to bring about a proper understanding between the two communities which Providence has brought together under one flag.

The advantages to the *Indian community* in subscribing to and supporting this paper would be —

(i) It would have a newspaper that would advocate its cause as well as give to all sections its news in their own languages.

(ii) It would contain news specially affecting Indians of all parts of South Africa, besides local and general information.

(iii) It would contain an epitome of events happening in India.

(iv) It would give commercial intelligence.

(v) It would contain contributions from competent writers, Indians as well as Europeans, on all subjects — Social, Moral, and Intellectual.

The advantages to the *European community* would be —

(i) The paper would give it an idea of Indian thought and aspirations.

(ii) It would acquaint it with such Indian matters as are not commonly known to it, and yet which should not be ignored by the true Imperialists.

To *Europeans* and *Indians* alike, it would serve as the best advertising medium in those branches of the trade in which Indians are especially concerned.

The rate of annual subscription is 12s. 6d. in the Colony, and outside the Colony 17s. payable in advance.

Single copies are sold at 3d. each.

Advertising charges can be had on application to the undersigned.

V. MADANJIT
Proprietor, *Indian Opinion*
113, Grey Street, Durban.

As indicated, the foolscap sized, three-column journal started publishing South African Indian news and views. It was filled with discriminatory law cases involving Indians, and which Gandhiji used to plead, or letters to the editors of local newspapers correcting false and mistaken reports concerning Indians. Important happenings in India were also displayed. Besides, there were contributions from ' competent writers ' on subjects ' social, moral and intellectual '. Gandhiji tried his hand on intellectual and aesthetic subjects as well. Here is an example, being the extract of an article on ' Indian Art ' — published in the issue of the journal of September 17, 1903.

" ... The Hindu palace-architecture of Gwalior, the Indian-Muhammadan mosques and mausoleums of Agra and Delhi, with several of the older Hindu temples of Southern India, stand unrivalled for grace of outline and elaborate wealth of ornament. The Taj Mahal at Agra justifies Heber's exclamation, that its builders had designed like Titans, and finished like jewellers. The open-carved marble windows and screens at Ahmedabad furnish examples of the skilful ornamentation which beautifies every Indian building, from the cave monasteries of the Buddhist period downward. They also show with what plasticity the Hindu architects adapted their Indian ornamentation to the structural requirements of the Muhammadan mosque. English decorative art in our day has borrowed largely from Indian forms and patterns. The exquisite scrolls on the rock-temples at Karla and Ajanta, the delicate marble tracery and flat wood-carving of Western India, the harmonious blending of forms and colours in the fabrics of Kashmir, have contributed to the restoration of taste in England. Indian art-work, when faithful to native designs, still obtains the highest honours at the international exhibition of Europe."

Gandhiji was not only contributing articles for the journal but money as well. Journalistic adventure became increasingly expensive for him. During the first year he had to spend £ 2,000 from his own pocket. This state of things could not be allowed to continue. The venture had either to be stopped or he had to assume the full responsibility for it. Shri Madanjit also entreated him to take over the journal as well as the press in lieu of the money he had invested. He agreed. It was rather a formal hand over — the ' de jure ' recognition of the ' de facto '. Both Europeans and Indians in South Africa knew very well that he was the man responsible for the journal's management and policy, though not the editor in name. As he, in his autobiography, re-called in a reminiscent mood : " I had to bear the brunt of the work, having for most of the time to be practically in charge of the journal."[3]

But financial burden was too much for a young barrister yet to set up lucrative practice. Nor did he realize how costly the journal, at the initial stage, could be. As he confesses, after getting wiser, " I had no notion that I should have to invest any money in the journal."[4]

But he was not sorry for all this. In his letter of January 13, 1905, to his political guide and philosopher, Shri Gopal Krishna Gokhale, Poona, he wrote : " When I saw that Mr. Madanjit could not carry on the paper without pecuniary assistance and as I know that he was guided by thoroughly patriotic motives, I placed at his service the bulk of my savings . . . . I have already become responsible to the extent of nearly £ 3,500."[5]

In the same letter he indicated that he assumed the responsibility for the journal round about October, 1904. " Three months ago, I took over the whole responsibility and management. Mr. Madanjit still remains nominally the proprietor and publisher, because I believe that he has done much for the community. My own office is at present being worked in the interests of the *Indian Opinion....*"

Shri Mansukhlal Hiralal Nazar, a journalist from Bombay was appointed the editor in which post he continued till his death in January, 1906. In a signed obituary note in the *Indian Opinion*, Gandhiji, among other things wrote : " Without him this journal would never have come into being. In the initial stages of its

---

[3] M. K. Gandhi : *An Autobiography or The Story of My Experiments with Truth* (Navajivan Publishing House, Ahmedabad, 1956), p. 285.

[4] Ibid., p. 285.

[5] *Gandhi Marg* (Gandhi Smarak Nidhi, Rajghat, New Delhi, 1960), Vol. IV, p. 234.

struggle, Mr. Nazar took up almost the whole of the editorial burden, and if it is known for its moderate policy and sound news, the fact is due, to a very large extent, to the part that Mr. Nazar played in connection with it."

But that was much later. In December, 1904 the *Indian Opinion* entered into a new phase. Under the caption ' Ourselves ' reminding the readers of the first editorial under the same caption of June 4, 1903, the *Indian Opinion* of December 24, 1904, informed the public that the paper " enters upon the third stage of its career in the short space of the 18 months of its existence ". It also gave an account of how the paper, during the period, was run. The proprietor " had to depend for the editing of the paper purely on voluntary and unpaid assistance ". More urgent was the task of enlisting paid subscribers. The Natal Indian Congress and the British Indian Association came to the rescue, but " the paper continued, octopus-like, to devour all it received and wanted more ".

Only " a novel and revolutionary project ", said the editorial, could save the situation. The workers " were to look not to the present but to the future ; not to their pockets but to the paper first ". Gandhiji rather demanded this from the workers when the declared policy of the journal was service. " It was to educate public opinion, to remove causes for misunderstanding, to put before the Indians their own blemishes ; and to show them the path of duty while they insisted on securing their rights."

The future plan was also unfolded in the same article. " If a piece of ground sufficiently large and far away from the hustle of the town could be secured, for housing the plant and machinery, each one of the workers could have his plot of land on which he could live."

Thus the Phoenix settlement — 14 miles away from Durban town and 2½ miles from the Phoenix Railway Station — came into being. The *Indian Opinion* was transferred there from Durban and the first issue, in one sheet, was printed on a treadle machine on the due date, i.e. December 24, 1904. In the farm everyone had to work, drawing the same living wage — £ 3 per head — and attending to the press job work in spare time.

In the issue of December 31, 1904, the Gujarati edition of the *Indian Opinion* published brief notes on the three Englishmen who were assisting in the printing and publication of the paper.

Mr. West owned a printing press in Johannesburg. But he joined the struggling group with 24 hours' notice. " Now he takes from us just enough for his bare needs, but stays on with us in the faith that there will be profits eventually. He toils in from morning to evening looking upon the work as his own."

Mr. Kitchin was an electrical contractor. He joined the *Indian Opinion* as " he felt that the objectives of *Indian Opinion* were worthy ". Then there was Mr. Polak. " Since he is a man of much simplicity and believes that he can freely express his feeling against oppression through *Indian Opinion* he has informed his chief of his intention to resign, and he will arrive here towards the beginning of next year. Meanwhile he has started writing for the journal ".

In 1905 there was the outbreak of plague in Johannesburg. Gandhiji with a band of volunteers was fighting against this deadly disease. Throughout this period he was writing editorials, publishing news items and letters, drawing the attention of the Town Council as also the Indian community to the seriousness of the plague. He stated that he was serving a trinity of interests, viz. " truth, public weal and my own countrymen ".

Gandhiji was also continuously fighting against the disabilities suffered by the Indians in South Africa. These disabilities were many and varied. There were restrictions on immigration and trading ; on travelling in trains and cabs ; on walking on footpaths and what not. These were the result of racial arrogance and trade policy. The columns of the *Indian Opinion* were full of cases dealing with these disabilities and pleadings for sanity from the ruling power.

"... In protesting against the importation of indentured Asiatic labour and against the attempt to reduce ' free ' Asiatics to sub-human serfdom, Gandhiji was moved, not by abstract theory, but by instinctive sympathy and profound concern for the welfare of future generations. It was this love of humanity (European as well as Chinese) — and not political or economic theory — which inspired his criticism of Mr. Skinner's report on Chinese labour for the mines, and which also evoked his appreciation of Mr. Creswell's action in resigning his post as manager of a gold mining company because he could and would employ well-paid white labour, while the owners, caring only for profits, insisted on his employing cheap imported labour."[6]

[6] *The Collected Works of Mahatma Gandhi* (The Publications Division, Delhi, 1960), Vol. IV, preface, p. vii.

Narrating his experiences of those struggling days, Mr. Henry Polak, who left his cosy job in the *Critic* and joined the group, wrote :

" The printing press, where the typesetting was done by hand, was run by a decrepit oil engine which frequently broke down. When this occurred, the settlers had to resort to hand-power to turn out the paper in time for the usual despatch of mails, often until the middle of the night. More than once, when this happened during one of his occasional visits — he could not permanently reside there, as his public and professional work in the Transvaal then occupied almost all his energies — I can recall Gandhiji literally putting his shoulder to the wheel as energetically as any of us."[7]

His wife, Mrs. Millie Polak, had also recorded interesting facts about the printing arrangement.

" The printing press, at this time, had no mechanical means at its disposal, for the oil-engine had broken down, and at first animal power was utilised, two donkeys being used to turn the handle of the machine. But Mr. Gandhi, ever a believer in man doing his own work, soon altered this, and four hefty Zulu girls were procured for a few hours on printing day. These took the work in turns, two at a time, while the other two rested ; but every male able-bodied settler, Mr. Gandhi included, took his turn at the handle, and thus the copies of the paper were 'ground out '."[8]

" I remained a dunce to the last ", merrily recalled Gandhiji after many years.

Like so many experiments which shaped Gandhiji's thought and belief, the experiment in running the paper revealed many a novelty to him so much so that he devoted one full chapter, in his autobiography, on his experience on the first night. It not only shows his intimate knowledge of the working of the printing press at that time, but also speaks of his masterly grip on every detail.

Shri Prabhudas Gandhi adds further details of the working in the press-room of the *Indian Opinion.*

" Friday nights were of importance for the weekly *Indian Opinion* was despatched by Saturday. The material for the paper was composed by mid-day on Friday. It was evening by the time the paper went to the press. There were no servants, peons or other labour. The press workers themselves had to print the paper, fold it, paste the addresses, make bundles and take them to the station. The work would take the whole night and there would still be something left to do after day break. Under such pressure of work Gandhiji

[7] H. S. L. Polak : *Incidents of Gandhiji's Life,* ed. by Chandrashankar Shukla (Vora & Co., Bombay, 1949), p. 240.

[8] Millie Graham Polak : *Mr. Gandhi : The Man* (Vora & Co., Bombay, 1949), p. 40.

along with others would keep awake all night. To encourage the staff rice-pudding would be served at mid-night."[9]

Mr. Polak was earlier instrumental in introducing Ruskin's work — *Unto This Last* — to Gandhiji while he was on a journey by train. The book changed Gandhiji's ideas profoundly. Not only Ruskin, but other thinkers and philosophers like Thoreau, Emerson, and Tolstoy had great influence on him. Their teachings, in turn, influenced his writings in the *Indian Opinion*.

As Gandhiji admitted : " So long as it (*Indian Opinion*) was under my control, the changes in the journal were indicative of changes in my life. The *Indian Opinion* in those days, like the *Young India* and the *Navjivan* today, was a mirror of part of my life."[10]

His writings on the philosophy of Satyagraha served as inspiration for the Satyagraha movement he launched.

What were the main items in the paper ? These were varied, covering many topics. Two or more editorials and a few short editorial comments dealing with mostly Indian problems or discriminatory law cases involving Indians, were the weekly features. It had a small correspondence column. In the issue of January 27, 1906, the following reply, in the said column, was given : " G. D. L. (Over port). Your letter is quite unsuitable for publication."

The same issue made an important announcement regarding the suspension of Tamil and Hindi editions for want of " editors and compositors ".

The paper contained reproductions from other journals — mostly relating to Indian problems. There was sometimes, ' Our Weekly London Letter ' column.

Gandhiji was looking for reliable correspondents in other countries, particularly in England. His letter of December 10, 1904, to Mr. Dadhabhai Naoroji, will be read with interest in this context :

DEAR SIR,

Indian Opinion has entered on a third stage in its career. I would not weary you with the important step that has been taken in connection with it. You will see the full particulars published in it in the course of this month. It is now intended to have a weekly or a fortnightly letter from England of

[9] Prabhudas Gandhi : *My Childhood with Gandhiji* (Navajivan Publishing House, Ahmedabad, 1957), p. 45.

[10] M. K. Gandhi : *An Autobiography or The Story of My Experiments with Truth* (Navajivan Publishing House, Ahmedabad, 1956), p. 286.

16

general interest but also dealing particularly with the Indian question, in South Africa, as it may have effected (sic) from time to time in London. Could you recommend anyone who would undertake the work and if so, at what rate ? I have nothing special to report on the question this week."

In his letter on January 13, 1905, to Shri Gokhale, reference of which has been made earlier, he requests for correspondents to write for the *Indian Opinion.* " I am also anxious to secure either honorary or paid correspondents who would contribute weekly notes in English, Gujarati, Hindi and Tamil."

January 6, 1906 issue of *Indian Opinion* contained the following interesting news item :

Congratulation — It is with great pleasure that we announce the marriage of Mr. H. S. L. Polak and Miss M.G. Downs (who recently arrived from London), at Johannesburg on Saturday last. Mr. Polak is the Transvaal representative of *Indian Opinion,* and Mrs. Polak is in thorough sympathy with the cause of Indians in South Africa. We offer our heartiest congratulations and best wishes to the happy pair.

Sometimes photographs were published. A black bordered full page photograph of Shri Mansukhlal Hiralal Nazar was published in the same issue carrying an obituary written by Gandhiji, to which reference has already been made. Photos of the then Amir of Afganisthan, (1907), Shri Gokhale (March 10, 1908) and Gandhiji, when he was leading the South African delegation to London, were, among some others, published from time to time.

There were other interesting news items, which gave a glimpse of the life at the settlement. An example : " Many thanks. We have much pleasure in thanking Messrs. G. H. Miankahan and Co., for the gift of a splendid cricket set and a football, presented to the Indian Opinion Athletic Club ".

The editor was a sports enthusiast as well. In the post script of the letter written to Shri Chhaganlal Gandhi, from Johannesburg, dated April 20, 1907, Gandhiji wrote : " I am sending you three numbers of *The Times of India.* After you have seen and admired pictures I want you to cut out Gaekwar, the Jam and the Cricket Team. We might one of these days want to reproduce these pictures as supplements, and it would be better for you also to file any other picture you may come across and consider good enough for use."

Here is another piece of news item :

Visitors at Phoenix. The International Press was visited on Wednesday last, by Messrs M. K. Gandhi, H. O. Ally, Dawad Mahomed, Omar Haji, Amod Johari, M. C. Anglia, Peeran Mahomed and H. L. Paul. The various

17

departments were inspected with interest and the visitors expressed pleasure at what they saw.

Some of the headlines of the *Indian Opinion* will interest modern journalists. Both these were printed on March 31, 1906.

" IN THE IMPERIAL PARLIA —

MENT

SYMPATHY FOR INDIAN GRIEVANCE

INDIAN FOR TRANSVAL MISSION."

A typography-conscious editor would not put ' Parlia ' and ' ment ' like this.

" SENSATIONAL
POTCHEFSTROOM CASE

DUTCHMAN BLACKMAIL AN INDIAN
MR. JUSTICE WESSELS ON JUSTICE AND COLOUR "

Examples of a few other captions are given below from the *Indian Opinion*, dated July 25, 1906. These were neither ' catchy ' nor would they provide a ' lead '

" ANOTHER REGISTRATION CASE

MAGISTRATE'S CURIOUS DECISION "

" THE INDIAN STRETCHER BEARER CORPS

AN INTERESTING RECORD "

Or take the case of the following double column headlines which appeared in the December 29, 1906 issue of the journal :

" SOUTH AFRICA BRITISH INDIAN COMMITTEE

COMPLIMENTARY BREAKFAST BY DELEGATES "

" LORD REAY AND SIR RAYMOND WEST ON THE
OBLIGATION OF THE EMPIRE

DELIGATES LETTERS : NO OPPOSITION TO COLONISTS "

In spite of various checks adopted in the press, there was
a spelling mistake in *deligates*, an unfortunate thing. We should
not judge journalistic efficiency by the twentieth century standard.
But still the insertion of ' breakfast ' in a double column headline
should sound atrocious now-a-days.

Sometimes Gandhiji had to get into dangerous journalistic pit-
falls known as " printer's devil." One such interesting episode
was narrated by Mr. Henry S. L. Polak. Paul Kruger, Ex-President
of the South African Republic, died in July, 1904 while in exile in
Europe. His mortal remains were to be buried at Pretoria, Africa.
Mr. Polak was to cover the funeral proceedings. He was a
fastidious journalist and did not like errors in the *Indian Opinion*.
As such he asked Gandhiji to see the proof himself before it was
printed. Mr. Polak's opening sentence was " He is dead and
buried ". But the *Indian Opinion* published, " He is dead and
burnt ". Mr. Polak was shocked and annoyed and wrote to
Gandhiji immediately lest the mistake might create misunderstanding among the orthodox Boers. Gandhiji, however, explained
that the word ' burnt' seemed natural to him, a Hindu, whose
dead were habitually cremated.

No wonder, Gandhiji was, in his letter of March, 1907, advising
Shri Chhaganlal : " While reading the proofs, compare them
with the original book. Do not depend for spelling, etc., on the
copy sent by me. Please send me the proofs before printing.
Printing has to be done after deciding about the *format*, etc., of the
book. And I believe it is desirable to print off after composing
as much material as we have types for. Types necessary for job
work, etc., should be kept apart."

Not only " printer's devil," the enthusiastic journalist had
had other troubles as well. In one of his lectures on Hindu
Religion at Johannesburg, Gandhiji referred to the spread of
Islam and said that the majority of converts came from the lower
classes. It created a stir among the local Muslims and many letters
of protest were sent to the editor of *Indian Opinion*. He had to

19

publish letters in the Gujarati issue of the *Indian Opinion* on June 3, 1905 and June 17, 1905, with a view to apologizing and clarifying the objections raised. He was also misunderstood while publishing a life sketch of Prophet Mohammad. This had to be stopped because of protests from Muslim members of the Indian community.

Through the columns of the *Indian Opinion*, Gandhiji was reproducing biographies of great men and women of the world. His idea was to inspire his fellow countrymen so that they could emulate their examples. " ... We hope that the readers of this journal will read their lives and follow them in practice and thus encourage us. We have suggested earlier, that each one of our subscribers should maintain a file on *Indian Opinion*. We remind of it on this occasion."[11] The biographies were of people like Tolstoy, Lincoln, Mazzini, Elizabeth Fry, Florence Nightingale, Ishwar Chandra Vidyasagar.

While writing these biographies, Gandhiji committed a few mistakes. In the life story of Abraham Lincoln he wrote that the assassin was torn to pieces by ' people who witnessed the dreadful deed ', when he was shot dead in the special box at the theatre. In fact, the assassin, Mr. Booth, was killed in a barn which was set on fire by the soldiers in pursuit of him. In the biography of Washington he writes that he was elected President for a second time in 1892–1893. In fact, it was in 1792–1793.

Similarly, in the life of Wat Tyler who was fighting against the unjust taxes imposed by the King of England, he wrote that " Wat Tyler lived in the 12th century ". But he lived in the 14th century.

Under the caption —

' THE DEPUTATION,

A REMINDER '

the *Indian Opinion* carried a photograph of Gandhiji and the following news item in its issue of October 13, 1906.

" In connection with Mr. M. K. Gandhi's departure for England as one of the delegates for the Transvaal, it is of interest to recall the circumstances of his departure for India from Natal, in 1901. At that time, a committee was formed to present Mr. Gandhi with an address from the British Indian

---

[11] The *Indian Opinion*, Durban-Phoenix, South Africa, August 19, 1905.

Community of Natal and invitations were issued to the heads of European community. Amongst the replies received was the following interesting letter from the late Sir John Robinson, at one time Prime Minister of the Colony of Natal :

I beg to thank you for your kind invitation to the meeting at the Congress Hall this evening (October 15, 1901). It would have given me great pleasure to have been present on the occasion of so well earned a mark of respect to our able and distinguished fellow citizen Mr. Gandhi, but, unfortunately, my state of health prevents me going out at night, and I am, for the present, debarred from taking part in any public function ; so I must ask you kindly to excuse my inability to attend.

Not the less heartily do I wish all success to this public recognition of the good work done, and the many services rendered to the community by Mr. Gandhi."

This is crude publicity. To bring in the ex-Prime Minister of Natal in a very roundabout way, was not in good journalistic taste. The only excuse was that Gandhiji was at the time away in England.

Whatever might be the size, shape, content or policy of the paper, it was making a good headway in the realm of journalism. The *Cape Argus'* leading article on the *Indian Opinion* was published in the journal in its issue of January 5, 1907. It, *inter alia*, stated :

" They (Natal Indians) have an able organ, *Indian Opinion*, printed in English and Gujarati, and it is from Natal that the champion of South African Indians' interests mostly came ".

Under a sub-heading — ' An Indian Poetess ' — the *Indian Opinion* of March 2, 1907, reproduced the following paragraph from the journal *Indian People* :

" The Ladies Conference at Calcutta brought to prominence a lady orator, Mrs. Sarojini Naidu, already known as a poet of considerable distinction. Mrs. Naidu is a Bengali lady by birth and has married a Madrasi gentleman. She spoke without notes and made an impressive and most eloquent speech. It is further stated that she is not accustomed to speak in public. It is a very hopeful sign of the times that our ladies are coming to the front and are taking active part in the great work of national reform. A gifted lady like Mrs. Sarojini Naidu, with her persuasive and attractive eloquence, should be able to render important service to the women of India."

This was the first eulogistic reference made in public of Sarojini Devi whose friendship with Gandhiji lasted till death separated them.

Struggle against Registration ensued soon and the *Indian Opinion* became the mouthpiece of this resistance movement. Its editorials struck a new note : " Amidst a whole heap of bad coins, if there

is one true sovereign, the heap will be worth that one sovereign...
if you produce one civil resister of merit he will pull things through.
Do not start the struggle...unless you have that stuff."

Satyagraha movement or passive resistance was launched in
reply to the South African Government's insistence on the registration of Indians and other Asians. Under this, all such people
were to note down important physical identity marks and put
thumb impression on the certificates. A date was fixed by which,
all Indians were to register their names, failing which they were
to forfeit their right of residence and be liable to be fined or
imprisoned.

The *Indian Opinion* for the benefit of the large number of Indians,
translated the ordinance into Gujarati. There were meetings of
protest against this Black Ordinance. The struggle continued for
a long time, with intermittent lull. Some sort of agreement was
reached with the Government but the pledges of the Government
were soon broken. The *Indian Opinion* of May 3, 1913, wrote :

"Inspite of the bill being rushed forward a stage further, we imagine that it
will never reach the third reading stage. But it is well for passive resisters to
keep themselves in readiness. It is to be hoped that, if the struggle revived
the impending third campaign will be the purest, the last and the most brilliant
of all. We share the belief with Thoreau, that one true passive resister is
enough to win victory for right. Right is on our side."

The *Indian Opinion* of September 20, 1913, wrote :

"Hitherto passive resisters have challenged arrests by crossing the Transvaal
border. That is how, the present struggle too, has been commenced. We
may, on this question of crossing of the border, at once say this method of
resistance does not mean that we are asking for breaking of the provincial
boundaries. On the contrary as soon as the struggle ceases, those who will
have crossed the borders from different provinces will return to the province
of their domicile ".

The struggle continued and streams of people joined Gandhiji
in their fight for justice. Because of Gandhiji's earlier personal
contact with the editors in England and India, there was widespread
support for his movements.

Gandhiji was writing incessantly boosting up the morale of the
civil resisters. " During 10 years, that is until 1914, excepting the
intervals of my enforced rest in prison, there was hardly an issue of
Indian Opinion without an article from me," wrote Gandhiji.
He was thrown in prison in 1908 and again in 1909.

The political situation in India was not bright either. Earlier in 1907, the Indian National Congress split up between the extremists and the moderates. The Morley-Minto Reforms of 1909 offered little to the Indians. The newspaper, *Leader*, started publication under the guidance of national leaders. The Press Act of 1910, was passed empowering the Government to demand security from the Press.

The Satyagraha struggle continued till 1914, when on Shri Gokhale's advice Gandhiji left South Africa. With his Phoenix settlers, he reached India in the midst of World War I.

The Satyagraha movement without the *Indian Opinion*, as Gandhiji admitted, would not have become a success. It awakened the Indians to their rights and privileges.

The paper was solely used for the movement. Directives to resisters were issued ; news of successful boycott of Registration was published ; The ‘ Weekly Diary ’ of the *Indian Opinion* was eagerly read by Indians ; views of different aspects of the Satyagraha movement were displayed. The number of subscribers rose from 1,200 to 3,500. But the financial sting was still there.

In a letter to Shri Gokhale, April 25, 1909, Gandhiji wrote : " I gave you also the approximate summary of monthly expenses : office here £ 50, office in London £ 40, *Indian Opinion* £ 50, distressed families £ 25." Expenditure on the *Indian Opinion* was like that on any other item during the Satyagraha movement.

In the same letter he wrote that debt due to the *Indian Opinion* up to 20th instant was £ 1200. He ran the *Indian Opinion* " at a loss in the interest of the struggle ". " I have devoted to the continuance of *Indian Opinion* and the establishment of Phoenix all my earnings during my last stay in South Africa, that is nearly £ 5000."

Voteless Indian settlers in Johannesburg were paid compensation if removed from the segregated areas. " The municipality's offers were frequently so inadequate that the victims engaged Gandhi to take their claims to the appellate tribunal. He charged nominal fees and allocated half the costs allowed by the tribunal to the rising expenses of *Indian Opinion*."[12]

But he could bear it on without regrets. " It was never intended to be a commercial concern ", he said.

The paper was reorganized to meet the situation arising out of

[12] H. S. L. Polak, H. N. Brailsford, and Lord Pethick-Lawrence : *Mahatma Gandhi* (Odhams Press Ltd., London, 1949), p. 47.

the Satyagraha movement. A few workers, it was arranged, would not join the struggle, but would run the paper instead. The size was reduced from 16 to 8 pages. It was brought out on Wednesdays instead of Saturdays so as to catch the English mail at Cape Town.

Gandhiji was giving indication of the shape of things to come. In his letter to Shri Maganlal Gandhi, dated November 27, 1909, written in Gujerati, he said : " Phoenix will be put to test now. Probably we may not get money from Johannesburg. Our pledge is that we shall bring out at least a one-page issue of *Indian Opinion* and distribute it among the people as long as there is even one person in Phoenix." Within a week he again wrote to Maganlal Gandhi, in Gujerati : " It is the duty of those who have devoted themselves to Phoenix to improve the life there and do their best to develop *Indian Opinion*: for through *Indian Opinion* we have been imparting education and doing public good. We need not be disheartened if some of us in Phoenix do not put in their best, waste our resources or are quarrelsome."

Immediately before the size of the *Indian Opinion* was changed, he wrote a letter to Mr. A. H. West, on or before December 29, 1909[13], saying :

" The size (of the *Indian Opinion*) should be changed as suggested. No apology need be offered in the paper for it. The English columns should be reduced. No leading matter of opinion (be) given for the present except explanatory notes. All matter should be severely condensed. Energy should be devoted to the art of condensing. It may be divided into Passive Resistance, Natal notes, Cape notes, etc. Reports of Bombay and other meetings may be considerably shortened . . . . The English columns then should simply give news on the disabilities throughout South Africa and about matters we are interested in . . . . The Gujerati columns ought not to be reduced; but if the Gujerati subscribers fall off, even that may be reduced almost to any extent, you there, in Mr. Polak's and my absence, being the sole judge."

Though Gandhiji said that no apology need to be offered, the *Indian Opinion* of January 1, 1910, published the following under the heading ' Ourselves ':

" With the present issue, this journal appears under a somewhat changed

[13] *The Collected Works of Mahatma Gandhi* (Vol. X), the Publications Division, Ministry of Information & Broadcasting, Government of India, p. 107.

dress. The size, too, has been reduced. The Transvaal struggle has put a very severe strain on our resources. It has now become too great for us to continue the old form and size. It is within the knowledge of most of our readers that our publication is not a commercial concern, but our capacity for the service of the community to whose interests *Indian Opinion* is devoted is limited, and our limitation has necessitated the change the readers will notice in its appearance. We part very reluctantly by way of retrenchment with the cover whose colour was very specially selected. Though the size has been reduced, we hope that we shall be able by means of condensation to give the same amount of information. Our readers who are interested in the ideals we endeavour to promote can render useful service by finding subscribers for the journal which they may call their own. It is our desire to give more varied matter as our resources increase. It is, then, for the readers to say when they shall have a better service of news."

The size of the paper was reduced. Still Gandhiji had the problem of finances. In his letter to Shri Maganlal dated January 20, 1910, Gandhiji wrote :

" It is desirable not to give more than a month's credit for *Indian Opinion*. You should only take a limited risk. Let the amount be debited to your account. It will not be deducted from your current allowance. You should never take liability for more than ten subscribers. Even that is, perhaps, too much. However, whatever liability you have taken upon yourself in the Cape Colony is binding on all as you did not know the new rule. The new rule is, I believe, very good—at least for the present. "

" We will have to carry many (fresh) burdens ; it is, therefore, better to cut down these. This (not allowing too much credit) seems to be the prevalent practice of newspapers. As people gradually get used to it, they will follow it of their own accord. We pay the licence fee in advance because of compulsion, i.e., physical force. That we shall take the subscriptions in advance will be on the strength of soul-force. That soul-force consists in making *Indian Opinion* interesting and for that the only course open to us is to put in maximum effort. The subscriptions will then come in automatically. I have no time now to dilate upon this "

The Gujerati edition of the *Indian Opinion*, in its issue of September 4, 1912, published the following :

" It is more than seven years ago that this journal began to be printed at Phoenix. We are now taking a step forward. So far the legal proprietor has been Mr. Gandhi, but the ownership is now being transferred to (a board of) Trustees, and the objectives which will govern the management of Phoenix have been precisely laid down. We feel this is a step in the right direction and we are sure our readers will feel the same.

" The paper has never been in a position to pay its way. It is here needless to go into the reasons for that. It, however, need to be recalled on this occasion that the paper would have been in dire straits if Mr. Tata's generous help had not been drawn upon to meet its needs.

" When the workers decided to settle in Phoenix and start a journal there, it was expected that the income from it and the land would not only give them enough to live on but also enable them to put by substantial savings, for they were to be the masters of whatever profit might accrue from the enterprise. Experience has shown that the assumption was incorrect. We realised that the Phoenix way of life could not be reconciled with monetary gain. And so, for the last several years, the Phoenix settlement has been worked on that basis.

" Our principal object was that, while living by agriculture, we should give of our best in the service of the people and publish the paper for them. We have not so far succeeded in that aim.

" We gave up job-work many years ago. We now feel that we should also discontinue the practice of publishing advertisements. We believed then that advertisements were a good thing to have but on reflection we see that the practice is wholly undesirable. Advertisements are inserted by people who are impatient to get rich, in order that they may gain over their rivals. They are also much in fashion these days that any and every kind of advertisement is published and paid for. This is one of the sorriest features of modern civilization, and for our part we wish to be rid of it. If however, we published non-commercial advertisements, which serve a public purpose, free of charge, they would fill the entire number each time, so we shall only accept them against payment. Other advertisements, we shall stop publishing forthwith. As for advertisements which we have on hand, we shall try to negotiate with our clients and free ourselves of the commitments. We shall then be able to work more on the land and more effectively fulfil the main object of the Trust Deed which we publish in this issue.

" We believe that the proposed changes will enhance our capacity for public service. We also hope that we shall be able to publish worthier and more valuable (reading) matter in the journal. It has been our endeavour daily to add to its value as an instrument of moral education. There are two, and only two, reasons for its existence : to strive to end the hardships suffered by Indians in this country and to promote moral education. The second purpose can be best served by our improving our way of life. That is why we are doing our best to eschew the commercial aspects of our work, such as jobbing and advertisements. Progressively as we live up to the ideals enumerated in the title deed, we shall be able to give our readers more useful material. We want all Indians to help us in this."

The Phoenix Trust Deed was published in the *Indian Opinion* dated 14 September, 1912. Under the title, ' Ourselves ', the following was published :

" The Trust Deed which we publish in this issue, and which is in course of registration, marks a step forward in our work. Mr. Gandhi ceases to be the sole legal owner of the concern known as the International Printing Press, where this journal is printed. Nearly eight years ago we migrated to Phoenix, the idea being that the workers might be able to look more to the land for their sustenance than to the proceeds of the sale of *Indian Opinion* and the advertisements inserted in it. During this period we have not given that attention to the land which it was thought we should be able to give, and we have certainly not been able to pay our way by means of agriculture. That the journal itself has not been self-supporting is a widely known fact. The assistance received by it from Mr Tata's gift of 1909 enabled it to tide over a crisis in its career.

" We have also come to the conclusion that, consistently with our ideals, we could not accept advertisements for paying our way. We believe that the system of advertisement is bad in itself, in that it sets up insidious competition, to which we are opposed, and often lends itself to misrepresentation on a large scale : and that, if we may not use this journal for the purpose of supporting us entirely, we have no right to cater for and use our time in setting up advertisements. We have always used our discrimination and rejected many advertisements which we could not conscientiously take. Our friends and well-wishers, who have hitherto extended their support to us, will not, we hope, take it amiss if we discontinue the practice of inserting advertisements. The object of issuing this paper is two-fold: to voice and work to remove the grievances of the British Indians of South Africa, and to do educative work, by publishing matter of an elevating character. We hope that our readers will appreciate our position, and continue to give us their support, by subscribing to the paper. "

There were more changes in the Gujerati edition of January 4, 1913. The following information was given to the readers :

" In this issue readers will notice a few changes. We believe these to be an improvement ; we have made them because we thought that, if the journal was printed in two columns instead of three, it would look better. It would (also) be more convenient if the articles had to be published in book form. Our purpose is to publish, from time to time, articles of permanent value so that readers who like to preserve copies can later have them bound into a volume. It is our intention to continue providing the same (reading) matter (as before), but in as short a form as possible. By so doing we will be able to fit in more material within the same space or even less. Beginning this time, we have reduced the number of Gujerati and English pages, but we wish to provide more information, though not more words within these pages. It is our hope to reduce the work of the compositor while increasing that of the writer.

" Our venture is more than eight years old. We have published information about rates (and prices) of interest to merchants and have also discussed serious topics. Matter varying from four to twentyfour pages in length has appeared in the Gujerati Section of *Indian Opinion*. We now hope to print, for the most part, writings of two kinds : those which will provide the community with full information, in so far as that is possible, of the hardships we suffer, and we will (also) consider and suggest remedies; secondly, those that deal with an ethic of public conduct or contain, in essence thoughts of great men of this problem. We hope that *Indian Opinion* will thus become an instrument of education."

In the Gujarati edition of the *Indian Opinion* of December 31, 1913, the following remarks were made :

" The satyagraha campaign, as carried on this time and still continuing, has hardly a parallel in history. The real credit for this goes to the Hindi and Tamil speaking brothers and sisters living in this country. Their sacrifice has been the highest of all. Some of them have even lost their lives : killed by the bullets of the white soldiers. As a tribute to their memory, we have decided to give Hindi and Tamil news in this paper. Some years ago, we used to bring out this paper in these two languages as well, but we had to discontinue the practice owing to some difficulties. Those difficulties are not yet over. And yet, we resume publication in these languages for the duration of the struggle, that being, in our judgment, the least that we must do, even at some inconvenience to ourselves, in honour of communities whose members have made such sacrifices in a struggle of this kind. It is not with a commercial motive that we are publishing in these languages. Whether or not to continue the practice after the struggle is over we can only decide in the light of the circumstances then prevailing."

Gandhiji left South Africa. The *Indian Opinion* continued to be published. In his absence, it naturally, lost much of its weight.

B. 'SATYAGRAHA' AND 'YOUNG INDIA'

The *Indian Opinion* was a weekly paper, publishing news of interest from the South African Indian point of view. Journals that Gandhiji subsequently edited in India were viewspapers. His ideas, social, political or economic, as well as the plan of action to achieve those, were now in the process of crystallization. He wanted political emancipation first as that would help elevating 'mass consciousness'. Masses, once awakened, cannot rest till social and economic emancipation is achieved. Gandhiji plunged himself in all these activities side by side. For that purpose he wanted a proper vehicle to transmit his ideas. As he wrote, " newspaper, if otherwise well edited, can become a most powerful vehicle for transmitting pure ideas in a concise manner...". The transformation was already taking place ; from newspaper it was going to be, as the new journals he edited showed, a viewspaper.

This fitted in remarkably with the journalistic trend in India. Mrs. Annie Besant's *New India*, Maulana Mohamed Ali's Weeklies, Maulana Abul Kalam Azad's *Al Hilal*, Shri Balgangadhar Tilak's *Kesari*, Shri Surendra Nath Banerjee's *Banga-*

basi, all veered round respective personalities. As M. Barns put it : " In India, from Raja Ram Mohan Roy to Keshub Chunder Sen, Gokhale, Tilak, Feroze Shah Mehta, Dadabhai Naoroji, Surendranath Banerjea, C. Y. Cintamni, M. K. Gandhi and Jawaharlal Nehru, there is a distinguished line of public men who have used, and are using, the press as a medium for the dissemination of their ideas of moral values."[14]

But with Gandhiji it was much more. The story of his viewspapers is the story of Indian struggle for independence. They stood for the struggle on behalf of humanity, against the manmade bondage. They initiated and nourished a political movement that upheld moral values.

When Gandhiji arrived in India on January 9, 1913, journalism did not establish itself as a profession, excepting in case of the Anglo-Indian Press. Advertisement did not play that important part as it plays today. By and large papers had to depend on sales promotion and, more important, on monetary help from individuals. The Anglo-Indian Press was technically, from production or news coverage angle, superior ; but it was not popular with the Indian reading public. On the other hand the Indian newspapers were popular, but the quality of printing, etc., were not up to the mark. Newspapers were printed normally in two sizes — the seven columns and five columns.

Incidentally, in 1913, the Criminal Law Amendment Act was passed in India. The First World War started in 1914 and with its outbreak, the Defence of India Regulations came into force. Both these Acts were, among others, aimed at silencing criticism of the Government and stopping any sort of political agitation. The Press Association of India, formed in 1915, submitted a memorandum in which it pointed out that by 1917, 22 newspapers were asked to furnish security. Of the 22, 18 preferred to close down than to submit to the Government orders. Between 1917 and 1919 coercive action was taken against 963 newspapers and printing presses. In addition, 173 new presses and 129 newspapers were killed at birth by demand of heavy security. Nearly rupees five lakhs were collected by the Government by way of securities and forfeitures alone. The Association also pointed out that over 500

[14] Margarita Barns : *The Indian Press* (George Allen and Unwin Ltd., London, 1940), p. xv.

29

publications were proscribed within that period. It added : " The total number of orders under the Defence of India Act to which presses and papers were subjected for purposes unconnected with the pursuit of the war were very large, varied, arbitrary, contradictory and often ludicrous to a degree."[15]

On the advice of Shri Gokhale, Gandhiji, after reaching India, was touring the country and meeting people but the *Indian Opinion* was very much in his mind. In a letter to Mr. J. B. Petit, Secretary, South African Indian Fund, on June 16, 1915, Gandhiji wrote : " The Journal *Indian Opinion* has never been and can never be an entirely self-supporting proposition. The English portion of it is mainly of an educative character for the European public amongst whom it is distributed gratis. It was a powerful weapon in the armoury of Passive Resistance and continues to be the only recorder of accurately sifted facts about our countrymen in South Africa and of Passive Resistance movement. It is in no sense a commercial enterprise."

Expenditure of the *Indian Opinion* was like any other item of the Phoenix settlement. In his letter to A. H. West, from Ahmedabad, dated August 3, 1915, Gandhiji wrote " Allocation of £ 3,000 to Phoenix settlement includes assistance to *Indian Opinion*. This enables you to report cases of hardship and to help such cases also. You may even open a branch office in Durban and collect information about hard cases of immigrants and give them free help, you can engage men for reporting cases, etc. The expenses will be justified only as far as you use the paper to attend (to) local relief."

Gandhiji did not like the price of the *Indian Opinion* to be reduced further. In his letter to Maganlal Gandhi, from Ahmedabad, before September 26, 1915, he wrote " The price of *Indian Opinion* has been reduced to one penny. It seems he (Chhaganlal) has been hasty."

Gandhiji was worried over Chhaganlal. In his letter to Mr. A. H. West, from Ahmedabad, dated October 31, 1915, he wrote : " All I know is this that you must continue I.O. even if you have to labour in the streets and if you burn your boats, so much the better. If you cannot, you and your family, so long as you are at

[15] S. Natarajan : *The History of the Press in India* (Asia Publishing House, Bombay, 1962), pp. 172-173.

Phoenix turning out the paper, will be supported at all costs."

Gandhiji was not quite sure whether donations for the Phoenix settlement will go towards meeting the expenses of the *Indian Opinion*. It appears there had been some dissentient voices on this. In his letter to Mr. A. H. West, from Ahmedabad, December 12, 1916, he wrote : "The Committee here will at the most just tolerate the withdrawal of funds for sustaining *Indian Opinion*, and the Public there will also look upon such support with strong disfavour. In the circumstances, we can only fall back upon local support or failing that reduce the paper to any extent we choose."

While quitting South Africa, Gandhiji left the *Indian Opinion* to the able hands of Mr. Polak. But there was no one to look after the Gujarati section of the paper and Gandhiji was approached for advice. In 1916, he sent his second son, Shri Manilal Gandhi, aged 23, to take charge of the edition and assured him his constant guidance from India. He was doing it regularly, even in midst of his ' Know India Tours,' through letters written in Gujarati. Here is an extract from one such letter : " If your aim in running the press is to acquire wealth, you will be serving your own self interest. If that is not your aim you will be serving the public. If you suffer exile with the knowledge that the paper your father was conducting was good and that the spirit underlying it has benefited the country, you will be rendering a great social service."[16]

Towards the end of 1917, Mr. A. H. West suggested that the *Indian Opinion* should be shifted from the Phoenix Settlement to Durban. In his newsletter of December 10, 1917. Gandhiji wrote to Mr. West: "My view is that if you can turn out *Indian Opinion* only by removing to Town, you should suspend publication. I do not like the idea of your competing for jobs or advertisements. I think that when that time comes, we shall have outlived our purpose." The next day he wrote to Mr. Govindswami, engineer in the Phoenix settlement, about the same question. "Mr. West has asked me whether it may not be advisable to shift to Town. My answer is in the negative. I would feel deeply hurt if you cannot keep up *Indian Opinion* in Phoenix. In any case you should not remove the works. If you cannot turn out the Paper

[16] *The Indian Opinion—Mahatma Gandhi Memorial Number*, Durban-Phoenix, South Africa, March, 1948.

in Phoenix, it must be stopped. You should then try to get a living from agriculture alone devoting the whole of your time to it."

Mr. West wired back: "Agriculture impossible. Will you lend Sam, myself, jobbing plant, papers, each living Durban? Ultimately complete independence. Paper published English, Gujarati, Phoenix. Management editorship same time being. Cable reply."

Gandhiji cabled back on or about February 24, 1918: "You may enforce your Plan. Good Luck."

In his letter to Mr. A. H. West, July 17, 1919, Gandhiji wrote: "Recently I wrote to Mani Lal about *Indian Opinion*. He asked me to supply him with funds or to let him revert to advertisements and business printing. I still retain the view I held there and the more I see of the jobbery that goes on here, the indiscriminate manner in which advertisements are taken, the more I think how these advertisements, etc. are nothing but an insidious method of indirect voluntary taxation, how all these debases journalism and how it makes of it largely a business concern, I feel more and more convinced of the rightness of my view. Anyway, it would not be proper to blow hot and cold. Either you must make *Indian Opinion* a business concern and then not expect the public to take a philanthropic or patriotic interest in it, or to make it merely an organ representative of Indian aspirations in South Africa, and then rely entirely upon public support and goodwill. I have dissuaded Mani Lal from making it a business concern. I have not sent him there to do business but to render public service. I feel that *Indian Opinion* has served this purpose if only partially."

In India, Gandhiji was not indulging in much journalistic activity. "I was not editing any journal at that time, but I used occasionally to ventilate my views through the daily Press."[17]

He sent the following article for publication in the Gujarati daily *Hindustan* published from Bombay.

"I promised the Editor a contribution for the Diwali 1 Number of *Hindustan*. I find that I have no time to make good the promise, but, thinking that I must write something, I place before the readers my views on newspapers. Under pressure of circumstances, I had to work in a newspaper office in

[17] M. K. Gandhi : *An Autobiography or The Story of My Experiments with Truth*, (Navajivan Publishing House, Ahmedabad, 1956), p. 456.

South Africa and this gave me an opportunity to think on the subject. I have put into practice all the ideas which I venture to advance here.

" In my humble opinion, it is wrong to use a newspaper as a means of earning a living. There are certain spheres of work which are of such consequence and have such bearing on public welfare that to undertake them for earning one's livelihood will defeat the primary aim behind them. When, further, a newspaper is treated as a means of making profits, the result is likely to be serious malpractices. It is not necessary to prove to those who have some experience of journalism that such malpractices do prevail on a large scale.

" Newspapers are meant primarily to educate the people. They make the latter familiar with contemporary history. This is a work of no mean responsibility. It is a fact, however, that readers cannot always trust newspapers. Often, facts are found to be quite the opposite of what has been reported. If newspapers realized that it was their duty to educate the people, they could not but wait to check a report before publishing it. It is true that, often, they have to work under difficult conditions. They have to sift the true from the false in but a short time and can only guess at the truth. Even then, I am of the opinion that it is better not to publish a report at all if it has not been found possible to verify it.

" The reporting of speeches in Indian newspapers is generally defective. There are very few who can take down a speech verbatim, so that speeches are generally found to be a mere hotch-potch. The best thing to do would be to send the proofs of the reported speech to the speaker for correction and the paper should publish its own report of the speech only if the speaker does not correct anything in the proofs sent to him.

" It is often observed that newspapers publish any matter that they have, just to fill in space. This practice is almost universal. It is so in the West, too. The reason is that most newspapers have their eye on profits. There is no doubt that newspapers have done great service. Their defects are therefore overlooked. But, to my mind, they have done no less harm. There are newspapers in the West which are so full of trash that it will be a sin even to touch them. Many, full of prejudices, create or increase ill-will among people. At times they produce bitterness and strife even between different families and communities. These newspapers cannot escape criticism merely because they serve the people. On the whole, it would seem that the existence of newspapers promotes good and evil in equal measure. "

War ended. Instead of Home Rule, India got the Rowlatt Bill. The whole country rose against it. Gandhiji was very much in the midst of this movement. From a loyal supporter of the British Empire, he was emerging as a rebel in the eyes of the Englishmen.

The Rowlatt Bill, among other things introduced important changes in the criminal law of the country. Not only the

33

publication of ' seditious document ' but its mere possession was made a punishable offence.

As a protest, an unregistered weekly, the *Satyagraha*, under the editorship of Gandhiji, started publication from April 7, 1919. It was to be published on Mondays and the price was one pice.

The following are the contents of the *Satyagrahi** the unregistered newspaper, which Mahatma Gandhi issued on Monday in defiance of the Indian Press Act:

(Please read, copy and circulate among friends; and also request them to copy and circulate this paper) No. 1. Price : one pice.

Satyagrahi

(Editor: Mohandas Karamchand Gandhi, Laburnum Road, Gamdevi, Bombay.)

Published every Monday at 10 A.M.

Bombay, 7th April, 1919.

NOTICE TO SUBSCRIBERS

" This paper has not been registered according to law. So there can be no annual subscription. Nor can it be guaranteed that the paper will be published without interruption. The editor is liable at any moment to be arrested by the Government and it is impossible to ensure continuity of Publication until India is in the happy position of supplying editors enough to take the place of those arrested. We shall leave no stone unturned to secure a ceaseless succession of editors.

" It is not our intention to break for all time the law governing publication of newspapers. This paper will, therefore, exist so long only as the Rowlatt legislation is not withdrawn."

OUR CREDENTIALS

"Our credentials are best supplied by answering the question what will the *Satyagrahi* do ? *Satyagrahi* has come into being for the sake of ensuring withdrawal of the Rowlatt legislation. Its business, therefore, is to show the people ways of bringing about such withdrawal in accordance with the principles of satyagraha. The satyagraha pledge requires the signatories to court imprisonment by offering civil disobedience by committing a civil break of certain laws. This publication can, therefore, show the best remedy in one way and that is by committing civil disobedience in the very act of publishing this journal. In other forms of public activity, the speaker is not obliged to act as he preaches. The object is to draw attention to this contradiction as a fault. It is a method of doing public work. The method of satya-

* The first issue appeared under the title *Satyagrahi*.

graha is unique. In it example alone is precept. Therefore, whatever are suggested herein will be those that have been tested by personal experience, and remedies thus tested will be like well-tried medicine more valuable than new. We hope, therefore, that our readers will not hesitate to adopt our advice based as it will be on experience."

NEWS

" Yesterday many great events took place : but none was as great as that owing to the ceaseless efforts of satyagrahis the mill-hands celebrated the National Day by working in their respective mills as they were unable to get permission of their employers."

Defiance was everywhere — in all spheres. The whole country was ablaze. Situation was going out of control of the leaders. In the *Satyagraha* of May 6, 1919, Gandhiji cautioned people, citizens of Bombay particularly, to understand fully the significance of ' hartal ' before they would observe it to show " outward evidence of their deep affection for Mr. Horniman ", the fearless editor of the *Bombay Chronicle*, who was forcibly being deported from the country.

Mass upheaval continued and very soon the Jallianwalla Bagh massacre took place. Popular violence followed suit. Leaders were stunned at this development. Was the rebel editor, Gandhiji, inciting the masses ? Was the message of his ' Satyagraha ' falling on deaf ears ? Was the country fully prepared to abide by the message of the new ' Messiah ' ?

On April 12, Poet Tagore wrote to Gandhiji : " I know your teaching is to fight against evil by the help of good. But such a fight is for heroes and not for men led by impulses of the moment." Gandhiji agreed : " My error lay in my failure to observe this necessary limitation. I had called upon the people to launch upon civil disobedience before they had thus qualified themselves for it.... "

Satyagraha was called off temporarily and Gandhiji launched an educating campaign, mostly through leaflets, on the true meaning of ' Satyagraha '. But he was soon to utilize a bigger and better forum.

Mr. B. G. Horniman, formerly of the *Manchester Guardian* and the *Statesman*, and then the editor of the *Bombay Chronicle* was deported to England for his bold writing on the Indian situation. Directors of the paper — many of them were now colleagues of

Gandhiji in the political field — approached him with the request to take up the editorship. Gandhiji hesitated. Commenting on this situation Gandhiji said : " But the Government came as it were to my rescue, for, by its order, the publication of the *Chronicle* had to be suspended."[18]

Gandhiji was then 50. It was certainly a great honour to edit a paper like the *Bombay Chronicle*. Why was he hesitating ? Was it because the responsibility was too heavy ? Or was the personality of the veteran journalist Mr. B. G. Horniman creating a complex in his sub-conscious mind ?

Undoubtedly, he wanted a journal to preach what he believed. He got the chance too.

World War I enriched the Gujarati businessmen. Commercial firms, not only in big cities of India but in Africa as well, became prosperous, so to say, overnight. They gave Gujaratis a " new sense of power and importance ". They also soon realized that without political power, economic prosperity cannot be sustained. " A band of young Gujaratis...started an English weekly, *Young India* : organised the Bombay Branch of Home Rule League... carried on an intensive agitation in Bombay and Gujarat."[19] The editorship of the *Young India* was offered to Gandhiji. He agreed and immediately transformed it from a weekly to a bi-weekly, to be converted again into a weekly.

He said in this connection :

"I was anxious to expound the inner meaning of ' Satyagraha ' to the public and also hoped that through this effort I should at least be able to do justice to the Punjab situation. For, behind all I wrote, there was potential ' Satyagraha ', and the Government knew as much.[20]

" By the courtesy of *Young India* syndicate, composed as it is largely of ' Satyagrahis ', since the deportation of Mr. Horniman, I have been permitted to supervise the duty of the journal. I asked for such supervision .... I have hitherto written some leading articles in the usual editorial style .... "

The Gujarati monthly, the *Navajivan*, under the same management, was also placed at his disposal. Writing in Gujarati, in the *Navajivan Ane Satya* Gandhiji wrote in July, 1919 :

[18] Ibid, p. 473.

[19] K. M. Munshi : *Gandhi : The Master* (Rajkamal Publications Ltd., Delhi, 1948), p. 43.

[20] M. K. Gandhi : *An Autobiography or The Story of My Experiments with Truth* (Navajivan Publishing House, Ahmedabad, 1956), p. 473.

" At the time of Horniman's deportation, *Young India,* published from Bombay in English, was a weekly. Simultaneously with his deportation, *The* (Bombay) *Chronicle* was put under censorship.

" In the circumstances, the management stopped publication of the *Chronicle.* Thereupon the management of *Young India* decided to make it a bi-weekly, so that it might serve, partly, the purpose which the *Chronicle* had served and entrusted me with supervision of its contents. Though the *Chronicle* has now resumed publication as usual, *Young India* continues to be brought out as a bi-weekly. Some friends posed a question to me whether it was not my duty, seeing that I was burdening myself with the supervision of an English paper, to bring out a similar paper in Gujarati. This same question had occurred to me. I think I have a service to render to India by delivering a message to her. Some ideas I have come by as a result of my thinking are such as will advance us towards our welfare. It has ever been my endeavour to explain these. I have not succeeded as well as I should have liked to for want of ability or time or favourable circumstances. For instance, even about satyagraha I see a great deal of misunderstanding prevailing yet. I am convinced that I have no gift better than this for India. I have always been avid of placing before the people this priceless thing, and several others of which I have had ample experience. One powerful modern means for this purpose is the newspaper. The founders of *Navajivan anc Satya* have agreed to place it under my supervision and undertaken to secure facilities for its publication as a weekly. Shri Indulal Kannaiyalal Yajnik is a busy man in the public life of Gujarat. Even so, he has pledged himself to make *Navajivan* his chief concern and help it to the utmost. These circumstances are no mere accident. I would be ashamed not to welcome them. And so, though my health is not what it used to be a year ago, I have ventured to assume the burden of running *Navajivan.* I seek the blessings of Gujarat in this and invite the help of its men of letters in running the paper and of others in ensuring a wide circulation for it, and I am perfectly confident that I shall get it.

" *Navajivan* will be published every Sunday and arrangements have been made to see that it is available on the same day at a number of places in Gujarat.

" The management has no desire to run the paper for profit. Accordingly, it has decided to keep the rate of subscription as low as possible, at Rs. 3-8-0 a year including postage. This is the very figure which had been decided upon for the monthly *Navajivan* from its July issue onwards, with some increase in its size. A copy of *Navajivan* will be priced at 1 anna and the first number will be issued on Sunday, September 7.

" The subscription rate mentioned above is regarded as the minimum for the reason, mainly, that the weekly will carry no advertisements. I realized from my experience of running *Indian Opinion* in South Africa for many years that advertisements bring little profit to the people. Ultimately, they are paid for by the public itself, and all sorts of them appear, moral and immoral. For this reason, *Indian Opinion* has been running for years without carrying any advertisements. For the present, *Navajivan* will have eight pages of foolscap size. As circulation increases and facilities improve, the size, too, will be enlarged.

" Those, other than subscribers of the monthly *Navajivan* who desire to enrol themselves as such should send their names to the Manager at Ahmedabad. I earnestly hope that *Navajivan* will have a great many subscribers."

It was soon converted into a weekly. The *Young India* was brought from Bombay to Ahmedabad where there was the facility of a press at the disposal of the editor. The *Navajivan* first appeared on October 7, 1919. The *Young India* followed suit after a day. Gandhiji was editor of both and Shri Mahadev Desai and Shri Shankerlal Banker were publisher and printer respectively. The journals were priced at one anna each.

Gandhiji soon made his personality felt through the columns of the *Young India* and the *Navajivan*. The impending change was visible from the very beginning. He turned these into his views papers. " They enabled me freely to ventilate my views and to put heart into the people," he said.

In the editorial, ' To the Subscribers and the Readers ', appearing in the first issue of the *Young India* under the new editor, Gandhiji enunciated the policy of the journal.

Readers, in this context, may recall that the objective of the *Indian Opinion*, as declared in the paper, was a " desire to promote harmony and good-will between the different sections of the one mighty Empire". But by the time Gandhiji became associated with the *Young India* and the *Navajivan*, his hopes in British justice, in the course cf the last sixteen years, were shattered. He was becoming more and more conscious of the true nature of the colonialism and was preparing the country to fight injustice with the ' Satyagraha ' as he had practised it in South Africa.

He wrote :

" A word as to the policy of *Young India*. Apart from its duty of drawing attention to injustices to individuals, it will devote its attention to constructive ' Satyagraha ' as also sometimes cleansing ' Satyagraha '. Cleansing ' Satyagraha ' is a civil resistance where resistance becomes a duty to remove a persistent and degrading injustice such as the Rowlatt Act."

He further told his readers :

" *Young India*, from this week, enters upon a new stage. It became a bi-weekly when Mr. Horniman was deported and the *Chronicle* was strangled. Ever since the *Chronicle's* rebirth, the syndicate and I have been considering the advisability of reverting to the weekly issue. The conversion of *Navajivan* into a weekly and its coming under my charge has hastened the decision. The burden of conducting a bi-weekly and a weekly is too great a strain on me and a weekly *Young India* will now serve almost as well as a bi-weekly. The annual subscription will now be Rs. 4 instead of Rs. 8 and the price of single copy will be one anna instead of two, without postage."

This reduction was at a time when printing materials, immediately after the war, were difficult to procure at a reasonable rate. Margarita Barns calculated that during the First World War and immediately after that, the cost of newsprint alone increased seven-fold.

Incidentally, a year earlier, the Central Publicity Bureau of the Government of India, of which the Press Information Bureau is the successor today, was formed. An Indian Press party, for the first time, was also taken out to the front to get first-hand information of the war which was nearing its end.

The editor had something more to tell his readers.

"The editing of *Navajivan* has been a perfect revelation to me. Whilst *Young India* has little more than 1,200 subscribers, *Navajivan* has 12,000. The number would leap to 20,000 if it would but get printer to print that number. It shows that a vernacular newspaper is a felt want. I am proud to think that I have numerous readers among farmers and workers. They make India. . . . The English journals touch but the fringe of the ocean of India's population."

Gandhiji was, he said, editing the English journal mainly for the benefit of his friends in the Madras Presidency. But, he warned, "I will not be a party to editing a newspaper that does not pay its way. *Young India* cannot pay its way unless it has at least 2,500 paying subscribers."

"But *Young India*... sold more copies than the combined totals of several newspapers in India There was not only a new thought but a new language in newspaper writing, and what he wrote was...finest in journalistic writing," wrote Mr. A. S. Iyengar, the veteran journalist.[21]

At one time the circulation reached the figure of 40,000. What was more, Gandhiji's articles were now freely reproduced in most papers in India. Moreover, the *Young India* and the *Navajivan* were made "free from the curse of advertisements". If his journal aimed at the service of the community and the country, the countrymen should see that the paper pays its way through.

The front page article in the same issue, under the title 'No

[21] A. S. Iyengar : *All Through the Gandhian Era* (Hind Kitabs Ltd., Bombay, 1950), p. 28.

Security ', gives an insight into the condition of the press during these days.

" . . . *Navajivan* when it became a weekly, was subjected to a security of Rs. 500. *Young India* escaped security, because the printer was also the keeper of the press where it was published. The press in Bombay was itself under security . . . . Where security makes no difference to a journalist, a waiver really enhances his sense of responsibility. So long, therefore, as the objectionable features of the Press Act continue to disfigure it, exemption from security, whilst it is creditable for the Government, it can hardly be matter for congratulation for the controllers of any particular organ so exempted."

Though Gandhiji was getting more and more involved in Indian politics—and within a couple of years he was at the pinnacle of his political glory—he found, as he was touring the country, that " freedom lies in the economic and social emancipation of the ' teeming millions ' in the country ". So, in the midst of the political turmoil—the Khilafat Agitation and the non-cooperation movement —he was, through his masterly editorials, focussing the attention of the nation to other equally important problems. Week after week he was writing on ' Swadeshi', spinning wheel, Hindu-Muslim Unity, non-violence, place of vernaculars, etc.

At times he was poetic. On July 21, 1920, he wrote about the spinning wheel : " Not on the clatter of arms depends the revival of her (India's) prosperity and true independence. It depends most largely upon re-introduction in every home of the music of the spinning wheel. It gives sweeter music and is more profitable than the execrable harmonium, concertina and accordion."

Lokamanya Tilak passed away on August 1, 1920. Obituary written by Gandhiji—and obituaries written by him were unsurpassed—in the *Young India* is worth repeating.

" . . . . A giant among men has fallen. The voice of the lion is hushed . . . . His patriotism was a passion with him. He knew no religion but love of his country. . . . His courage never failed him. His optimism was irrepressible . . . . In the battle for freedom he gave no quarter and asked for none. . . .

" It is blasphemy to talk of such a man as dead. The permanent essence of him abides with us for ever. Let us erect for the only Lokamanya of India an imperishable monument by weaving into our own lives his bravery, his simplicity, his wonderful industry and his love of his country."

The August issue of the *Young India* contained many articles which reflected his political thinking in unambiguous terms. Though in a whirlwind tour of the country, he always made it a point to write for the paper. He would explain his ideas of non-cooperation, accepted by the Calcutta Congress, to his countrymen patiently and persuade them to accept his view-point.

As an editor of a different character, Gandhiji, whose duty was to weigh the opposite point of view, would publish the arguments of his critics. In the December 18, 1920, issue of the *Young India* Gandhiji wrote : " . . . . The columns of *Young India* are open to all who have any grievance against non-cooperation." He was giving detailed instructions side by side to non-cooperators. He was also replying to some of the criticisms published in other papers.

Gandhiji, it may be mentioned, did not get the support of the press from all over the country. The *Independent* of Allahabad and the *Servant* of Calcutta were supporting Gandhiji wholeheartedly. The *Swarajya* of Shri T. Prakasham was later published in 1922 for propagating his teachings of non-cooperation. But the press in Maharashtra were critical. So were the Bengali press, particularly the *Bengalee* and the *Nayak*. But the most formidable was Mrs. Besant, through the columns of the *New India*. In her statement to the Press Laws Committee, more about which later, Mrs. Besant said :

"Mr. Gandhi in *Young India* is allowed every week to excite hatred and contempt against the Government in language compared with which criticisms of Government, that have ruined many papers, are harmless ; he is even allowed to approach perilously near high treason by saying that he would, in a sense, assist an Afghan invasion of India : papers that one has never heard of, wielding little influence have their securities forfeited or heavily enhanced. An administration which with flagrant injustice allows the main offender and inspirer of hatred, who proclaims 'war against Government,' speaks of 'paralysing' it or 'pulling it down', to go scot free, while crushing small offenders encouraged by his example, undermines in the community all respect for law and the authority of the Government. . . . I rejoice that the Government is strong enough to treat Mr. Gandhi's vapourings with contempt instead of bestowing on him the martyrdom he courts. But I urge that a Law not enforced against the influential should not be allowed to crush the weak."[22]

The correspondence between the two great men of the age—Mahatma Gandhi and Poet Tagore—is worth reproducing in this context. According to the Poet, non-cooperation was a doctrine of separatism, exclusiveness, narrowness and negation. According to Gandhiji, it was "a protest against unwitting and unwilling participation in evil". He would even go a step further and

[22] S. Natarajan : *The History of the Press in India* (Asia Publishing House, Bombay, 1962), pp. 200–201.

declare " non-cooperation with evil is as much a duty as cooperation with good ". In the *Young India* dated June 1, 1921, he wrote,
" An India prostrated at the feet of Europe can give no hope to
humanity. An India awakened and free has a message of peace
and goodwill to a groaning world."

He was careful in correcting newspaper reports likely to create
misunderstanding between him and the Poet. In the February 9,
1922, issue of the *Young India* he mentions a *Bombay Chronicle*
news item regarding Gandhiji's alleged disrespectful remarks about
' Santiniketan ' of Poet Tagore. He was very much pained by that
report and concluded : " I wish the unknown friend had never
thought of reporting it. The report does not convey the central
truth of it."

Young Manilal, looking after the *Indian Opinion* in Phoenix,
South Africa, would get, from time to time, journalistic advice,
from Gandhiji. The editor has to be patient and seek for the truth
only, he advised. Like the famous Joseph Pulitzer, he could say :
" Accuracy is to a newspaper what virtue is to a lady ". His earlier
acquaintance with Mr. Saunders of the *Englishman* taught him that:
" We win justice quickest by rendering justice to the other party."

" You should write what is the truth in *Indian Opinion* ; but do
not be impolite and do not give way to anger. Be moderate in your
language. If you err, do not hesitate to confess it,"[23] wrote the
veteran journalist-father to the budding journalist-son.

But moderation in language is a relative term. There have been
exchanges of intemperate language—though not from the pen of
Gandhiji—in the *Young India*. Shri J. C. Kumarappa narrated
the following interesting incident :

" When I was in editorial charge of *Young India*, some over-zealous person,
who was anxious to attain non-violence in a hurry, in his own fashion, in thought,
word and deed, suggested that my language of criticism was severe and that
Gandhiji should ask me to tone down. Gandhiji replied with a smile : ' Kumarappa comes from Madras. You must allow for the chillies in his blood.' "[24]

What a humorous way of easing a situation. This sense of
humour, which he did not lose till the last day, cleared many a
tense atmosphere.

[23] *The Indian Opinion—Mahatma Gandhi Memorial Number* (Durban-
Phoenix, South Africa, March, 1948).

[24] J. C. Kumarappa : *Incidents of Gandhiji's Life*, Ed. by Chandrashanker
Shukla (Vora & Co., Bombay, 1949), p. 142.

The whole country was turned into a prison in 1921. Gandhiji, in the *Young India* would publish, week after week, names of those in prison, " His Majesty's hotel ", as he called it. Gandhiji warned : " Starvation, or its alternative canine food, no covering much less any worth the name to protect against the severe winter, microbe infected, lice-laden blood-stained tatters, the worn-off relics of common felons ", were in store for the patriots courting jail.

The country was now moving towards a Civil Disobedience Movement. Earlier on October 6, 1921, the *Young India* published the manifesto on Freedom of Opinion. The signatories were led by Gandhiji, and stated that " . . . it is the inherent right of every one to express his opinion without restraint about the propriety of citizens offering their services to or remaining in the employ of the Government . . . . "

In the same issue, under the title ' Expression of Opinion ', he wrote: " When in any movement violence is religiously eschewed, it becomes a propaganda movement of the purest type. Any attempt to crush it is an attempt to crush public opinion, and such the present repression has become."

He had to agitate on the subject as a number of papers were closed because of too heavy security money being demanded by the Government. He was pained to see " The *Independent* is no longer a printed sheet. The *Democrat* is no more. And now the sword has descended upon the *Pratap* and *Kesari* . . . . The *Bande Mataram*, Lalaji's child, has warded off the blow by depositing Rs. 2,000 as security."

He further said, ". . . . I believe that an editor who has anything worth saying and who commands a clientele cannot be easily hushed so long as his body is left free. He has delivered his finished message as soon as he is put under duress. The Lokamanya spoke more eloquently from the Mandalay fortress than through the columns of the printed *Kesari*."

He was further suggesting " a heroic remedy meant for heroic times ". He suggested the publication of hand-written news-sheets. He said : " Let us use the machine and the type whilst we can give unfettered expression to our thought. But let us not feel helpless when they are taken away from us by a ' paternal ' government watching and controlling every combination of types and other movements of the printing machine." To him " the restoration of free speech, free association and free press is almost the whole Swaraj ".

Shri Pyarelal, Secretary of Mahatma Gandhi, narrated the following incident in this connection :

" On reaching Allahabad I found that a notice was served upon the *Independent* demanding security under the Press Act, and the paper had to close down. What was to be done next ? We asked for instructions. Back came the reply by wire : Run it as a cyclostyle, or even as a hand-written sheet.

"This was done. Mahadev was arrested a few days later. But the manuscript *Independent* continued with the significant motto, ' I change, but I cannot die'."[25]

Incidentally, Sir Tej Bahadur Sapru when he was Law Member of the Viceroy's Council, appointed a committee with himself as the Chairman, in 1921, to scrutinize the existing Press Laws. A few statements by the editors, as witnesses before the Committee, are of great interest as they reveal discriminatory treatment meted out to the Press in India. Mrs. Besant, editor of the *New India*, a veteran journalist, said : " An Anglo-Indian editor in Madras was allowed to make the most violent attacks on Indians who advocated the reforms that are now Law. But if an Indian paper replied to the attack, it found itself accused of exciting hatred. A Christian paper attacked the Muslims in an insulting way but the Government took no notice, while a Muslim paper was censured for attacking Christians."

The Sapru Committee found out some more interesting facts about the Indian Press of that time. Nine-tenths of the editors in Northern India, were semi-educated. The Chairman remarked that, " excepting one or two, they were men with scarcely any culture about them ".

In the Central Government a Department of Publicity had been set up under Dr. Rushbrook Williams on the recommendation of Mr. Stanley Reed, who had organized the Government's wartime publicity. Dr. Rushbrook Williams deposed to the Press Laws Committee that his work was to keep in touch with editors, and to remove misconceptions. " The Department (of Central Bureau of Information) which for the sake of convenience is a sub-section of the Home Department, is really a link between the Government and the Press. The most important part of my duties is to examine the current Press with the object of finding out topics in which the

[25] *Illustrated Weekly of India* (Bombay, October 20, 1957), p. 25, .

public is interested and on which it requires information, and of finding out matters in connection with which the action of Government is criticised . . . . Our duty is then to extract the more important of these statements and to bring them to the notice of the departments concerned. . . . " [26]

The Press Laws Committee recommended the repeal of the 1908 and 1910 Acts, the Amendment of the Registration of the Press and Books Act.

Gandhiji was now pouring out fire through his pen. He felt keenly that the alien government had no right to govern. So it was his duty, he held, to propagate the so-called sedition. If the articles were not seditious enough did it not mean that his pen was weak ? [27]

In passing, it may be mentioned that Gandhiji at the helm of affairs in the Indian National Congress, was also in charge of publicity for the organization. The Congress Working Committee earlier resolved in favour of foreign propaganda during this critical period and asked Gandhiji to finally decide on the matter and take necessary steps. Gandhiji, in the *Young India* of March 9, 1922, expressed his views against publicity abroad. His points were: (*a*) people in the country will be made less self-reliant as they will depend on outsiders to help in their struggle ; and (*b*) independent interest of other countries about the Indian condition will cease. He gave an instance of the Italian newspapers who were showing interest in collecting news of their own. He would, as a journalist, rather prefer interest being created. He had other objections, too, on administrative and organizational grounds.

The reader will like to compare this situation with the one when he, more than once, visited India and England to get the support of newspaper editors and public men on the South African question. Now he was relying more and more on his and his countrymen's strength. Moreover, he was convinced, that justice, was with him.

The British Government was unwilling to allow any more of this stuff in printing. On March 11, 1922, the editor of the *Young India* along with the printer was produced before the court for writing

[26] S. Natarajan : *The History of the Press in India* (Asia Publishing House, Bombay, 1962), p. 201.

[27] B. Pattabhi Sitaramayya : *The History of the Indian National Congress*, Padma Publications, Bombay, 1946), Vol. I, p. 238.

seditious articles like ' Tampering with Loyalty ', ' The Puzzle and its Solution ', and ' Shaking the Mane '.

Gandhiji was sentenced to six years imprisonment. For two years the flow of Gandhiji's invigorating and inspiring articles in the *Young India* and the *Navajivan*, were missed. The circulation also came down from 21,500 to 3,000.

How was Gandhiji spending his time in prison? Though a civil disobeyer outside, he was a model prisoner abiding punctiliously the prison rules. In his letter to Hakim Ajmal Khan, his close associate, on April 14, 1922, he gave a glimpse of his life in Yeravada prison.

" . . . . My cell is in itself, decent, clean and airy. The permission to sleep in the open air is a great blessing to me, as I am accustomed to sleeping in the open. I rise at four to pray. . . . At six I begin my studies. . . . At seven in the evening, when it is too dark to read, I finish my day's work. At eight I betake myself to rest after the usual ' ashram ' prayer. My studies include the ' Koran ', the ' Ramayana of Tulsidas ' ; books about Christianity, excercises in Urdu and much else. I spend six hours on these literary efforts. . . . "

In prison he read about 150 books on religion, literature, social and natural sciences. He read the whole of the *Mahabharata* and the six systems of Hindu philosophy in Gujarati. He also read Bhuler's *Manusmriti* and Max Muller's *Upanishads*, as also Paul Carus' *The Gospel of Buddha*, Rhys Davids' *Lectures on Buddhism*, Amir Ali's *The Spirit of Islam* and *History of Saracens*, Shibli's *Life of the Prophet*, Dr. Mahomed Ali's *Koran*, Dean Farrar's *Seekers After God*, Moulton's *Early Zorastrianism*, Henry James' *The Varieties of Religious Experience*, Hopkin's *Origin and Evolution of Religions*.

He read Gibbon's *Decline and Fall of the Roman Empire*, Bacon's *Wisdom of the Ancients*, Buckle's *History of Civilization*, James' *Our Hellenese Heritage*, Kidd's *Social Evolution*, Motley's *Rise of the Dutch Republic*, Wells' *Outline of History*, Gedde's *Evolution of Cities*, Lecky's *European Morals* and Roseberry's *Life of Pitt*.

He also read Goethe's *Faust*, Tagore's *Sadhana*, Shaw's *Man and Superman*, and Kipling's *Barrackroom Ballade*.[28]

Gandhiji wrote a primer, and a Urdu manual. He intended to write in prison, his autobiography. But could not do it. Instead, he wrote most of the manuscript of ' Satyagraha in South Africa '.

[28] D. G. Tendulkar : *Mahatma* (V. K. Jhaveri and D. G. Tendulkar, Bombay, 1951), Vol. II, p. 147.

After his release in April 1924, he wrote a series of articles in the *Young India* giving details of his prison life. Friends advised him to take a few months rest as he was still convalescing from the recent appendicitis operation. But he felt that the " editorial job would be for him rather a kind of mental recreation than a task ". It was his channel of communication with his beloved people. He appealed from ' Juhu ' rest house : " If all my time and energy were taken up seeing and entertaining you, it will not be possible for me to edit the weeklies in the way I desire."

In the first article after release in the *Young India*, dated April 3, 1924, under the caption ' For the Readers—Past and Present ', he wrote : " It is not without much hesitation that I resume the editorship of *Young India*. In taking up the editorial control of *Navajivan* and *Young India*, I am following the Light as far as I see it. . . . There will be no new method or policy developed in the pages of *Young India*. I hope they will not be stale. *Young India* will be stale when Truth becomes stale."

He was not only devoting himself to the editor's job, but was also suggesting others to take up the honourable profession of journalism. On September 15, 1924, he wrote to Shri Jawaharlal Nehru : " Why may you not take up remunerative work ? After all you must live by the sweat of your brow even though you may be under father's roof. Will you be correspondent to some newspapers?"[29] He was thinking on the same lines regarding his son, Shri Devadas, whom he earlier introduced to the editor of the *Times of India*.

As usual he was writing on all subjects not merely politics. Louis Fischer remarked : " Great editor that he was, Gandhi dedicated the entire May 29, issue of *Young India* to his 6,000-word article on ' Hindu-Moslem Tension, its causes and cure '."

The liberty of the Press was constantly in his mind. The *Bombay Chronicle* had to pay a fine for a defamation suit. Under the caption ' Below the Belt ', Gandhiji, wrote in the *Young India* on August 7, 1924 : " The Press law is gone only to be replaced by new activities under the laws of sedition and libel . . . . The editor of a daily newspaper when he begins writing his leading article does not weigh his words in golden scales. He may be

[29] Jawaharlal Nehru : *A Bunch of Old Letters* (Asia Publishing House, Bombay, 1958), p. 41.

47

betrayed into a hasty word. Must he pay for it even though he did it obviously in good faith without malice and in the public interest ? These libel actions are calculated to demoralize Indian journalism and make public criticism over-cautious and timid. I am no lover of irresponsible or unjustifiably strong criticism. But the caution to be beneficial must come from within and not superimposed from without."

He knew when to highlight a matter or ignore it. For example, Lord Irwin succeeded Lord Reading as Viceroy on April 1, 1926. " But the fateful change ", records Mr. Louis Fischer, " was not mentioned in *Young India.*" Gandhiji was then busy writing on the question of the killing of dogs under the caption ' Is this humanity '.

But his silence on the political changeover was much more eloquent.

Though his Congress Presidential work—he was elected for Belgaum Session—exacted much of his time, he was trying to answer hundreds of questions through the columns of his paper. Seldom did any editor handle such voluminous correspondence. Issues of the *Young India* were then full of questions from readers, both from the country and outside. To the editor no question that affected man and society, should be treated lightly. The same issue, would sometimes carry articles on the economics of ' Charkha ' or the ideal diet or hydropathy, side by side with the most important political problem of the day. A reading of the journal, from the title to the printer's name, would open to the reader an enormous world to be explored.

His advice to his correspondents were human and touching. Here is an example quoted from an issue of the *Young India* of a later date. Under the headline ' An unnatural father ', Gandhiji reproduced a letter of a young married man who went abroad. During his absence, a friend of his got intimate with his wife and as a result the wife conceived. His wife was now very repentant. The father suggested an abortion. Under the circumstances, the young man wanted advice from Gandhiji.

Gandhiji readily gave it. He suggested that the new born babe should be accepted as the man's child. When the wife is repentant, the matter should be forgotten.

On October 28, 1926, he addressed a note ' To journalist

friends ', saying that requests are pouring in asking for his articles for publication in other papers. Gandhiji had two alternatives. Either to edit the *Young India* and the *Navajivan* or to write for other papers. He preferred the first course and so stopped writing for others. In a modest tone he added : " My field is very limited and even on the subjects I am familiar with, I cannot always be original, I have no false notions about the efficacy of my writings."

There are instances when he wrote for others. But that was very rare and on very special occasions. One such was a signed article by him written for the *Forward,* the paper of Shri C. R. Das, in Bengal. The article, an obituary, was published on June 20, 1926, under the caption ' Long Live Desh Bandhu.'

The Press in India were under great difficulties. A number of them had to close because of securities demanded. The *Forward* was one such. Under the caption ' A Brilliant Career,' Gandhiji wrote on May 9, 1929, about the closure of the paper which proved a thorn in the side of Government. He concluded " *Forward* is dead. Long Live *Forward*."

In June 6, 1929, issue, Gandhiji wrote an editorial under the caption ' Atrocious ' wherein he criticized the Government for conducting searches in the office of the *Modern Review*, Calcutta, and the residence of the editor.

In the *Young India* of January 12, 1928, Gandhiji wrote :

" . . . . I long for freedom from the English yoke. I would pay any price for it. I would accept chaos in exchange for it. For the English peace is the peace of the grave. Anything would be better than this living death of a whole people. This satanic rule has well nigh ruined this fair land materially, morally and spiritually.

" . . . . My ambition is much higher than independence. Through the deliverance of India, I seek to deliver the so-called weaker races of the earth from the crushing heels of western exploitation in which England is the greatest partner. . . . "

The same year, i.e. 1928, the *Young India* was publishing Shri Jawaharlal Nehru's articles on Russia. It, incidentally, reflected the new spirit that was growing in the country under the leadership of Shri Nehru. In 1929 Gandhiji's name was proposed for the Presidentship of the Indian National Congress. He declined and suggested the name of Shri Nehru. He wrote :

" Older men have had their innings. The battle of the future has to be fought by younger men and women. And it is but meet that they are led by one of themselves. . . . Pandit Jawaharlal has everything to recommend him. He

G—4

has for years discharged with singular ability and devotion the office of secretary of the Congress. By his bravery, determination, application, integrity and grit he has captivated the imagination of the youth of the land. He has come in touch with labour and the peasantry. His close acquaintance with the European politics is a great asset in enabling him to assess ours."[30]

When Shri Jawaharlal's name was accepted, Gandhiji said :

". . . . In bravery he is not to be surpassed. Who can excel him in the love of the country ? 'He is rash and impetuous,' say some. This quality is an additional qualification at the present moment. And if he has the dash and the rashness of a warrior, he has also the prudence of a statesman. A lover of discipline, he has shown himself to be capable of rigidly submitting to it even where it has seemed irksome. He is undoubtedly an extremist thinking far ahead of his surroundings. But he is humble and practical enough not to force the pace to the breaking point. He is pure as crystal, he is truthful beyond suspicion. He is a knight *sans peur et sans reproche*. The nation is safe in his hands."

Gandhiji had his problems with fellow journalists as well. On August 22, 1929, under the heading 'Reporters, a Nuisance' he informs the readers how some reporters have circulated a story about his weight being reduced to 80 lbs. and that he was so ill that he fainted. This was baseless. He commented : "Often has my anger against them got the better, for a moment, of my non-violence." He suggested to the agencies that "they warn their reporters that they would be fined or dismissed for repeated offences of the character I have described."

Independence, as the ultimate goal for the country, was accepted by the Lahore Session of the All India Congress in 1929–30. A student of Indian Independence movement will be interested to know, that Senator Blaine moved a resolution in the U.S. Senate, for recognition by the United States, of the Indian Independence. It *inter alia* stated :

"Whereas the people of India are today spontaneously moving towards the adoption of self-government under the constitutional form with popular approval, and seeking national independence, therefore, be it resolved that the Senate of the United States, mindful of the struggle for independence, that gave birth to our republic, participates with the people with deep interest that they feel for the success of the people of India in their struggle for liberty and independence."[31]

Gandhiji was preparing India for the civil disobedience movement. But he was not quite sure what form it should take. It soon

[30] D. G. Tendulkar : *Mahatma* (V. K. Jhaveri and D. G. Tendulkar, Bombay, 1951), Vol. II, p. 488.

[31] Ibid., (1952), Vol. III, p. 1.

occurred to him that breaking of Salt Tax might be the first item under disobedience movement. Salt is consumed by all. Gandhiji wrote in the *Young India*, February 1930 : " There is no article like salt, outside water, by taxing which the State can reach even the starving millions, the sick, the maimed and utterly helpless. The tax constitutes, therefore, the most inhuman poll tax the ingenuity of man can devise."

On January 9, in the *Young India* he wrote : " . . . . I would far rather be witness to chaos in India . . . than that I should daily witness our gilted slavery." The tone of his writings was definitely changing. He started his famous ' Dandi march ' on March 12, 1930, to make salt with his own hands from water nature had given in plenty. Even at that age of 61, and after fatiguing journeys, he would, at the end of the day, write for the *Young India*.

The Viceroy promulgated an Ordinance on April 27, reviving the Press Act of 1910. On the Press Act, Gandhiji made a statement which was published after his arrest, in the *Young India* of May 8, 1930 :

" . . . . Act contains additional provisions making the whole piece more deadly than before . . . it is a veiled form of Martial law. . . . The pressmen if they are worthy representatives of public opinion, will not be frightened by the ordinance. Let us realise under the wise dictum of Thoreau that it is difficult under the tyrannical rule for honest men to be wealthy. . . . I would therefore urge pressmen and publishers to refuse to furnish securities and if they are called upon to do so, either to cease publication or to challenge the authorities to confiscate whatever they like . . . . They may confiscate type and machinery, they will confiscate pen and still less speech . . . . There is hardly a man or woman breathing in India who with every breath does not breathe disaffection, sedition, disloyalty, and whatever other terms one may use to describe the mentality of the nation which has set its mind on destroying the existing system of Government."

The press responded magnificently. As M. Barns says : " Never before had the press played so important a part in the national campaign and enthusiasm was kindled and maintained by the vigorous action of the Nationalist newspapers. . . . Indeed, all the methods which a nationalist press might be expected to use in a country at war were employed by the journals supporting the movement." [32]

Government fell upon the press with a heavy cudgel. By July

[32] Margarita Barns : *The Indian Press* (George Allen and Unwin Ltd., London, 1940), p. 373.

1930, 67 papers and 55 printing presses were shut down under the Press Ordinance. The Manager of the Navajivan Press was advised not to pay, if Government demanded, any deposit money. Soon the press was forfeited and with it, the printing of the journals stopped. The *Young India* began to appear in cyclostyle form till the truce with the Government was signed.

In prison, Gandhiji had more or less the same programme as during the previous term. Every minute at his disposal was properly utilized. He wrote a line or two to every inmate of the *ashram*. Addressing the children as ' little birds,' he wrote :

" Ordinary birds cannot fly without wings. With wings, of course, all can fly. But if you, without wings, will learn how to fly, then all your troubles will indeed be at an end. And I will teach you. See, I have no wings, yet I come flying to you every day in thought. Look, here is little Vimla,-here is Hari, and here Dharmakumar. You also can come flying to me in thought. There is no need of a teacher for those who know how to think. The teacher may guide us, but he cannot give us the power of thinking. That is latent in us. Those who are wise get wise thoughts. . . . " His weekly letters to other inmates appeared in the *Young India* and were subsequently published in book form—*From Yeravada Mandir*. His other literary activity in prison, was the translation of the hymns from the Upanishads and other Sanskrit scriptures.

The famous Gandhi-Irwin Pact was signed in 1931. In the notification issued by the Government of India dated March 5, 1931, it was agreed that the Civil Disobedience Movement would be stopped. " The publication of News-sheets in support of the Civil Disobedience Movement " will be discontinued. On March 6, Gandhiji gave an interview to the Pressmen, when the following question and answer took place :

" Q. Do you intend bringing out *Young India* again ?

A. As soon as I can. It all depends on the putting into effect the settlement, which implies the return of machinery, etc., which was confiscated under the Press Ordinance. I would certainly be eager to resume the printing of *Young India*. Of course, *Young India* has continued to be published on a cyclostyle. We have suspended the publication of this week's issue to fulfil the terms of settlement, which includes the discontinuance of unauthorised news-sheets."[33]

The paper resumed publication next week.

[33] B. Pattabhi Sitaramayya : *The History of the Indian National Congress* (Padma Publications, Bombay, 1946), Vol. I, p. 450.

In the first issue of March 12, 1931, he wrote that it had again been possible to resume publication of the *Young India* ' under the law.' He informed the readers how typed sheets were brought out when the Government put its ban on printing. Thousands of copies could be distributed due to ' brave and self-sacrificing ' staff of the *Young India* and the *Navajivan*. He further added : " I hope that the public will join me in the tangible manner they can, namely by patronising *Young India* and what is more, fulfilling the mission for which *Young India* stands. The readers know that *Young India* and *Navajivan* do not exist for a commercial purpose. They are published for the sole purpose of educating the nation to win ' purna swaraj ' through truthful and non-violent means."

The objective of the *Young India* and the *Navajivan* was to reach that goal. His mighty pen was directed for that purpose. Freedom did not only mean attaining political independence. It was freedom from want and hunger—economic freedom as well. It should further aim at social justice. Unless political freedom was attained, equitable justice could not be ensured.

It will not be out of context to reproduce the following conversation narrated by Mr. H. C. Perry of the *Times of India*. [34]

" This is my son—he wants to be a journalist," said Mahatma Gandhi, as he smilingly introduced young Devadas. . . . ' And what do you want ? ' I couldn't resist asking the father. ' I want my country to be free,' said Gandhi senior."

In August 1931, Gandhiji sailed for England to attend the Round Table Conference. Here he came in touch with the newspapers which did not conform to his own ideal—papers devoted to truth. He became disappointed with the twentieth century journalism. To his great dismay he found that newspapers could twist matters to suit their convenience. Service to self-interest and not the interest of humanity was the prevailing trend.

Incidentally, in England he met Mr. Charlie Chaplin, the great comedian. In the October 8, 1931, issue of the *Young India*, Shri M. Desai narrates how innocently Gandhiji asked who Mr. Charlie Chaplin was.

On his return to India Gandhiji wrote under ' A Retrospect ' (the *Young India* December 31, 1931) : " Never since taking up the

[34] *The Times of India* (Bombay, November, 1956).

editorship of *Young India* have I, though not being on a sick bed or in a prison, been unable to send something for *Young India* or *Navajivan* as I was during my stay in London . . . . Fortunately, Mahadev Desai was with me and though he too was over-worked, he was able to send a full weekly report for *Young India.*" Gandhiji was soon arrested on reaching India.

C. HARIJAN

" . . . . In view of consideration stated in Mr. Gandhi's letters of October 18th and October 24th. . . in connection with the problem of untouchability, they (Government) are removing all restrictions on visitors, correspondence and publicity in regard to matters which, in Mr. Gandhi's own words, ' have no reference to civil disobedience and are strictly limited to removal of untouchability . . . .' ," thus ran the Government order conveyed to Gandhiji on November 3, 1932, in prison, where he was detained in connection with the Civil Disobedience Movement.

He was now thinking in terms of a new weekly. It would be devoted to the cause of the ' Harijans ' or men of God as Gandhiji called the untouchables. He would engage himself fully for eradication of this social evil. The wizard was again wielding his pen for a great cause.

In a letter dated January 8, 1933, to Shri G. D. Birla, the industrialist, Gandhiji wrote : " . . . . I have revived my suggestion that the English edition at least should be published in Poona, and it can be published, not simultaneously with the Hindi, but on Fridays, if the Hindi is published on Mondays. The English edition may then be issued under my supervision . . . . " [35]

The paper *Harijan* first appeared on February 11, 1933, and was priced at one anna. Shri R. V. Sastry became the editor and the weekly was published under the auspices of The Servants of Untouchables Society. Ten thousand copies were printed for the first issue.

It carried an English rendering by Poet Tagore of a Bengali poem of Shri S. Datta, entitled ' Scavenger.' Tagore's poem on the same theme was also published in a subsequent issue of the

[35] G. D. Birla : *In the Shadow of the Mahatma* (Orient Longmans, Bombay, 1953), p. 89.

Harijan. There were news items giving information regarding temple opening for 'Harijans'. The main editorial was devoted exclusively to untouchability. Next there was a column, 'To the Reader,' in which explaining the importance of the newly launched movement, Gandhiji said, " since the movement has a world-wide significance and seeks the sympathy, if possible, of the whole humanity, it is necessary to keep the world acquainted with its implications and progress ". The paper, he made it clear, would be devoted for the service of 'Harijans' and would highlight all efforts for the removal of untouchability.

" You will note," he commented, " that no advertisements are being taken for the upkeep of the paper. It has to depend solely upon the subscriptions received." The page ended with a notice to the subscribers reminding them that " subscriptions should be paid strictly in advance."

In a signed article in the *Harijan* dated February 25, 1933, Gandhiji explained that the Hindi edition was to be published first. But as there was delay, the English came out earlier. "I am happy to be able to inform the reader that the Hindi edition will have been out before this is in his hands. Arrangements are proceeding as fast as possible for the publication of provincial editions in the provincial languages e.g. in Bengali, Marathi, Tamil, Guzrati etc."

Explaining the term 'Harijan', Gandhiji wrote :

"It is not a name of my own coining. Some years ago, several ' untouchable ' correspondents complained that I used the word ' asprishya ' in the pages of the *Navajivan.* ' Asprishya ' means literally untouchable. I then invited them to suggest a better name, and one of the untouchable correspondents suggested the adoption of the name ' Harijan ', on the strength of its having been used by the first poet-saint of Guzrat. . . . I thought that it was a good word. ' Harijan ' means a man of God. All the religions of the world describe God pre-eminently as the Friend of the friendless, Help of the helpless, and Protector of the weak. The rest of the world apart, in India, who can be more friendless, helpless or weaker than the forty million or more Hindus, who are classified as untouchables. . . . "

Gandhiji was conducting the paper from the prison in Poona. He was released on May 8, 1933. On May 13, he wrote : " All should know that even though I am supposed to be a free man, *Harijan* will continue to be edited as if I was in prison. It will still be solely devoted to the ' Harijan ' cause and will scrupulously exclude all politics."

He was again taken to prison, but was given the facility, by the Government, of sending instructions or contributions to the *Harijan* editor three times a week. He was released on August 23.

In September 1933, Gandhiji moved to the Wardha *Ashram*, and devoted himself more and more to the ' Harijan ' cause. Though still weak, he would contribute regularly to the journal. He reiterated: " *Harijan* will remain what it has been ever since its inception. It will rigorously eschew all politics."

The *Harijan* became the mouth-piece for the 'Harijan' movement and village industries. There were criticisms for this. Gandhiji explained (*Harijan*, December 21, 1924): " . . . . Any problem connected with the welfare of villages as a whole must be intimately related to the ' Harijans,' who represent over a sixth part of India's population. Those who complained of monotony were perhaps not sufficiently interested in the cause. No doubt it would be true criticism, if I were told that the columns of *Harijan* were not as interesting as they might be made. There are causes for this which are inherent in the movement itself."

Again he was demonstrating, if it at all needed, that service should be the motto of journalism. He was serving the cause of India's teeming millions. It was much more. He was serving humanity.

There was a complete black-out of important political news of the day in the *Harijan*. It made no mention of the Congress session, nor of his retirement from politics. The Government of India Act which got Royal assent in 1935, did not have any place in the journal. On the other hand there were more and more articles on village-made ' gur,' hand-pound rice, village cleanliness, nutritious food, cow's milk vs. buffalo's, from waste to wealth through night soil, etc.

He started village reconstruction work, particularly the revival of cottage industries, in nearby villages. Scientific facts were made known on importance of honey, fresh vegetables, tamarind, etc. There were researches on nutrition and balanced diet. Snakes were divided into poisonous and non-poisonous ones and treatments for snake bites were explained. Village sanitation was vigorously publicized.

Books on rural problems were reviewed. Useful extracts from books were published for the benefit of all. To enlighten the rural workers, rural uplift programmes in other countries were narrated.

Wardha, like ' Sriniketan ' of Poet Tagore, soon became a laboratory for rural work.

Anything indigenous or country-made was worthy of recommendation. He gave a letter of appreciation—a very rare one—to a barber. It was dated November 25, 1939, ' Anand Bhavan,' Allahabad. He wrote: " Munnilal has given me a fine shave with devotion. His razor is country-made and he shaves without soap."

In a leading article in the *Harijan*, Gandhiji, in a simple lucid style, spoke about the rural development programme in a village.

"Anantpur is a little village in Saugar district, C.P., containing 177 houses with a population, roughly, of 885. It has no post office or telegraph office. There is a weekly service from the nearest post office, Relly, twelve miles from Anantpur. It is a typically poor village of poor India. The villagers are occupied not more than four months in the year. There was hardly any supplementary occupation for the villagers as a whole before an event that happened four years ago. . . .

"It was in 1929 that a young man, with a single-minded zeal seldom surpassed, chose Anantpur for his experiment, after one year's travelling in search of such a village. . . . His name is Jathalal Govindjee. He does not know English. He is no Gujarati scholar. Himself a town-bred man, by dogged pertinacity he has inured himself to the hardships of village life and lives like, and in the midst of, villagers. He has three companions with him. He is a thorough believer in one thing at a time and, therefore, will not pursue other social service, no matter how tempting it may be. If the spinning wheel is well established in every cottage, he thinks that all other problems that puzzle and drag down villagers will solve themselves. They visit every cottage and offer to teach them ginning, spinning, carding, weaving and dyeing. They improve their wheels and manufacture new ones for sale only from the material available in the village. This has given extra work to the village carpenter and the village blacksmith. Every item is well thought out. They have an almost complete record of the condition of every cottage and also its dwellers. They have made a fairly accurate study of the villagers' wants and woes, customs and manners, and they have published their report in Hindi. Their workshop is a busy hive. Work is being done in a neat and methodical manner. A common log-book is kept containing a day-to-day summary of the work done by each worker. I have mentioned only four foundation workers. Needless to say they have raised workers in seventeen villages they are now serving within a five-mile radius of Anantpur. . . ."

Anantpur was a ' Harijan ' village. Anything connected with ' Harijan ' was getting due publicity. Sometimes, he would go to the farthest to espouse the cause of ' Harijans '. The earthquake of 1934, he said, was due to the sin of caste Hindus against untouchables. This brought a sharp rejoinder from Poet Tagore.

'It has caused me a painful surprise ", wrote the poet, " to find Mahatma Gandhi accusing those who blindly follow their own social custom of untouchability, of having brought down God's vengeance upon certain parts of Bihar, evidently specially selected for His desolating displeasure. It is all the more unfortunate, because this kind of unscientific view of phenomena is too readily accepted by a large section of our countrymen. I keenly feel the indignity of it, when I am compelled to utter a truism in asserting that physical catastrophies have their inevitable and exclusive origin in certain combination of physical facts. Unless we believe in the inexorableness of the universal law in the working of which God Himself never interferes, we find it impossible to justify His ways on an occasion like the one which has sorely stricken us in an overwhelming manner and scale."

Following an interview with Mrs. Sanger, he devoted a few articles on family planning. He advocated self-restraint against contraceptives. " What has been possible for you is not possible for all young men. I can restrain myself. But my wife cannot," read a frank letter to the editor. The editor advised : " If he is sincerely desirous that his wife should be weaned from the sexual desires, let him surround her with the purest love, let him explain the law to her, let him explain the physical effects of union without the desire for procreation, let him tell her what the vital fluid means."

It is of interest to note that while in England as a student, Gandhiji had not formulated definite ideas against artificial means for birth control. This was manifest when Dr. Allinson, who advocated artificial methods, stood for election for the committee of the Vegetarian Society. Dr. Allinson lost the election because of his views on birth control. Gandhiji resigned from the committee. " It is to be noted that he himself became a vigorous opponent, in later years, of artificial methods of birth-control, advocating self-control and continence." [36]

For a brief period, in 1936, he was not writing for the *Harijan*, due to ill-health. On February 29, he resumed writing. Under the title ' Nothing Without Grace,' he wrote:

" I am now able, by way of trial, to resume to a limited extent my talks with the readers of *Harijan*. I shall not carry on private correspondence with reference to the correspondents' personal problems or domestic difficulties, except those with which I have already concerned myself, and I shall not accept public engagements or attend or speak at the public gatherings. There are positive directions about sleep, recreation, exercise and food, with which the reader

[36] H. S. L. Polak, H. N. Brailsford and Lord Pethick-Lawrence : *Mahatma Gandhi* (Odhams Press Ltd., London, 1949), p. 15.

is not concerned and with which, therefore, I need not deal. I hope that the readers of *Harijan* and correspondents will cooperate with me and Mahadev Desai, who has in the first instance to attend to all correspondence, in the observance of these restrictions."

In the September 24, 1938, issue of the *Harijan*, Gandhiji wrote : ". . . . *Harijan* is not a newspaper, it is a viewspaper representing those of one man. Even Mahadev and Pyarelal may not write anything whilst I am alive."

He sought the indulgence of readers and correspondents if they were not served in time or at all. " For the time being—whilst Mahadev's illness lasts, readers will overlook the gaps they will notice in the editing of the *Harijan*." Much later in the July 19, 1942, issue, he explained further as to how a viewspaper differs from a newspaper. " Let it be known too that *Harijan* is a viewspaper as distinguished from a newspaper. People buy and read it not for amusement but instructions and regulating their daily conduct. They literally take their weekly lessons in non-violence."

As a protest against the British Government's action involving India in war without consulting her, Gandhiji started ' individual Satyagraha ' by asking people ' na ek pai, na ek bhai ' (not a farthing, nor a man) for the war efforts. On October 18, 1939, the editor of the *Harijan* and allied weeklies received a notice to the effect that " no account of incidents leading up to ' Satyagraha ' by Shri Vinoba Bhave and no aspect of his speeches or any subsequent development " should be given publicity to.

On October 24, he wrote in the *Harijan* : " I cannot function freely if I have to send to the Press Adviser at New Delhi every line I write about ' Satyagraha '. The three weeklies have been conducted in the interest of truth and therefore, of all parties concerned. But I cannot serve that interest if the editing has to be done under threat of prosecution. Liberty of the Press is a dear privilege . . . . I am unable to reconcile myself to the notice which, although in the nature of advice, is in reality an order whose infringement will carry its own consequence."

But he was all the time feeling that he might have to suspend the weeklies. He advised the people to carry the news from mouth to mouth. He blessed these ' walking newspapers ' and thought these more honourable than ' garbled, one-sided ' news-sheet.

' Bidding goodbye ' to the readers (the *Harijan*, November

10, 1938) Gandhiji sorrowfully remarked : " I shall miss my weekly talks with you, as I expect you, too, will miss them. . . . The suspension must, therefore, continue while the gagging lasts . . . . It constitutes a Satyagrahi's respectful protest against the gag."

In mid-December, 1941, he wrote a 25-page booklet ' Constructive Programme.' Now that the *Harijan* was suspended, it filled the gap to some extent. The *Harijan* and the other two weeklies resumed publication on January 18, 1942.

But things were not normal in the Press world. Government restrictions were being increasingly imposed on papers. As a journalist, he criticized, under the caption ' Draconian Order ' government instructions against the *Bombay Sentinel*, the *Jugantar* of Bengal, and the *Pratap* of Punjab in the *Harijan* of May 3, 1942. The Central Press Advisory Committee had earlier passed a resolution " viewing with grave concern the action of the three Provincial Governments, namely those of Bombay, Bengal and the Punjab against three daily papers." This was, it said : " A violation of the spirit of the agreement " between the Government and the Press. Gandhiji opined that the Press regulations were of such sweeping character that anything and everything could be brought under their operations.

By the time the article was sent to the Press, Government orders in case of the *Bombay Sentinel* and the *Jugantar* were rescinded.

But said Gandhiji: " What I have said has reference to the larger question of publication of news and the Standing Committee should take up a strong stand on the liberty of the Press to disseminate news in a sober and as far as possible accurate manner."

India was watching over a rapid succession of political events in the world—after Pearl Harbour—culminating in the British Government's proposal, through Sir Stafford Cripps. Gandhiji was now convinced that the British would not leave India of their own. He started with his writings in the *Harijan*, pleading with the British to leave India, ' Quit India.' There was urgency and passion in his writings. In his appeal ' To every Briton,' he begged " for a bloodless end of an unnatural domination and for a new era, even though there may be protests and wailings from some of us." (The *Harijan*, May 11, 1942).

Correspondents made enquiries whether Gandhiji was making

plans for launching a new movement. He said to them :

" I have never believed in secrecy, nor do I do so now. There are certainly many plans floating in my brain. But just now, I merely allow them to float in my brain. My first task is to educate the public mind in India and the world opinion, in so far as I am allowed to do so. And when I have finished that process to my satisfaction, I may have to do something. That something may be very big, if the Congress is with me and the people are with me. Naturally, I do want to carry the whole of the Congress with me if I can, as I want to carry the whole of India with me. For, my conception of freedom is no narrow conception. It is co-extensive with the freedom of man in all his majesty. I shall, therefore, take no step without the fullest deliberation."[37]

Gandhiji was also keeping the American public informed about the state of affairs in India. To Preston Gover of the *Associated Press of America*, he said, " I have every right to expect America to throw her full weight on the side of justice, if she is convinced of the justice of the Indian cause."

Gandhiji, it may be mentioned in passing, had been criticized, justly or unjustly, by his countrymen, for showing weakness for foreign journalists. Many of his important announcements were released through international news agencies. Much later, in the *Harijan* of April 21, 1942, he explained the position.

" An Indian journalist complains that our great men have a weakness for foreign journalists to the extent of excluding Indians at their Press conferences, and wonders whether I am myself free from this weakness. For myself, I can say, without fear of contradiction that I have never been guilty of such partiality. Having suffered a good deal for the crime of being an Asiatic, I am not likely to be guilty of such weakness. And I must say that I know of no such example as my friend adverts to, if only because public men can ill afford to face a boycott by Indian Pressmen. What has happened with me and, so far as I am aware, with others too is that they and I have found it necessary at times to give special interviews to foreign journalists when it has been found necessary in the interest of the common cause to get messages across the seas. It is impossible in the present circumstance to do otherwise. It would be as foolish to invite a boycott by foreign journalists and by Indian. An industrious person will find out that Indian journalists have been preferred by Indian public men again for the sake of the common cause. As a fellow journalist I would urge journalists, whether Indian or foreign to prefer their particular causes to their own or their employer's pockets or to descending to recriminations or personalities."

In July 19, 1942, issue of the *Harijan*, Gandhiji wrote :

" Anxious enquiries are being made as to what I would do if the *Harijan* was suppressed. . . . I would ask the enquirers not to be agitated if *Harijan* is suppressed. The *Harijan* may be suppressed, its message cannot be, so long

[37] D. G. Tendulkar : *Mahatma* (V. K. Jhaveri and D. G. Tendulkar, Bombay, 1953), Vol. VI, p. 3.

as I live. Indeed, the spirit will survive the dissolution of the body and somehow speak through the millions. . . .

" Let us see what *Harijan* is today. It is now published in English, Hindi, Urdu (two places), Tamil, Telugu (two places), Oriya, Marathi, Gujarati, Kanarese (two places). It is ready to be published in Bengali, only waiting for legal permission. Applications have come from Assam, Kerala, Sind. All but one have a large circulation compared to the other weeklies. I suggest that it is no small matter to suppress such a paper. The loss will be more Government's than the people's. They will incur much ill-will by suppressing a popular paper."

" And *Harijan*," he cautioned, " is not an anti-British paper. It is pro-British from head to feet. It wishes well to British people. It tells them in the friendliest manner where in its opinion they err."

" The Anglo-Indian papers, I know, are Government favourites. They represent a dying imperialism. Whether Britain wins or loses, imperialism has to die. It is certainly of no use now to the British people whatever it may have been in the past. In that sense, therefore, Anglo-Indian papers are really anti-British as *Harijan* is pro-British. They are disseminating hatred day by day by hiding the reality and bolstering imperialism which is ruining Britain. It is in order to arrest the progress of that ruin that, frail as I am, I have put my whole soul into a movement which, if it is designed to free India from the imperial yoke, is equally intended to contribute the mightiest war effort in their behalf."

Gandhiji's slogan of ' Quit India ' was followed by his call ' Do or Die ' for the country. He told the delegates to the Congress Committee in Bombay in the first week of August, 1942 : " Here is a mantra, a short one, that I give you. You may imprint it on your hearts and let every breath of yours give expression to it. The ' mantra ' is ' Do or Die.' We shall either free India or die in the attempt ; we shall not live to see the perpetration of our slavery. Every true Congressman or woman will join the struggle with an inflexible determination not to remain alive to see the country in bondage and slavery. Let that be your pledge . . . . "

There was a special request to fellow journalists.

" . . . . A word to the journalists. I congratulate you on the support you have hitherto given to the national demand. I know the restrictions and handicaps under which you have to labour. But I would now ask you to snap the chains that bind you. It should be the proud privilege of the newspapers to lead and set an example in laying down one's life for freedom. You have the pen which the Government can't suppress. I know you have large properties in the form of printing-presses, etc., and you would be afraid lest the Government should attach them. I do not ask you to invite an attachment of the printing-press voluntarily. For myself, I would not suppress my pen, even if the press was to be attached. As you know my press was attached in the past and returned later on. But I do not ask from you that final sacrifice. I suggest a middle way. You should now wind up your standing committee, and you may declare that you will give up writing under the present restrictions and take up the pen only when India has won her freedom. You may tell Sir Frederick Puckle that he can't expect from you a command performance that his press notes are full of untruth, and that you will refuse to publish them. You will openly declare that you are whole-heartedly with the Congress. If you do this, you will have changed the atmosphere before the fight actually begins."

He appealed, as well, to princes, to Government servants, to soldiers, to students with the request to help the struggle. But Shri H. Mukherjee, Deputy Leader of the Communist Party in the Indian Parliament criticizes : " No particular role was allotted to the workers and the peasants, and though they formed the over-whelming majority of the people they were expected simply to line up in the manner directed by their superiors. The priority given to journalists in Gandhi's order of appeal is perhaps not entirely accidental ; the Mahatma, with all his great courage and occa-sional sublimity, had throughout his life a shrewd eye to publicity whatever he thought or did."[38]

Gandhiji was arrested on August 8, 1942. The *Harijan* was closed down and all copies, old and new, confiscated by the Govern-ment. When Gandhiji asked for an explanation from the Govern-ment of Bombay, he was informed that : " The Government instructed the District Magistrate, Ahmedabad, to destroy all objectionable literature from Navajiwan Press such as the old copies of the *Harijan* newspapers, books, leaflets and other miscellaneous papers. . . . All the old files of *Harijan* since 1933 have been destroyed." [39]

Prison life this time, was eventful and tragic. He lost his Private Secretary, Shri Mahadev Desai, who was more than a son to him. His wife Kasturbai, breathed her last on February 22, 1944. On inquiry from the Government, Gandhiji expressed his wishes with regard to Kasturbai's funeral rites :

" Her body should be handed over to my sons and relatives which would mean a public funeral without interference from Government. If that is not possible, the funeral should take place as in the case of Mahadev Desai and if the Government will allow relatives only to be present at the funeral, I shall not be able to accept the privilege, unless all friends, who are as good as relatives to me, are also allowed to be present.

[38] Hiren Mukherjee : *Gandhiji—A Study* (National Book Agency Pvt. Ltd., Calcutta, 1958), p. 149.
[39] D. G. Tendulkar : *Mahatma* (V. K. Jhaveri and D. G. Tendulkar, Bombay, 1953), Vol. VI, pp. 228-229.

" If this also is not acceptable to the Government, then those who have been allowed to visit her will be sent away by me and only those who are in the camp—detenus—will attend the funeral.

" This has been, as you will be able to bear witness, my great anxiety not to make any political capital out of this most trying illness of my life companion. But I have always wanted whatever the Government did to be done with good grace, which I am afraid, has been hitherto lacking. It is not too much to expect that now that the patient is no more, whatever the Government decide about the funeral will be done with good grace."[40]

Gandhiji was released on May 6, 1944, and the *Harijan* was revived on February 10, 1946, after a lapse of three and a half years. Shri Pyarelal, Gandhiji's Secretary, described events leading to the reappearance of the journal thus :

" While in Madras Gandhiji decided to resume publication of the *Harijan* weeklies which had been suppressed after the commencement of the 'Quit India' struggle. The re-appearance was not without a dramatic touch. Gandhiji had hoped to post at Wardha the matter for the first issue to Ahmedabad, from where the weeklies were printed and published. It had been Gandhiji's pride that during half-a-century of active Journalism, not one issue of his various journals had ever failed to come out on time—even when he was roaming over the length and breadth of India, Burma and Ceylon, and even during his visit to England. But the special bringing him back from Madras, to quote a speaker in the Central Assembly, who compared it to a ' drunken caterpillar in the last stage of inebriety ', reached its destination at midnight, seven hours late, when the mail bound for Ahmedabad had already left Wardha. Gandhiji regarded it as a bad beginning. ' Let us get the first issue of the weeklies struck in Bombay,' he suggested. ' I once did like that in Phoenix in the case of the *Indian Opinion.*'
' But what about despatch? The subscribers' registers are all at Ahmedabad.'
' Let us wire the whole thing to Ahmedabad,' some one suggested.
" But the whole Hindustani and Gujarati copy would have to be transcribed in Roman script as the system of accepting telegrams in Indian scripts had not yet been introduced. That took up the better part of the morning. Then someone had a brain wave. ' Send the English articles by wire and the rest by a special messenger. If they can be through with the English earlier, the press will be able to catch up with the vernacular copy.'
" And so, a special messenger was despatched and all the three weeklies came out on time after all the misadventures."[41]

In the first issue, Gandhiji explained the reason for the revival of the *Harijan*. " Why is *Harijan* revived ? This question may have occurred to many as it has to me. I may tell the reader that no

---

[40] Ibid., p. 296.
[41] Pyarelal : *Mahatma Gandhi—The Last Phase* (Navajivan Publishing House, Ahmedabad, 1956), Vol. I, pp. 165–166.

special effort was made for its revival. An application for the removal of the ban was made on December 3, 1945, and the ban was removed on January 10, 1946. Many readers, including English and American, had all along felt a void and they began to feel it more after the defeat of the Fascist Powers. The reason for the feeling was obvious. They wanted my reaction, in terms of Truth and Non-violence, to the various events happening in India, if not in the world. I wished to satisfy this desire."

And again in February 24, 1946, issue he wrote :

" I have taken up *Harijan* at such a critical moment in our country's history that having undertaken to write I cannot wait in certain matters for publishing my thoughts till the next number of *Harijan* is out. Then, too, it is published not at the place where I reside but away from me. Thus exacting readers will forgive me if they find things in the columns of *Harijan* which have already been printed in the daily press. The reason for publication is obvious. *Harijan* goes to many readers who do not read the papers in which my statements may be published and in which accurate publicity can never be guaranteed. *Harijan* is not a commercial concern in any meaning of the expression. It is published purely in the interest of the cause of India's independence."

The next few issues of the *Harijan* were entirely taken up in discussing the food situation in the country. It was alarming and he felt that his attention should now be concentrated on this. He asked the Government—what he called a ' peace time war effort '— to engage the army and the navy in helping the production from land and water. He advised people to shake off inertia. He asked for the co-operation of all concerned to meet the calamity and said, " Grow more food was not a bad cry during the war. It is a greater necessity now. . . . Everything possible should be done to draw water from the bowels of the earth. . . . Cloth famine can and ought to be averted by telling the millions to spin and weave in their own villages, the State supplying them with cotton, where it is not grown or available, and with the simple instruments of production on hire or on long term purchase."

The Private Secretary to the Viceroy met the rebel and non-cooperator and the latter emphasized the need for closest co-operation in the face of the impending crisis. He suggested " . . . . Food should be grown on all cultivable areas, wherever water is or is made available. The flower gardens should be used for growing food crops. . . . All ceremonial functions should be stopped. Women can play the highest part in the alleviation of the present

65

distress by economising in their households. In nine-tenths of our activity, we can manage our daily affairs without the aid of the Government. . . . Panic must be avoided at all costs. We must refuse to die before death actually takes toll. . . . "

He also requested people to " confine daily wants regarding food to the minimum." He asked city people to depend more on milk, vegetable, oil and fruit so that the grains and pulses could be used by the villagers.

Some people criticized when Gandhiji suggested catching of fish to supplement food. " Does it not entail violence?" Gandhiji admitted that it does. " This kind of violence is inherent in all embodied life, therefore, in man too. . . . The man who coerces another not to eat fish commits more violence than he who eats it. . . . I do not consider it violence to permit the fish eater to eat fish. It is my duty to suffer it. Ahimsa is the highest duty. Even if we cannot practise it in full, we must try to understand its spirit and refrain as far as is humanly possible from violence."

Great political changes were in the offing. Independence of the country could be announced any time. But Gandhiji was busy with his own programme. He came to Bengal to tour round the villages, where, like in some other parts of India, Hindu-Muslim religious tension was continuing. He found his non-violence theory at stake and wanted to test it in Bengal's interior villages. He decided to stop all work in connection with the *Harijan* and other weeklies. Time permitting he agreed to send occasional contributions for the weeklies.

He came back to Delhi in April 1947. His mind was full of tales of woe of what he saw or heard in Bengal. He cautioned the newspapers against misleading news. He even went to the extent of advising people not to read newspapers.

On June 2, 1947, Gandhiji wrote in the *Harijan* :

" Readers must have noticed that last week I started writing for the *Harijan*. How long I shall be able to continue it, I do not know. God's will be done in this, as in other things . . . the circumstances under which I had stopped writing for the *Harijan* have not altered. Pyarelalji is far away from me and, in my opinion, is doing very important work in Noakhali. He is taking part in what I have called the ' maha yagna '. Most of the other helpers are also unable to help under the stress of circumstances or other causes. To resume writing for the *Harijan* under these adverse conditions would be ordinarily considered madness. . . . "

There were communal disturbances at places. The newspapers, he felt, were through irresponsible reporting, helping in creating panic. They were not at all serving the community. On the other hand, Government was trying to suppress information. He did not like that either. On March 20, 1947, he wrote to the Prime Minister, Shri Nehru : " I would like you. : . to tell me what you can about the Punjab tragedy. I know nothing about it save what is allowed to appear in the Press which I thoroughly distrust. Nor am I in sympathy with what may be termed by the old expression of ' hush hush policy. ' It is amazing how the country is adopting almost the very measures which it criticised during British ad ministration. Of course, I know the reason behind it. It makes no appeal to me."

India was divided and the communal frenzy was at its height. Pakistan Press was exaggerating reports of riots. One such was regarding Kathiawad. Gandhiji sent his workers to investigate the matter. It was found out that reports were mostly false. The local Muslim leaders admitted, through a wire to Gandhiji, that there had been much exaggeration about communal riots. Gandhiji narrated this in his prayer meeting on December 5, 1947. " The proper thing," he said, " is to trust truth to conquer untruth." Later on, in his prayer speech, he gave a practical suggestion as to how to report on communal disturbances and avoid exaggeration. There should, he said, be a joint board to which all reports about communal troubles would be submitted for scrutiny. The board, if necessary, may refer such cases to State Ministers before giving publicity.[42]

For sometime past he was thinking of closing down the *Harijan*. In a letter to Sardar Vallabhai Patel, in July 1947, he wrote : " . . . . I also feel that *Harijan* should now be closed. It does not seem to me to be right to give contrary guidance to the country." He was sick at heart when he did not see eye to eye with the activities of some of his colleagues.

To the Manager of the *Harijan*, he wrote : " Perhaps we may have to decide to close *Harijan*. . . . My mind rebels against many things that our leaders are doing. Yet I do not feel like actively opposing them. But how can I avoid it if I am running a

[42] D. G. Tendulkar : *Mahatma* (V. K. Jhaveri and D. G. Tendulkar, Bombay, 1954), Vol. VIII, p. 61.

paper ? You do not want to run it without me, nor does the ' Sardar '."

Addressing the readers of the *Harijan*, Gandhiji said : " It occurs to me that now that freedom from the British rule has come, the *Harijan* papers are no longer wanted." He was for the last few months contributing, on an average, only one and a half columns for a week. The columns of the paper were filled with his prayer speeches. This, to him, was " hardly satisfactory." He, therefore, asked his readers' frank opinion as to the need of the publication.

Some correspondents wanted him to retire and close down the weeklies. " I detect anger in this advice . . . . My life line is cast in public service. I have not attained the state which is known as ' action in inaction '. My activity, therefore, seems at present to be destined to continue till the last breath. Nor is it capable of being divided into watertight compartments. The root of all lies in Truth, otherwise known to me as Non-violence. Hence the papers must continue as they are. ' One step enough for me '." Thus he wrote in the *Harijan* of September 28, 1947.

Under the caption ' My Duty,' he summarized the replies and wrote in the *Harijan* : " A fair number of replies have been received in answer to my query. The majority of the readers, with only a few exceptions, want the papers to be continued. The purpose of these letters is that the readers desire my views on the present day topics. This means that, probably, after my death, these will no longer be required."

Soon Gandhiji had to go to Noakhali, now in East Pakistan, on a peace mission, to restore confidence among the Hindus who lost lives and properties at the hands of the Muslims. The charge of the *Harijan* was temporarily vested in two of his colleagues. They soon resigned. In spite of the heavy burden, Gandhiji was prepared to take up the full responsibility provided the Trustees agreed. Earlier they expunged some of his remarks in a prayer meeting from the text reproduced in the *Harijan*. He wrote to one of the Trustees : " I fully realise *Harijan* does not belong to me. It really belongs to you who are conducting it with such diligence. Whatever authority I exercise is moral."[43]

It reads like a pathetic confession from one who not only built

[43] Pyarelal : *Mahatma Gandhi—The Last Phase* (Navajivan Publishing House, Ahmedabad, 1956), Vol. I, pp. 598–599.

up the morale of the people through his writings but led the nation to Independence. The colleagues in whom he had explicit faith, followers whom he made national leaders, people whom he made ministers were, on many occasions disagreeing with him on fundamental issues on which he felt his theories were based and his life principle dedicated. He was noticing the change and silently withdrew from the active field.

Gandhiji came to Delhi in May, 1947, and resumed writing for the *Harijan*, after a lapse of over six months. He wrote till the end, which came on January 30, 1948. He was killed by an assassin's bullet while going to conduct a prayer meeting in Delhi. The frail voice which moved and inspired millions of people stopped suddenly.

The next issue of the *Harijan* dated February 3, 1948 carried a photograph of Gandhiji on the front page. In a signed editorial— 'Out of the Ashes'—Dr. Rajendra Prasad, later elected President of the Republic of India, wrote :

" Mahatma Gandhi is no more in flesh and blood to speak to us, to console us, to guide us. But did he not tell us often that the body is mortal and transient, that the ' atma ' alone is immortal and imperishable ? Did he not tell us that God would keep his body so long as He had any use for it ? May be that his spirit freed from the limitations of the body will work all the more freely and create instruments to complete and fulfil what remains unaccomplished. May be that out of the ashes on the banks of the Jamuna will arise forces that will blow off all the mist and cloud of misunderstanding and distrust and establish the kind of peace and harmony for which he lived and worked and alas ! at last victim to the assassin's bullet. . . . "

" My life is my message," said Gandhiji. The life was gone ; so how messages could be poured through the columns of the *Harijan* ? The Journal announced the following item on February 15, 1948, under the signature of C. Rajagopalachari, the then Governor-General of India.

" The *Harijan* was Bapu's voice. And when his body has been consigned to the elements, the *Harijan* cannot go on. Any attempt to continue it must take a different shape."

It continued for some time. But the journal ceased publication soon.

3 / Running the Desk

" THE post card is now finished and slipped into the basket. Again he turns to the khadi stationery case. It is evidently an article that he is going to write, because he extracts a number of odd sheets, with writing on one side, but unused on the other. These are his ' pusti ' sheets, carefully collected from the blank pages on the backs of letters and other communications which come in endless numbers by each post. Bapu begins to write. The article seems to be of a serious nature, probably on some burning problem of the day, for a concentrated, even stern, look appears on his countenance. Before the article is finished he begins to feel sleepy. The pen is laid in the stand, and the tiny tin top is placed on the balm bottle. The ' pusti ' sheets are carefully put on one side, and Bapu turns and lies down on his *gaddi*. He removes his glasses, places them by the side of his pillow, and in one or two minutes he is fast asleep, and breathing as peacefully as a little child."[1]

Thus described Miss Mirabehn, the editor of the *Young India* and the *Harijan* running the desk.

In his book *Seven Months with Mahatma Gandhi* Shri Krishnadas gave another pen picture of the editor, in a different setting :

" As I found Mahatmaji looking grave at all times, I rarely went to him unless sent for. I suppose he assumed this seriousness in order to get through his work.

" Once or twice, I had even seen him cooling his forehead and head with ice. And yet everyday, whether in his room or in the train, he would go on calmly and patiently writing articles for the *Navajivan* and the *Young India*, while all round him people were making noise and the crowds were howling outside. Such complete mastery over the mind seemed to me unique. When he had done with the report of the Sasaram speech, he took up that of his Gauhati speech, but put it by, having looked through it a little."[2]

Unfortunately nobody has recorded a graphic picture of Gandhiji

---

[1] Mirabehn : *Incidents of Gandhiji's Life*, Ed. by Chandrashankar Shukla, (Vora & Co., Bombay, 1949), pp. 186–187.

[2] Krishnadas : *Seven Months with Mahatma Gandhi* (S. Ganesan & Co., Madras, 1928), p. 34.

while editing the *Indian Opinion* in South Africa. Whatever titbits we get, are from his own writing or passing references made by Mr. Henry Polak. But we can visualize a short and thin man, dressed in European attire, sitting on a chair, busily jotting down notes for publication in the next issue of the *Indian Opinion*. To Shri Chhaganlal, he wrote on October 26, 1906, from London :

" I have not a moment to spare. It is now 8-30 P.M. and I have not touched the Gujarati letter. If I can, I want to give you one leading article and one correspondence letter in continuation of what I have sent you already."

Gandhiji as we had seen, would insist on objective writing. As model, he had before him the example of the *Times*, London, as it used to be published in his student days. Gandhiji who started reading newspapers only in England, had a strong liking for the way the *Times* was edited. It was moderate in tone, accurate in presentation of news.

Mr. Henry Polak recalled many incidents showing Gandhiji's high standard of responsibility while running the *Indian Opinion*. " He was always exact in his facts and he would never magnify his case for the sake of argument."[3]

Once Mr. Polak commented vehemently " and somewhat acidly " on certain reports, appearing in other papers, relating to the Indian community in South Africa. Gandhiji advised him, to quote Mr. Polak, " . . . it would be much better for me, as a matter of professional self-discipline, and would have more desirable results for the cause of what we were both seeking to serve, if I were to model my style rather upon the moderation and objectiveness of the London *Times* than upon the more picturesque if less accurate ways of the ' cheaper,' press. " And Mr. Polak followed his advice.

He would, in turn, not hesitate to accept good advice from his colleagues. " I remember telling him once, with mock editorial gravity, that I could not send his ' copy ' to the printer unless he rewrote it, which he did with due humility and with an amused twinkle in his eye, " recalled Mr. Polak. Gandhiji had not yet acquired that commendable command over English which he

³ H. S. L. Polak : *Incidents of Gandhiji's Life*, Ed. by Chandrashankar Shukla, (Vora & Co., Bombay, 1949), p. 236.

developed in later years. Nor did he develop that news sense in that early period of his journalistic life.

But from the very beginning he was against stunt in journalism. He hated false or exaggerated reports. He abhorred discourtesy in writing. In an editorial note captioned ' Journalistic Courtesy ' in the *Indian Opinion* of November 3, 1906, he criticized the *Natal Advertiser* saying : " There are times when mockery is permissible, when one is desirous of defeating another's argument, but there can never be an excuse for vulgarity. We fear very much that our contemporary has overstepped the limits of journalistic courtesy in what purports to be a reply to our article on ' Durban and its unemployed ' published in the issue of the journal of 20th ultimo."

Under an unsigned short note—' What is journalism ? '— the *Indian Opinion* of January 19, 1907, wrote : " The *Natal Advertiser* continues to bestow attention upon us, even if it be at times without acknowledgment. We have read with great pain our contemporary's remarks on Mr. James Godfrey's address to the London Indian Society. We have always necessitated that the one true test of journalism is that it gives facts to the public. We are constrained to say that our contemporary ignominiously failed in conforming to the first days in the article we have referred to." The short note then gives facts about the case.

Under the sub-heading ' Back-door Journalism,' the *Indian Opinion* of February 2, 1907, criticized the paper, the *Natal Witness*, for misrepresentation of facts which *inter alia* said : " Without the Act practically no restrictions would have existed upon the back-door competition of the Arab Trade."

Again on February 9, 1907, the *Indian Opinion*, under the sub-heading ' Journalism of a Sort ' wrote : " Last week I called my readers' attention to the back-door methods of the *Witness*. This week the *Ladysmith Gazette* has made itself conspicuous. It refers to the *Indian Opinion* as being ' one of the mouth-pieces of nasty, cheap, coloured labour of Natal.' This seems to show that the editor does not read this journal or else he would have seen, on 29th December last, a leading article advocating repatriation of Indian indentured labourers and offering its cooperation in the matter. But I suppose we must not expect an editor to read a journal which he vilifies."

During Mr. Henry Polak's visit to India, in 1909–10, Gandhiji wrote : " Keep your standards right. Everything else will follow."

To his son Shri Manilal, Gandhiji wrote, as mentioned earlier, " You should write what is the truth in *Indian Opinion.*" What is truth in journalism ? How does it differ from accuracy ? Are they the same thing ? Truth is not only a question of knowledge. It means more. It means the balancing of judgment in a most disinterested manner. It may be achieved in a weekly ; but it is very difficult to be truthful in the daily newspaper. When we consider the condition in which it is produced, the number of agencies through which the news passes, and the speed with which it is gathered from all parts of the world, translated, transmitted, selected, sub-edited, and printed.

" Further, it is dependent on the time factor. In the hustle of a daily newspaper with a pull of conflicting interests always present and the necessity of pleasing a wide public never out of mind, truth in the sense of careful and balanced presentation can only with luck, and occasionally, emerge. Even the most highly trained and best informed journalist must be conscious as he writes that his thought and knowledge are not sufficiently mature and that had he not been writing to the habitual length and pattern of the particular publication, he might not have taken just precisely the view he did take. Whether his article is a report of complex events or an editorial comment on the significance of these events, to test it only by the accuracy of the facts it contains is to show an abysmal ignorance of the art of journalism. Any practised journalist can write a column which contains no single mis-statement of fact and which is yet a damned lie from the first word to the last. Similarly, incidental inaccuracies in fact or expression may occur in an article by an honest reporter or editorial writer who, with the sweat of his brow, attempts to reach the truth by a careful balancing of the fact and vigorous expression of his convictions."[4]

This is no apology for incorrect news or views. This is a point of view arising out of peculiar circumstances caused by the vast technological improvement which has completely revolutionized newspaper and turned it into a big commercial proposition.

In one of the unauthorised leaflets of the *Satyagraha* published

[4] Kingsley Martin : *The Press the Public Wants* (The Hogarth Press, London, 1947), p. 114.

between April 16 and April 28, 1919, Gandhiji wrote about the poems that were attributed to him. He denied his authorship. " My writings cannot be poisonous, they must be free from anger. . . . There can be no room for untruth in my writings. . . . My writings cannot but be free from hatred towards an individual. . . ."

Gandhiji, as an editor, would correct himself publicly if he found that some untruth had crept in his writings. To cite a typical example, he compared the Jallianwala Bagh massacre, immediately after the First World War, to that of Glenco. A correspondent drew his attention saying that the latter was much more horrible. In the next issue of the *Young India*, Gandhiji corrected the statement.

Mr. Jack C. Winslow narrated a similar incident during his first visit to Gandhiji as arranged by Mr. C. F. Andrews : " One characteristic incident of that visit remains with me. Charlie and I had left Bapu lying on the verandah, and Charlie was telling me about an article he had just written for the *Manchester Guardian* about the Satyagraha movement then in progress in Travancore. In glowing terms he had described how all eyes were now concentrated on this wonderful movement and no one was interested any longer in the proposed Government reforms. ' I will just go and show it to Bapu,' said Charlie, ' before I send it off ! ' Presently he returned, thoroughly crest-fallen. What did Bapu think of it ? I asked. ' Oh, ' said Charlie, Bapu said : ' Charlie, it is what you would like to be true : but it isn't true.' With all Bapu's idealism went a strong strain of realism, which Charlie Andrews sometimes lacked." [5]

Why are papers chary to the idea of correcting mistakes or publishing protests against misrepresentations ? A man can be misrepresented, his ideas may be twisted. He has to read such reports every day and cannot do anything unless he takes legal action against this deliberate action. It is even difficult to persuade a paper voluntarily to print even a letter of protest or correction.

The reason is psychological. No human being would like admitting himself in the wrong. Partly it is due to the papers' belief that today and tomorrow are news, but yesterday is history. They do

[5] Chandrashankar Shukla (Ed.) : *Reminiscences of Gandhiji* (Vora & Co., Bombay, 1951), p. 217.

not want to pin-point attention to old news, particularly if it was inaccurate. They desire to like their readers to assume that they are infallible. And often they get the desired result. To Gandhiji correction had a different meaning. In the *Harijan* of January 16, 1937, he wrote : " I know there are readers of *Harijan* who study many articles that appear from time to time in *Harijan*. The weekly is not published for providing momentary amusement or pleasure for the reader. It is designed to be a serious contribution to the *Harijan* cause in the widest sense of the term. It, therefore, often contains writings of more than transitory value. Hence serious errors need to be corrected. Such an error was detected in the *Harijan* of the 9th inst. at page 383, 2nd Column, line 2. Read ' sub-human ' for ' human '. "

Though he was well conversed with the subject he was writing about, he would invariably check the information. " Gandhiji loved beauty of language too and always appreciated a well-written article or letter. He was meticulous where his weekly articles for the *Harijan* were concerned. They were always given in the first instance to one of us to read and suggest any verbal or other amendments, and then finally edited by himself before being sent to the press."[6]

He would also try to guess the public reaction, whether that would hurt the feelings of the people. "I always aimed at establishing an intimate and clean bond between the editor and the readers," said he. He would not allow unfair criticism to be published in his journal. That, to him, constituted violence. He would not attack even when he was hit below the belt. Mrs. Annie Besant, in her journal the *New India*, for weeks, wrote slanderous articles against him. She went, as we saw, to the extent of advising the Government to arrest Gandhiji and stop his seditious activities once for all. In reply, Gandhiji did not say or write anything.

The British Press was at its worst critical mood so far as Gandhiji and Indian National Congress were concerned, during the period Gandhiji was in England, attending the Round Table Conference. The well-known British journalist, Mr. Solocombe, represented Gandhiji as prostrating himself before the Prince of Wales.

" Mr. Solocombe, " Gandhiji only remarked, " this does not do any credit to your imagination. I would bend the knee before

[6] *Illustrated Weekly of India* (Bombay, October 20, 1957).

the poorest scavenger . . . much less before the Prince of Wales, for the simple reason that he represented insolent might." [7]

He was called a ' simpleton.' Truth, to which he tried to clinch, was dismissed as humbug. British papers were full of indecent cartoons of Gandhiji.

" I referred to the vicious attacks upon him in certain of the London newspapers and expressed the hope that they did not trouble him unduly. ' No,' he said, ' they do not trouble me, but they pain me terribly. Think of how fully and freely I have talked to the reporters. I have told them everything. And yet they print these slanderous lies. It hurts me that such things can be done.' ' But,' he continued with a smile, ' I don't let them worry me. They do not harm. Nothing can injure truth.' " [8]

But he was disappointed in British journals. The *Times*, London, could no more serve as his ideal.

He was always ready to weigh opposition points of view. Here is a typical example of his approach to controversial topics.

Under the caption ' No and yes,' he wrote in the *Young India* : " Comrade Saklatwala is dreadfully in earnest. His sincerity is transparent. His sacrifices are great. His passion for the poor is unquestioned. I have, therefore, given his fervent appeal that close attention which that of a sincere patriot and humanitarian must command. But in spite of all my desire to say ' yes ' to his appeal, I must say ' no ' if I am to return sincerity for sincerity and if I am to act according to my faith."

" On occasions, Gandhiji wrote to individual editors, sometimes acknowledging the weight of a point in criticism and at other times explaining his point of view in great detail with an earnestness which clearly showed his anxiety to remove misunderstanding rather than silence criticism." [9]

Gandhiji thus won over, even the hostile press. He encouraged the editors to express their views freely. Through his weeklies he would argue with them if they opposed his views on non-coopera-

---

[7] C. Rajagopalachari and J. C. Kumarappa (Ed.) : *The Nation's Voice* (Navajivan Publishing House, Ahmedabad, 1947), p. 116.

[8] John Haynes Holmes : *My Gandhi* (George Allen & Unwin Ltd., London, 1954), p. 44.

[9] India Government : *Report of the Press Commission, Part II*, Comp. by J. Natarajan (Manager of Publications, Delhi, 1954), p. 155.

tion. " The variety of subjects he touched on quickened public discussion and as he always struck an unusual note, the arguments had a perennial interest."[10]

Another great quality of Gandhiji, the editor, was his direct and forthright manner in conveying things. Direct presentation was the beauty of all his writings. He had a clear thinking and knew well what he was going to say. He would put forth his ideas and arguments in crisp short sentences, pregnant with meaning. From the *Indian Opinion* to the *Harijan* was a long way and we discover with the passing of each year a mature journalist in him.

" 'Who wrote these two articles,' asked Gandhiji, pointing out the editorials from the latest issue of the *Young India* when Shri Prabhu, the *de facto* editor of the journal went to hand over the charge.

" He signified his preference for one ; the other he criticised. Giving his reasons he said :

' In the first, you have said all that you wanted to say in a direct manner, while the writer of the second article indulges in all sorts of innuendoes and says things which he does not really mean.'

' When you want to say a thing, don't beat about the bush, don't indulge in euphemisms and pin-pricks, but tell it in a straight-forward way,' he advised."

But he was in a devastating mood when he wrote the following letter to a young journalist on June 7, 1919 :

" It is dangerous to call me 'Revered Father' as you will see presently. I have no doubt about your prodigality. The very slovenliness of your writing is eloquent proof of it and it certainly requires a prodigal son to write to his adopted 'Revered Father' a letter containing almost as many corrections as there are lines in it written anyhow and unrevised. A son frugal in his adjectives, obedient in reality, would write to his father, especially when he is deliberately adopted, a careful letter written in his best handwriting. If he has not enough time, he will write only a line, but he would write it neatly.

" Your article on Mr. Jamnadas was ill-conceived and hurriedly written. It could not be printed in *Young India*, nor is it worth printing in any other paper. You will not reform Jamnadas by letters of that character, nor will you benefit the public thereby. Your second article is not much better. . . . You really lose yourself in the exuberance of your own verbosity. If you will give more attention to the thought than a mere lengthening out of your story, you will produce readable matter . . . . "

Shri Krishnadas narrated the following incident :[11]

" Today being Monday, Mahatmaji's day of silence, I have to be constantly by his side ; but as I had to write the article I could not spend much time with

[10] Ibid., p. 203.

[11] Krishnadas : *Seven Months with Mahatma Gandhi* (S. Ganesan & Co., Madras, 1928), p. 115.

him. At three in the afternoon he sent for me through Devadas. He had given me a second Urdu message concerning the Moplah rebellion from the pen of Maulana Azad Sobani to translate into English. Knowing, as I did, that he had not been particularly impressed by the Maulana's first message on the same subject, I had not yet taken up the second. When I said that, he wrote down for me the words, ' Just condense the whole into a single paragraph.' This I did. I wanted also to explain my article ' Under Swaraj ', as I had written, as also a note on the arrest of Shri Sengupta of Chittagong. He looked through them and wrote the following remarks : ' Under Swaraj is shaping itself all right ; you should finish it. The Chittagong note is not bright enough, and is somewhat censorious.' I explained that it was my intention to complete ' Under Swaraj ' with one more paragraph. He wrote in reply, ' As it is, it does not read complete, or as if it is ending with two or three sentences—but try.' I said that I was under the impression that the article was growing too long, and I had therefore thought fit to cut it short. But now I would write rather elaborately. Mahatmaji nodded assent."

Shri Sri Prakasa, a colleague of Gandhiji, was sent to Jodhpur, much later in 1942, to collect first-hand information of certain happenings over there. He visited the place, met people and prepared a statement which was submitted to Gandhiji. The rest may be put through the pen of Shri Sri Prakasa.

" Within this period of my stay at Sevagram, Monday, the day of keeping silence, came on which he would speak to nobody. Same day he devoted in writing articles for the *Harijan*. After reading my report, he prepared a brief for the *Harijan* and sent it to me for checking whether he had not missed any point. I remember that my type-written report was spread into 14 or 15 sheets, of foolscap size from which he had prepared the brief for the *Harijan* in only half a column. I was surprised how he had put in all the facts contained in my long report in a few lines. I read his brief several times but I could not say that he had missed any of the points presented by me in the report."[12]

" As was his wont, he would write a great deal for the *Harijan*. Anything written by someone else was published in that paper only after being closely scrutinised by him."[13]

Shri A. S. Iyengar recalled Gandhiji's deep consideration for the press. He went through all the reports of the All India Congress Committee proceedings and would make necessary changes in each copy submitted. " As for the corrections he made in the copy, I must say that they were very vital and essential, revealing his superior knowledge of editing including grammar and punctuation,

[12] Sri Prakasa : *The Navabharat Times* : *Sunday Supplement* (Delhi, June 2, 1963).
[13] Rajendra Prasad : *At the feet of Mahatma Gandhi* (Hind Kitabs, Bombay, 1955), pp. 238-239.

and all this he did whilst the proceedings were on, and whilst he was thinking out his own speech." [14]

On October 20, 1921, after the prayers, Gandhiji said :

"When lately all sorts of rumours of my arrest were in the air, I expressed the wish that the publication of *Young India* should be suspended. But since then (and even so recently as the day before yesterday), many friends have approached me and given me their assurance that there was no need to worry over *Navajivan* and *Young India* and that they would be able to conduct both in a manner worthy of their past, during my absence in gaol. I am not particular about *Navajivan*, but my belief is that it would not be easy to preserve the style and individuality of *Young India*. But the thing may be possible if I can give the necessary training to people from now. For this I have chosen Pyarelal and Krishnadas. Every one of us here in the Ashram should think it his duty to become responsible for, and specialise in, some particular work."[15]

Rajkumari Amrit Kaur, writing in the *Harijan* of April 11, 1948, after Gandhiji's death mentioned :

" To those of us who had the privilege of working with Gandhiji every week when the *Harijan* was being edited by him, it seems strange to be writing for its columns without submitting the same to the searching gage of that prince of journalists. The care and thought he bestowed on whatever he himself wrote, the eagle eye with which he vetted every word of what even a man like Mahadev Desai wrote, his insistence on right expression, on the adherence to the truth where facts were concerned, on the necessity of not using one word more than necessary, his appreciation of a good literary style, his ruthless weeding out of much or wholesale discarding of what one thought was good, all these are never-to-be forgotten lessons. But the remembrance of them makes one pause and wonder whether any one of our poor efforts can ever come up to the high standard of journalism which was one of Gandhiji's incomparable contribution to public life. . . . "

No subject was big for Gandhiji's editorial : none was too small. Louis Fischer, the celebrated journalist, said that Gandhiji would attach equal importance to a letter written to President Roosevelt as much to an article on the subject of rape.

Gandhiji was very much laconic in speech. He seldom used a superfluous word. Each comma or colon conveyed something or the other. Moreover, his expression was much less than his profound thinking on the subject. It was like an iceberg, nine-tenth beneath the water and only one-tenth above. He had suggestions to give on each item published in the journal. Everything he wrote

---

[14] A. S. Iyengar : *All Through the Gandhian Era* (Hind Kitabs Ltd., Bombay, 1950), p. 98.

[15] Krishnadas : *Seven Months with Mahatma Gandhi* (S. Ganesan & Co., Madras, 1928), p. 108.

was with a purpose. He never jotted a line for mere writing's sake.

In preaching an ideal, Gandhiji would go deeper in the matter. He would suggest living up to the principle enunciated. In the May 13, 1939, issue of the *Harijan*, he wrote : " The propagation of truth and non-violence can be done less by books than by actually living those principles. I do not say that we may not issue books and newspapers . . . we must make a sincere effort to enter into his mind and to understand his view-point . . . without that book and newspaper propaganda is of no avail."

It was more. It was a self-educative process. The Editor has much more responsibility in conducting a viewspaper. He wrote in the *Young India* of July 2, 1925:

" I have taken up Journalism not for its sake but merely as an aid to what I have conceived to be my mission in life. My mission is to teach by example and precept under severe restraint the use of matchless weapon of ' Satyagraha ' which is a direct corollary of non-violence and truth. I am anxious, indeed I am impatient, to demonstrate that there is no remedy for the many ills of life save that of non-violence. It is a solvent strong enough to melt the stoniest heart. To be true to my faith, therefore, I may not write in anger or malice. I may not write idly. I may not write merely to excite passion. The reader can have no idea of the restraint I have to exercise from week to week in the choice of topics on my vocabulary. It is a training for me. It enables me to peep into myself and to make discoveries of my weaknesses. Often my vanity dictates a smart expression or my anger a harsh adjective. It is a terrible ordeal but a fine exercise to remove these weeds. The reader sees the page of *Young India* fairly well dressed up and sometimes, with Romain Rolland, he is inclined to say ' what a fine old man he must be.' Well, let the world understand that the fineness is carefully and prayerfully cultivated."

Newspaper or viewspaper is a social institution. Its success, as is admitted, depends to the extent in which, through news and views, it prepares and educates the minds of the readers, who are educated, half educated or ill educated. Unfortunately papers mostly cater to the lower taste of the reader, through sensation mongering rather than educating him for better citizenship. A crime or sex story serves as an outlet for making imagination for such a readership. He pictures himself as a spy tracking the murderer or an out-law defying law and God. This kind of journalism satisfies a genuine craving in him. It is, in a way, an extension of his personality.

We often hear ' Readers want this.' This is how an average reader is led to think so. Newspapers have now become industries with the greater application of science and technology to boost its mass circulation. It is profitable, efficient, but costly. It cannot do without advertisements, rates of which have increased enormously. Old time newspapers or viewspapers found it difficult to maintain themselves. Editors like Sir Robert Donland, Mr. J. A. Spender and Mr. A. G. Gardiner lost their positions as they declined to adjust to the new pattern of thinking. Business Managers and Proprietors took their places. Papers changed their character. Headlines became catchy ; editorial superficial. In Great Britain serious papers, which depended so long for careful reporting and intelligent comments followed the methods of crime journals with a view to making these popular. Popular Press, thus, is an antidote to education. It gives the public news and views which they read on their breakfast table or in a train or bus coming tired from the day's work.

Gandhiji under the circumstances, had an uphill task. He belonged to the category of Spender and Gardiner, but unlike them, had to write mostly for half educated readers. To turn the scale, he was training a band of journalists inspired with ideals. He was trying to raise the level of his readers. But this proved transitory, as we saw the fate of his paper after his death. He could not, side by side with his educative role as an editor, change the curriculum for schools and colleges which could educate the younger generation with advanced political, economic and social ideas so as to appreciate a high level journal.

In this context Shri S. Natarajan's description of the condition of the press in India at a time when Gandhiji appeared on the scene, is worth quoting :

" Round about twenties had certain characteristics in that a small staff looked after the working of the newspaper. Commercial page or sports page were appearing though there were not much of specialisation. Cinema reviews were regular feature. There were advertisements but advertisers commanded very little influence with the press. The front page was a page of advertisements and not news as it is now-a-days. There was not much of theory or practice of journalism as was done in other countries. Even the reporters could not know shorthand. Horniman's claim that he could make a journalist out of any one, was the order of the day."[16]

The reader was no better. He cared more for sensational news.

[16] S. Natarajan : *A History of the Press in India* (Asia Publishing House, Bombay, 1962), p. 224.

G—6

Anything unusual was hot favourite with him. To him, to quote a well-known cliche, it was not news if a dog bit a man ; but if a man bit a dog, that was news. But Gandhiji's concept of journalism was different. He would give the reader correct stories. He would abide by truth. But Mr. Kingsley Martin said :

" . . . we must face the fact that comparatively few people have a passion for truth as a principle or care about public events continuously when these do not obviously affect their own lives. People want to be pleased, and truth is not always pleasing. The scientist may have a disinterested desire for knowledge in his particular science, but he rarely applies the discipline of the laboratory to politics. Newspapers have always depended on their public, and the public hands out fortunes, not to those who present the truest possible picture of public events, but to the show man who can provide the most entertaining kaleidoscope."[17]

Mr. Scott Mowrer does not agree that newspapers should function like a school—conducting study courses for the education of the people. The newspaper is to give the news of the day. In the selection of news editors have to be careful otherwise it might be one-sided. It is also to be balanced so as to give cheap news for it. Now there is a tendency on the part of the newspaper to have as many sections as possible so that each group of reading public gets the thing it wants.[18]

Incidentally, what did Gandhiji think about the sensational press ? We can get an idea from the following report. " In one of the voyages to England, his fellow passengers formed a club called ' Billy Boats ' and published a sheet, ' Scandal Times.' The name suggested the materials in it and they brought an issue to Gandhiji and asked for his opinion of it. He took the sheet, extracted the pin which fastened the leaves and told them that he had taken the most precious thing from the sheets."[19]

He was a serious and fastidious editor. Before starting the *Harijan*, Gandhiji in a letter to Shri G. D. Birla, wrote : " I would warn you against issuing the English edition unless it is properly got up, contains readable English material and translations are accurate. It would be much better to be satisfied with the Hindi edition only than to have an indifferently edited English weekly."

[17] Kingsley Martin : *The Press the Public Wants* (The Hogarth Press, London, 1947), p. 67.
[18] League of Nations : *The Educational Role of the Press* (Paris, 1934), pp. 43–44.
[19] B.B.C. Portrait : *Impressions of Mahatma Gandhi* (September 30, 1956).

Gandhiji by nature was quite shy. " It has taught me the economy of words," he admitted. It also helped him in disciplining his thoughts. " A thoughtless word hardly ever escapes my tongue or pen." [20]

He reminiscenced the South African days and said :

" Indeed the journal (the *Indian Opinion*) became for me a training in self-restraint, and for friends a medium through which to keep in touch with my thoughts. In fact the tone of *Indian Opinion* compelled the critic to put a curb on his own pen. . . . For me it became a means for the study of human nature in all its caste and shades. . . . It made me thoroughly understand the responsibility of a journalist. . . ."[21]

Gandhiji knew the power of the press very well. It could make or mar a case. If used judiciously, a paper could do immense good to the people and in the hands of irresponsible people, it would work havoc. Like Mr. A. G. Gardiner he could say : " There is nothing more tempting to the journalist than to be an incendiary." He knew that it was the short cut to success. It was always easier to appeal to the lower passions of men than to their better instincts. He was convinced—and throughout his life he followed it — that the aim of journalism was service.

He warned, " The newspaper press is a great power, but just as an unchained torrent of water submerges whole countryside and devastates crops, even so an uncontrolled pen serves but to destroy. It can be profitable only when exercised from *within*. If this line of reasoning is correct, how many of the journals in the world would stand the test ? But who would stop those that are useless ? And who should be the judge ? The useful and the useless must, like good and evil generally, go on together and man must make his choice."[22]

The year 1946 ushered in a new atmosphere surcharged with emotion. The Cabinet Mission came on an exploratory mission. Delhi became, in April, ' a seething cauldron of rumours.' Newspapers, which were indulging in kite flying got a rebuke from Gandhiji. " The newspaperman has become a walking plague," he told a prayer meeting gathering. " All that appears in the papers is looked upon as God's truth. . . . That is bad."[23]

Gandhiji had, of late, been greatly distressed at the general fall in the standard of the Press. He hated speculation. This was

[20] M. K. Gandhi : *An Autobiography or The Story of My Experiments with Truth* (Navajivan Publishing House, Ahmedabad, 1956).

[21] Ibid., p. 286.   [22] Ibid., p. 287.

[23] D. G. Tendulkar : *Mahatma* (V. K. Jhaveri and D. G. Tendulkar, Bombay, 1953), Vol. VII, p. 115.

sometimes mischievous and often misleading. He hated fabrication of news ; he disliked the emphasis often laid on things of little value. He did not believe in so called journalistic ' scoop '. As one who believed in the service to the community, he would advise against publication of doubtful news. It was, he felt, the duty of the press to withhold publication of it until it was released from authentic sources. He laid the greatest stress imaginable on the good or the bad influence the Press could wield on its readers.

Gandhiji was quick to reprove the Press, if there was too much of speculation. " If I were appointed dictator for a day in the place of the Viceroy, I would stop all newspapers ". " With the exception of *Harijan*, of course," he added. That was just before the transfer of power.

In an article, ' Standards of Journalism ', published in the *Harijan* on April 11, 1948—after the death of Gandhiji—Rajkumari Amrit Kaur, testified : " . . . . The *Harijan* was read over the whole of India and in many countries abroad not only because of the rich food for thought which Gandhiji's writings always give but also because readers knew that what facts they gleaned therefrom were cent per cent true. And after having read the *Harijan* there was always the satisfaction that one had learnt something that one did not know before. And how obvious that ' something ' often was. . . ."

He was against accepting anonymous articles for the journal, though, in earlier days in South Africa, he published many unsigned articles. " Why are you afraid of signed articles ? " he would ask contributors. He was the most well-informed editor with scores of self-styled correspondents sending despatches regularly. They were all unpaid. He read everything sent by them and replied to important ones. He shared joys and sorrows, ups and downs, with them. That is how he could feel the pulse of the nation through a fleet of self-styled correspondents. They would, sometime, bring to his notice important official documents. The most celebrated of them was the publication of the secret circular issued by the Government in 1942, under the direction of Mr. Puckle, the then Home Secretary. Gandhiji explained :

" I have had the good fortune to have friends who have supplied me with titbits of national importance, such as I am presenting to the public here. Mahadev Desai reminds me that such an occasion occurred some 7 years ago, when a friend had unearthed the famous Hallet circular. Such was also an occasion, when the late Shraddhanandji was given an important document, though not of the sensational character as the Hallet circular, or Sir Frederick Puckle's very interesting production and that of his lieutenant Shri D. C. Das. The pity of it is that the circulars were secret. They must thank me for giving the performance as wide publicity as I can. For, it is good for the public to know to what lengths the Government can go in their attempt to suppress national movements, however, innocent, open and above-board they are. Heaven knows how many such secret instructions have been issued which have never seen the light of day . . . let the public know that these circulars are an additional reason for the cry of 'Quit India ' which comes not from the lips but the aching hearts of millions. Let the masses know that there are many other ways of earning a living than betraying the national interests. Surely, it is no part of their duty to lend themselves to the very questionable methods as evidenced by Sir Frederick Puckle's instructions."

How could he manage the voluminous correspondence and newspaper reports ? Shri Pyarelal, his erstwhile Secretary, said, that he evolved, through experience, a quick and efficient method of scanning the items. Nothing escaped him ; nor did he spend much time on these. His talks with Shri Prabhu, when taking charge of the *Young India* and regarding which references had already been made, will be of interest in this context.

" Gandhiji looking at the page of *Young India* which was made up of news in brief, asked me who gathered those news items. Being told that I was responsible for them, he asked me whence I culled the news. I said I made the clipping from the latest issues of the various Indian journals which were received in exchange for *Young India* and the *Bombay Chronicle*.

" How much time do you spend in gathering these items ? " he asked.

" I replied that it took me hardly more than half an hour to clip and paste these news items required to make up the page.

' You spend only half an hour over them ', he remarked in surprise. ' Do you know ', he added 'when I edited *Indian Opinion* in South Africa, we received some 200 papers in exchange and I used to go through all of them carefully throughout the week and I culled each news item only after I was fully satisfied that it would be of real service to the readers. When one takes up the responsibility of editorship, he must discharge it with a full sense of one's duty. That is the only way journalism should be practised—don't you agree with me?"[24]

[24] *Gandhiji—His Life and Work*, Published on his 75th Birthday October 2, 1944. Edited by D. G. Tendulkar and others (Published by Karnatak Publishing House, Bombay), pp. 272-273.

4 / *Editor with a Difference*

GANDHIJI proved that style was the man. To him words flowed like the rippling rivulet. Like a bird he chirped at ease, and merrily too. His English was biblical. Some compared it with that of masters like Ruskin or Thoreau.

We had seen how meticulous he was about the use of English words ; how carefully he chose the correct word at the right moment. Above all, his sentences were simple and lucid. The fact that he wrote from his heart made his writings all the more absorbing.

This style was a complete departure from the one that was in vogue in India when he reached the country. Giants like Shri Surendranath Banerjea, Shri Bipin Chandra Pal, Shri Balgangadhar Tilak, Shri Aurobindo Ghose were writing in their Macaulayan style. These writings were heavy in form and content. Sentences were unusually long. For an average reader these were difficult to follow. The following, for example, from Shri Ambika Charan Mazumdar's presidential address before the Lucknow Session (1916) of the Indian National Congress will illustrate the point :

" There are, however, those who say ' not yet.' Not yet : Then ' when? ' — asks the Indian nationalist. But here the oracle is dumb and echo only answers— ' when! ' Edwin Bevan's parable of the ' Patient and the Steel Frame ' is cited and the people are strictly enjoined to lie in peace and possess their souls in patience until their political ' Nirvana ' is accomplished. Simile and metaphor are not safe guides in practical life, for all fables are but fallacies clothed in equivocal language which captivates the imagination and deludes the reason. For even the patient ' steel frame ' required a gradual relaxation and occasional re-adjustment of his splints and bandages and, above all, a steady, substantial improvement in his dietary arrangements, as after all it is the food and nourishment and not the splint and bandages, that are calculated to give him strength and cure him of his injuries. You cannot indefinitely keep him on milk and sago to help either the knitting of the bones or the ' granulation of the flesh.' Our critics however, would enjoin ' perfect quiet and repose ' without prescribing any kind of diet until the people shall have, in their spirit of quiescence, fully recovered themselves in their steel frame. If any illustration were actually needed, one might fairly suggest that the case of either the swimmer or the rider would probably furnish a more apposite object lesson. You cannot expect the one to be an expert jockey without training him on the back of a horse, as you cannot expect the other to be an expert swimmer without allowing him to go into the water. There must be repeated falls and duckings before any efficiency can be attained by either. . . . There is a school for the lawyer, the physician, the educationist and the engineer where he can obtain his passport and begin his profession ; but is there any school or college where an aspirant can be admitted to his degree for self-government ? It is through self-government that the art of self-government can be either taught or acquired. . . . In the words of Mr. Gladstone, it is the institution of self-government which constitutes the best training ground for self-government. . . . "

Compare this Macaulayan amplitude and richness of phrasing and weight of trajectory learning with Gandhiji's wisely utilitarian, clear and direct language. In his appeal to the people of Gujarat, in 1922,[1] he said :

" Let him who wants, come. Let him who can, join the fray. Everyone is invited, but the hungry alone shall come to the feast. Others, even if they come, will only be sorry. He who has no hunger, will not relish even a dry crust of bread. Likewise, those who understand non-cooperation can alone stand by it. He who understands finds things easy. For those who do not, everything is difficult. What is the use of a mirror to the blind ?

" The times are difficult. Let us not take a thoughtless step, lest we may rue it. . . . Civil disobedience of laws. We are no longer ignorant of it. Jail is its inevitable destination. And we can court it. Why can we not do as much ? It is not so difficult. But— ?

" But if martial law is declared ? If Gurkhas come ? If Tommy Atkins comes ? Suppose they bayonet us, shoot us, make us crawl ? They are welcome. Let them come. But if we are asked to crawl ? Then too, we must be ready to die rather than crawl. We shall then only die by the bayonet instead of the plague. We are not likely to run away, if we are fired on : we have now acquired so much strength that we will receive the bullets on our chests, like playthings. We shall convert the Gurkhas into our brothers. If not, what happiness is greater than dying at the hands of a brother ? Even we say this, we feel proud.

" But if—

" I am confident this time that timid Gujarati will show its mettle. But as I write, my pen is heavy. Whenever did Gujarati hear gunshots ? When did it see rivers of blood flowing ? Will Gujarata withstand shots fired like crackers ?

---

[1] K. M. Munshi : *Gandhi : The Master* (Rajkamal Publications Ltd., Delhi, 1948), pp. 52–53.

Heads broken like earthen pots ? If Gujarata sees others' heads broken, it will be immortal. Why do you want training ? Confidence ? You will never acquire confidence by a Congress resolution. It is God who helps the weak. God alone gives courage. Whom Rama protects, none can injure. He has given us the body. Let Him, if he wants, take it away. Even if you so desire you cannot treasure up your body. Like money, it has to be spent in noble acts. What is a nobler occasion for giving up life than when you are combating this atrocity ? Whoever believes thus sincerely, will receive bullets with his bare chest, his face smiling."

Or take another sample of his political writings:

" Politically India's status has never been so reduced as under the British regime. No reforms have given real political power to the people. The tallest of us have to bend before foreign authority. The rights of free expression of opinion and free association have been denied to us, and many of our country-men are compelled to live in exile abroad and they cannot return to their own homes. All administrative talent is killed, and the masses have to be satisfied with petty village offices and clerk-ships.

" Culturally, the system of education has torn us from our moorings, our training has made us hug the very chains that bind us.

" Spiritually, compulsory disarmament has made us unmanly, and the presence of an alien army of occupation, employed with deadly effect, to crush in us the spirit of resistance, has made us think that we cannot look after ourselves or even defend our homes and families from the attacks of thieves, robbers and miscreants."

While on the river Brahmaputra he wrote :

" The steamer is gliding on the river. We are all sitting on the deck. The river looks wide as the sea. We can see the banks, far away on either side ; the distance between the two may be two miles or a little over. The voyage will take about fifteen days. Sublime peace has descended on the river. The moon, hidden behind the clouds, spreads a soft light over the waters. The propellers, even as they cut their way through the water, hum sweetly. Except for this hum, peace is over everything and everywhere. I alone have no peace of mind. The steamer is not mine, the river is not mine. I travel in the steamer through the courtesy of the power of which I am tired, which has made India decrepit, lustreless, poor."

Or consider the obituary written by him, after the murder of Swami Shradhanand by a Muslim fanatic in Delhi :

"Death is no fiend. He is the truest of friends. He is like sleep. Though Shraddhanand is dead, he is yet living. He is living in a truer sense than when he moved about in our midst in his giant body. The family in which he was born, the nation to which he belonged, are to be congratulated upon so glorious a death as his. He lived a hero ; he has died a hero. But there is another side to the shield. The joy of his death is tempered by the sorrow that an erring, misguided brother has been the cause of it .... It does not matter to me what prompted the deed. The fault is ours. The newspaperman has become a walking plague. He spreads the contagion of lies and calumnies. He exhausts the foul vocabulary of his dialect and injects his virus into the unsuspecting, and often receptive, minds of his readers. Leaders, intoxicated with the exuberance of their own language, have not known to put a curb upon their tongues or pens. It is therefore we, the educated and the semi-educated class, that are responsible for the hot fever which possessed Abdul Rashid."

What a contrast was the peroration in the old Johnsonian style, by the 'Thunderer of Bengal', Shri Surendranath Banerjea. The occasion was the unveiling of the portrait of Dadabhai Naoroji in the Cowasji Jehangir Hall, Bombay, in 1919 :

" The truest memorial that we can have of the illustrious dead is to raise tabernacles in our hearts in their honour, to devote ourselves to the worship of those principles which were theirs and to the furtherance of those aims which were their lifework. Then will these great men, emancipated from the fetters of flesh and blood, live in our midst in a higher form of existence and be imperishable guides in our outward march which must lead to the accomplishment of our highest destinies. Dadabhai Naoroji will be one such leader. You may have your busts, your statues, your portraits. They serve a useful purpose, they remind us of their mortal existence and of their imperishable work. But let not our reverence, our affection and our esteem be confined to mere dead forms, but let them be a living source of inspiration to us. Let them raise us to the higher atmosphere fragrant with the breath of these immortals and inspire us with a resolve to incorporate into our daily life the ideals which they have left for our instruction and guidance. Let us imprint upon our minds the lessons of sobriety, moderation, of lifelong devotion to the Mother Land which Naoroji has taught us. Then we shall have raised in his honour a memorial more lasting than brass or marble, a memorial transmissible from age to age, that will become the lasting heritage of our people in the rich possession of those moral qualities which are the truest guarantees of continued and undying national progress."

Gandhiji not only revolutionized the political thinking of the day, but English writing of his countrymen as well. It had no screaming headline, no catchy sub-headings or magic typography. But it was universally read.

" His thunder acquires a serve majesty, his appeal its persuasiveness, his confession its poignancy, as much by proper use of the proper word as by his personality. Sometimes, he is slyly humorous or playful . . . . With him, beauty of expression has to be a humble housemaid to Truth."[2]

The *Harijan* was first published in 1933. Shri Jawaharlal Nehru got copies of it while under detention. " I was delighted," Shri Nehru wrote to Gandhiji, from Dehradun gaol, after reading the first two copies of the *Harijan*, " to see the old rapier touch of

[2] K. M. Munshi : *Gujarata and its Literature*, (Longmans, Green & Co., Ltd., Calcutta, 1935), p. 312.

overmuch kindness and inexhaustible patience which extinguishes, or as you say, neutralizes the opponent."[3]

Younger generation of writers got influenced by his style. They tried to emulate him. Gone were the days of pompous style or verbosity. Not only contributors to the *Young India* or the *Harijan* but those to other papers and magazines started writing in simple English. A new class of journalists were coming to the fore. More important than the style was the content of his writing. The subject-matter he chose was down to the ground. Gandhiji was able to divert the attention of the rising journalists and authors from cities to villages. He impressed on them the fact that India lived in her villages ; that the journalist's or author's job was to write about village and villagers. Thus he was able to put the village of India on the wider and lively canvas of Indian writing. The Gandhian era of writing — a golden era — came into existence.

Presiding over the Gujarat Literary Conference on November 2, 1936, Gandhiji asked :

". For whose sake are we going to have our literature ? Not certainly for the great gentry of Ahmedabad. They can afford to engage literary men and have great libraries in their homes. But what about the poor man at the well who with unspeakable abuse is goading his bullocks to pull the big leather bucket ? Years ago I had asked Narasimharao, who I am sorry is too aged and ill to be here in our midst, if he could give me something, inspired tunes or ditties, which this man at the well could lustily sing and forget for ever the filthy abuse ? I have hundreds of such folks for whom I want real life-giving literature. How am I to do so ? I live in Segaon today where in a population of six hundred a little over ten are literate. . . .

" I should have loved to bring with me a Segaon boy here, I have not done so. What would he do here ? He would find himself in strange world.

" As I am speaking to you just now, I think of Dean Farrar and his book on the life of Christ. I may fight the British rule, but I do not hate the English or their language. In fact, I appreciate their literary treasures. And Dean Farrar's book is one of the rare treasures of the English language. You know how he laboured to produce that book ? He read everything about Jesus in English language, and then he went to Palestine, saw every place and spot in the Bible that he could identify, and then wrote the book in faith and prayer for the masses in England, in a language which all of them could understand. It is not in Dr. Johnson's style but in the easy style of Dickens. Here have we men like Farrar, who will produce great literature for the village folk ? Our literary men will pour on Kalidas and Bhavabhuti, and English authors, and will give

[3] From a letter from Shri Jawaharlal Nehru to Gandhiji.

us imitations. I want them to go to villages, study them, and give something life-giving."[4]

The Gandhian impact on contemporary Indian literature was great. As regards the writer's choice of language, one result of the Gandhian influence had been a general preference for the mother tongue or the regional language, and occasionally a purposeful bilingualism, the same writer handling with mastery his own mother tongue as well as English. Besides, whatever the language medium chosen, the stress has been more on simplicity and clarity and immediate effectiveness than on ornateness or profundity and artistry ; and this has been as marked in English writing as in writing in the regional language. As regards the choice of themes and the portrayal of character, the Gandhian influence has been no less marked. There has been a more or less conscious shift of emphasis from the city to the village, or there is implied a contrast between the two — urban luxury and sophistication on the one hand and rural modes and manners on the other.[5]

Gandhiji, in fact, brought in many new elements which introduced a fresh life in the field of journalism. "As a result of his wide interest, his genius for simplification, his eagerness to reach the largest number of people, and the startling nature of his activities, there was a quickening of life in journalism. Many of his followers were moved to write and publish in the Indian languages, and in imitation of his own direct style they wrote a simple prose. Regional journalism began to acquire an importance and there was hardly an area of the country which did not have its newspapers." ?[6]

Gandhiji's English had been praised by knowledgeable persons. Did he ever make a mistake in the use of this foreign language ? The following piece appearing in the *Harijan* of December 23, 1939, should be read with interest.

Under the caption, ' My Handicap,' Gandhiji wrote :

" I wonder if all journalists, having to write in English, feel the handicap which I do. The reflection arises from a stupid use I made of the verb ' cavil ' in my note on a learned Englishman's letter partly reproduced in *Harijan* of 2nd

[4] D. G. Tendulkar : *Mahatma* (V. K. Jhaveri and D. G. Tendulkar, Bombay, 1952), Vol. IV, pp. 114–115.

[5] K. R. Srinivasa Iyengar : *Indian Writing in English* (Asia Publishing House, Bombay, 1962), p. 22.

[6] S. Natarajan : *A History of the Press in India* (Asia Publishing House, Bombay, 1962), p. 190.

December. In my comment I said, ' The writer seems to cavil at the demand for Independence as distinguished from Dominion Status.' The learned writer draws my attention to the meaning of the word ' cavil ' as implying captious criticism of which, he says, he was wholly unconscious. I take great care in the use of English words. With all my care, however, I cannot make up for my imperfect knowledge of a foreign tongue. I had never known the dictionary meaning of the word. I must have picked up the word in the course of reading or hearing. I had hitherto given it an innocent meaning in the sense of strongly objecting. Knowing the writer as I do, I could never think of him as raising captious objection. I have apologised to him for the unconscious error. It is good that he drew my attention to it. Heaven only knows how often, though wholly unconsciously I must have offended persons simply because of my ignorance of English language and its subtle idiom and usage. The language expands with the expansion of its people. I must struggle in the best manner I can and expect the indulgence of the English readers who, knowing my limitations, should believe that where my language seems to offend, the offence is wholly unintended."

Gandhiji undoubtedly introduced a new and a noble element in the field of journalism. It was his approach — his human approach — which gave his writings a character. He never looked upon the reading public as target for propaganda. He regarded them as living reality whose interests, tastes and foibles he willingly shared and fathomed in order to bring a real change in the country and the world. He belonged to the people by identifying himself with them and wrote about their feelings and aspirations. His voice was the voice of humanity — not the voice of a pamphleteer. He wanted to change the human character and would never be satisfied by changing a few laws or acts, here and there.

To whom should the journalist be loyal to ? To the proprietor, to one's own self or to the particular class he belongs to ? This has often been debated with different conclusions. But to Gandhiji, readers were the most important. A journalist may be a patriot, a party member, or a faithful employee ; but his loyalty according to him should primarily be to his readers. Public has the right to know the truth. He must be informed objectively as to what is happening. If the paper looses confidence of his readers, it has lost all that is worth in journalism.

Progress of science and education was continuously raising the intellectual level of the public. Certain papers were inspired to become promoters of ideals. This was particularly true in the Victorian era when the British press, by and large, started educating people on political and moral values. Gandhiji, when he first started journalism in South Africa, grew in this climate. Though industrial civilization later dominated every aspect of human life, Gandhiji was still preaching high standards and trying to introduce a sense of value through his writings.

The educational mission that the press is capable of accomplishing depends, in a large measure, upon the talent of those who write for the papers. If a journalist possesses personality, he can accustom his readers to follow him into almost every field and, in the end, impose upon them a veritable education. The public is fascinated by the radiation of his personality. The reader is automatically attracted by personal magnetism. In the field of journalism, this is, perhaps, the one axiom that does not admit of dispute. If a journalist, on the other hand, is strongly individual, he will, from time to time, make his articles almost always unreadable as he asks too much of the reader. To give his readers an elementary course of politics would demand a great deal of tact, and still more talent. He, perforce confines himself to writing in his usual style, which is incomprehensible for the public and often prevents it from taking interest in political happenings. In brief, the writer alone is in a position to link up with the very sources of life an important event, be it political, social or economic and in a few words, bring it into the strictly human domain which is accessible to all.

This was Gandhiji's magic. His treatment was like that. That was why his readers would read his writings as gospel truth. His personality would attract readers, his writings would elevate them to a higher plane, would help them in a holy communion with God, which, in his case was truth.

"There was not only a new thought but a new language in newspaper writing and what he wrote was the best in political thought and finest in journalistic writings. *No editor could escape being influenced by Gandhiji's writings.*"[7]

Gandhiji had sometimes reviewed books. That was done also from the point of view of service to the community. If he would come across a book which would prove useful to the people, he would write about it with his comments. He reviewed, at length

[7] A. S. Iyengar : *All Through the Gandhian Era* (Hind Kitabs Ltd., Bombay, 1950), p. 28.

Mr. F. L. Brayne's books on rural upliftment activities in Gurgaon district, Punjab. He pointed out the good points and the bad points of the book vis-a-vis a better solution as he thought of the rural problems.

He would ignore reference of books if these were not useful. Even in South African days when he had to compromise on small matters for the ultimate good of his paper, he was strict about reviews, in the *Indian Opinion*. In his letter to Shri Chhaganlal Gandhi, dated September 30, 1905, he wrote : "I have seen today the book written by Sheikh Mehtab. Do not take any notice of it in the *Opinion*." Sheikh, it may be mentioned, was his school mate.

At times he would be highly critical of harmful books. The best example is his review of Miss Mayo's *Mother India*. Under the title 'Drain Inspector's Report,' he wrote, in the *Young India* dated September 15, 1927 : "Miss Mayo has herself favoured me with a copy of her book . . . . The book is cleverly and powerfully written . . . . But the impression it leaves on my mind is that it is the report of a drain inspector sent out with the one purpose of opening and examining the drains of the country to be reported upon or to give graphic description of the stomach exuded by the opened drains." He wrote at length with supporting extracts from the book and concluded : "That a book like Miss Mayo's can command a large circulation furnishes a sad commentary on Western literature and culture."

Under the heading 'A vicious book,' Gandhiji, on July 25, 1929, mentioned about the book *Swami Dayanand — A critical study of his life and teaching*. The caption of the review was enough to indicate what Gandhiji wrote.

Gandhiji was a prolific writer. On way to South Africa from England, in 1909, he utilized his time in writing the manuscript of the book — *Hind Swaraj*. It is in the form of 20 brief dialogues between 'Reader' and 'Editor.' It covers subjects like India and England, Civilization, Swaraj, machinery, Hindu Muslim Unity, non-violence, Satyagraha, etc. What Gandhiji thought and said and did during 40 years of his active life i.e. from 1908–48, was epitomized in the book. The manuscript was found intact even after many years. Shri Prabhudas Gandhi said : "Turning over the pages of the manuscript, one realises Gandhiji's genius as a writer. In the 275 hand written pages only three lines have been scratched out. A few words here and there have been changed. When Gandhiji got tired of writing with his right hand, he wrote with his left."[8] He finished the whole manuscript in ten days time.

He was asked later as to whether he would like to make any change in the book. He made only one change. The word ' prostitute ' used in connection with Parliament was taken out. This was done to satisfy the sentiment of an English lady who was annoyed over the use of the word.

What was Gandhiji's attitude towards the vernacular press ? Did he like conducting English papers at the cost of vernacular ones ? Was he happy in communicating his ideas with readers through the medium of a foreign language ? These and many other questions will naturally crop up while discussing Gandhiji as a journalist. He had, as we will see, his definite view on the subject.

Kaka Saheb Kalelkar mentioned an incident which occurred immediately after Gandhiji came back from South Africa. A Parsi journalist interviewed him and as was the custom of those days, started asking questions in English. Gandhiji, politely but firmly replied, " Friend, you are an Indian and I, too, an Indian. Your mother tongue is Gujarati, and so is mine. Why, then, do you ask your questions in English ? Do you imagine that I have forgotten my native tongue because I lived in South Africa. Or do you consider it more dignified to talk in English because I am a barrister."[9]

Newspapers carried this story widely. In those days when affected English conversation and European dress were criteria for a successful politician, at least here was a man who was not ashamed to speak his language if he could.

Personally Gandhiji did not like to write much in English though he loved the language and developed, as we saw, a style of his own. He knew that English could not be the national language of India. But so long as the national language, Hindustani, was not developed, he had to choose a medium through which his message could be reached to the four corners of the country. Indian

[8] Prabhudas Gandhi : *My Childhood with Gandhiji* (Navajivan Publishing House, Ahmedabad, 1957), p. 87.

[9] Kaka Kalelkar : *Stray Glimpses of Bapu* (Navajivan Publishing House, Ahmedabad, 1950), p. 4.

publicists in those days had to be, of necessity, bilingual. Raja Rammohan Roy wrote in Bengali as well as in English. ' Lokamanya ' Tilak edited the *Kesari* in Marathi and the *Mahratta* in English. Sri Aurobindo Ghose edited the *Bande-mataram* and the *Karmayogin* in English and the *Dharma* in Bengali.

Discussing objectives of the *Young India*, the first journal he was going to edit in India, Gandhiji declared: " . . . I recognise that for a few years to come, until we have accepted ' Hindustani ' as the common medium among the cultured classes and until ' Hindustani ' becomes compulsory in our schools as a second language, educated India, specially in the Madras Presidency, must be addressed in English ".

There was a suggestion from a correspondent that the English edition should be stopped to help the growth of Indian language editions. Apart from that, should not he give a lead and propagate his ideas through the local language ? Otherwise how ' Hindustani ' would thrive ? Gandhiji was also, for sometime, thinking on that line. Once he resolved to write for the *Harijan* in nothing but Gujarati and Hindi, and the articles were to be translated into English. " I personally was sad and begged of him to write at least one small note in English because his English was quite remarkable and his writings will certainly be included in years to come as valuable contribution to English literature. But he was adamant. However, after a while letters from abroad came pouring in and in the end he could not resist the impassioned appeal of his foreign readers to write original articles in the English *Harijan*." [10]

Gandhiji explained the position thus :

" I can't stop the English edition for the reason that Englishmen, as well as the Indian scholars of the English language consider me to be to a good writer in the English language. My relations with the West are also increasing every day . . . . I do not wish to forget that language, nor do I wish all the Indians to give up or forget it."

Gandhiji's Gujarati style was as commendable as his English. It was much more. He set a new style in Gujarati literature about which Shri K. M. Munshi discussed at length, in the book *Gujarata and its Literature*.

[10] *Illustrated Weekly of India* (Bombay, October 20, 1957).

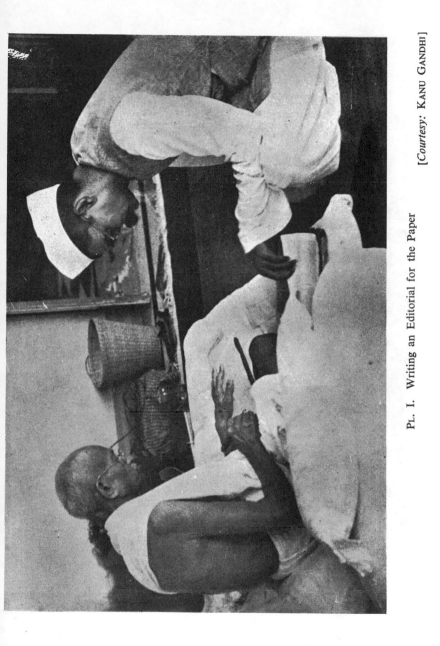

Pl. I. Writing an Editorial for the Paper

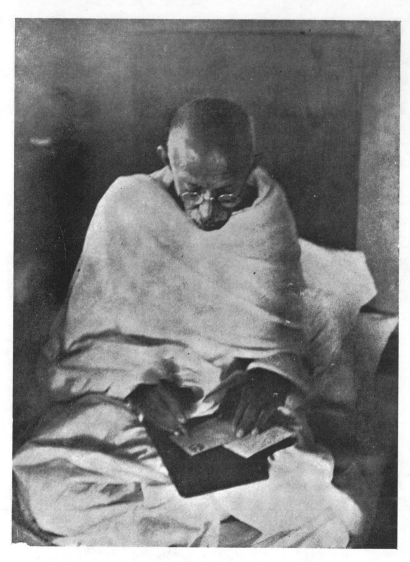

PL. II. Replying to Correspondents' Queries

[*Courtesy:* KANU GANDHI]

PL. III. Reading the Printed Copy
[*Courtesy:* KANU GANDHI]

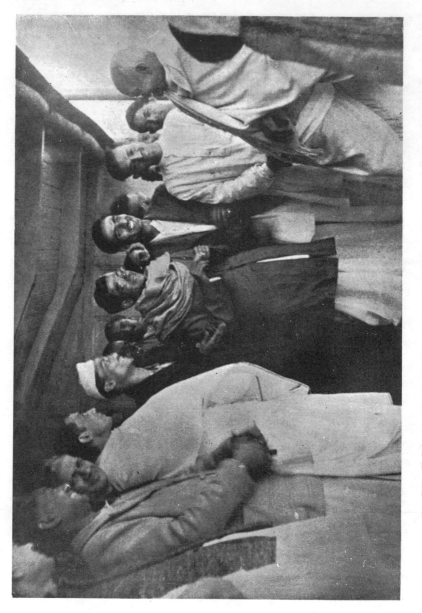

PL. IV. Talking to the Journalists on board the steam-launch in Noakhali, Bengal

[*Courtesy:* KANU GANDHI]

PL. V.   Papers that Gandhiji edited
[*Courtesy:* V. K. JHAVERI AND D. G. TENDULKAR]

Gujarati language is greatly indebted to Gandhiji. It had its heyday while he was editing and writing for the *Navajivan* and, later on, in the Gujarati edition of the *Harijan*. Even earlier he used to contribute Gujarati articles in the Gujarati section of the *Indian Opinion*.

His autobiography—*Atmakatha*—*Satyagraha in South Africa* (*Dakshina African Satyagrano Itihasa*), *Arogya Vise Samanya Jnana* were all written originally in Gujarati. So long there were two distinct trends of Gujarati literature. One was the Gujarati style and the other Saurashtra style. Both were pedantic, with liberal use of Sanskrit or Persian. Moreover there were unnecessary literary flourishes. Under Gandhiji's influence the Gujarati and Saurashtra were not only combined but were made into a powerful people's language. It was simple and direct. There was no verbosity in it. Nor were Sanskrit or Persian words unnecessarily mixed.

Shri Munshi wrote :

" . . . . Since he became the editor of the weekly *Navajivan* till it stopped in 1932, week after week, except when in jail, he has addressed to the Gujaratis his views and theories, his sermons, confidences, and battle-cries. Few other newspapers in the world have had a similar popularity and influence in their area of circulation as this small, unostentatious sheet which never screamed a head line and never published an advertisement. With many, it replaced the novel and the Purana in interest. A single copy of this weekly has often brought to a distant hamlet its only journal and gospel of life . . . . "[11]

His autobiography, originally written in Gujarati but appearing serially in the *Young India*, translated by Shri Mahadev Desai, is one of the best works in Gujarati. Though it lacks literary charm it is frank and inspiring. It rings with sincerity. Gandhiji's writing form should not be compared with that of a literary man. He developed his writing faculty as part of his communication with people. Understanding the people was more important to him than becoming a celebrated author. That makes his literary debut more welcome.

Mr. J. H. Holmes wrote :

" Gandhi's literary achievement is the more remarkable in view of the fact that he was never, in any sense of the phrase, a literary man. Unlike his great contemporary, Rabindranath Tagore, and his accomplished successor, Pandit Nehru, the Mahatma had no special grace of style. Seldom, if ever, in his

---

[11] K. M. Munshi : *Gandhi : The Master* (Rajkamal Publications, Ltd., Delhi, 1948), p. 49.

writings, did he rise to heights of eloquence and beauty. Memorable passages—i.e. memorable for their own sake—are rarely found. Gandhi's interests were never aesthetic, but rather pragmatic. He had no desire or ambition, no time, to be an artist. His one thought was of his own people, and his struggle to make them free. So he wrote with disciplined simplicity, seeking only to make himself clearly understood. The result was the one most important quality of literary art—namely, clarity. I doubt, if, in all his works, Gandhi ever wrote a sentence which failed to express with utter precision the thought he had in mind to convey. Gandhi mastered his medium. He wrought a style which was perfect for his purpose of communication. To read his writings is to think of content and not of style which means a triumph in the adaption of means to ends." [12]

Gandhiji's letters, small or big, official or personal, were pure gems. These were appropriately worded and spoken from heart.

" Many are playful ; some loving. Many administer a paternal rebuke ; some with indescribable restraint, hit, and hit well ; a few are intimates ; scarcely any throbs with the impulse of an unguarded moment. The author adjusts the tone, the language and the perspective of every letter with uncanny precision so as to have the desired effect on the addressee. These letters have provided him with his greatest instrument of controlling the conscience and conduct of his friends and adherents. No man has wielded so great an influence through his letters ; and few literary men have written theirs with such art." [13]

Not only did Gandhiji introduce style in Gujarati, he tried to do something for the children—for the coming generation—as well. Many do not know that Gandhiji tried to write primers for the children. This he did, as already referred to, in the Yeravada prison. It was a new style that he introduced—in the form of a dialogue—in telling things to the children. The dialogue was between the mother and the child, Gandhiji hoped that the mother in India will, in future, be her child's teacher.

Last but not the least was the initiative taken by him in establishing the ' Gujarat Vidyapeeth.' Not only the ' Vidyapeeth ' was to foster and see that the Gujarati language thrive but would also help in cultural promotions amongst the people.

Apart from Gandhiji's writing in original Gujarati, he took a great lead in translating other useful materials into Gujarati language. In fact he created a team of translation experts in the Navajivan Press. They translated many pieces and books and

[12] Homer A. Jack (Ed.) : *The Wit and Wisdom of Gandhi* (Beacon Press, Boston, 1951), preface pp. vii-viii.

[13] K. M. Munshi : *Gandhi : The Master* (Rajkamal Publications Ltd., Delhi, 1948), p. 56.

published them through the columns of the *Navajivan*. Shri K. M Munshi said : " Gujarat has taken a leaf out of Bapu's book and its insistence on a high standard of literature and on accuracy in translation has increased considerably. Before Bapu's influence changed its outlook, Gujarat abounded in shoddy translations of Bengali, Marathi and English books, in which the translators had calmly ignored all the difficult words and gave only half the meaning of difficult sentences."

Gandhiji was interested in the flourish of all Indian languages. Towards the end of his life he tried to learn Bengali. His own handwritings in Bengali can still be found. Even the day before he was killed he wrote a passage in Bengali and showed it to his teacher—Mrs. Ava Gandhi.

Early in his South African life Gandhiji started to learn Tamil so that he could easily communicate with the Tamil people residing in South Africa. In a letter to Shri Chhaganlal Gandhi, dated April 17, 1905, Gandhiji wrote : " I am studying Tamil very diligently and, if all is well, I may be able to fairly understand the Tamil articles within two months at the outside. I am rather anxious to get the Tamil books."

But Gandhiji made it his life's mission to make Hindustani the *lingua franca* of the people. As a nationalist he wanted a common language for the country and, though aware of the richness of the Gujarati literature, did not hesitate to support and foster the claim of Hindustani for this honour. He made all efforts to make the language acceptable in all India and for that he did not spare time, men or money.

5 / *Managing the Paper*

MANAGERIAL training for Gandhiji started with the *Indian Opinion*. In fact he from the beginning, showed a tremendous grasp over each detail in running the paper. That not only brought to surface his qualities for smooth and efficient management, but sharpened those faculties to greater extent. From type setting to printing, from packing to posting, from collecting of subscription to overall budgeting, he had a hand.

Being by birth and instinct a businessman—'bania', as he would call himself—he knew that efficient management of the business side of a paper was essential for its ultimate success. It called for right sort of coordination among workers, effective administration of office details and proper handling of correspondence. He was doing all these in the midst of his other preoccupations.

In fact, in the early days of the *Indian Opinion*, Gandhiji was practically doing almost everything single handed. In India, the volume of work increased many fold while running the *Young India* and the *Harijan*. But he was carrying on with his job magnificently with the help of a few trusted workers who were trained by him. And he was, as we had seen, keeping a watchful eye on each detail.

Gandhiji knew that the business side of a paper, however small it might be, must not be dealt in a slip-shod manner. All loose ends should be plugged. The success of a paper did not depend on the good editorials only ; it depended very much on efficient management.

No matter how excellent the editorial tone and selective the contents of a paper might be, they would avail little if circulation

100

was very much limited. As in a chain, there was no place for a weak link in a paper. It must be strong at each strategic point, i.e. writing, news editing, news selecting, printing and circulating. Newspaper running was largely a matter of timing.

Flow of copy to the press should be regular and adequate. Plans for selection of news and its placing must be done well in advance. Once that was taken care of, timely printing was assured. The foreman of the composing room, the head make-up and even the copy cutter could then keep the editor informed about the hourly development during the hours of production.

Because of its important and urgent nature, a paper should be particular in maintaining contacts with all. In fact it should set example in handling correspondence with parties. Gandhiji was in that respect a past master. He was not only prompt in answering business communications, but the quality of his letters was superb. He was corresponding on all matters with every one so to say. His correspondents were similarly keeping him abreast with all development.

Gandhiji introduced a new tone in his correspondence. Unlike the formal, stiff and highly artificial letters in an average newspaper office, his was couched in simple and direct language. It was brief and very much to the point. It was fashioned to suit the needs of the occasion. Being more natural, it was very much informal in tone. His letters were, as one writer said, a model for ideal correspondence : " Correct, artistic in appearance, conversational and informal in tone without sacrificing dignity, familiar without being bold or aggressive, definitive in purpose and, above all, courteous ".

Gandhiji not only planned, but executed the work along with other colleagues. When he was away from the scene, he would, through letters, etc., keep constant touch with them.

Gandhiji, later on, shifted to Johannesburg. He was, regularly from that place, advising on the management of the Press and the paper published from the Phoenix farm. He had an able assistant in Shri Chhaganlal Gandhi to whom he was writing constantly on matters of importance.

In the letter dated September 27, 1905, he wrote : " There is a letter from Hemchand to-day saying that a notice dispensing with his services has been served on him. I have thereupon sent a

101

telegram asking that he be not discharged. I do not relish the idea of discharging even Ramnath." In the same letter he confessed : " I do not think I shall be able to train Gokuldas for Gujarati in two months. He seems to be very weak in Gujarati."

Shri Chhaganlal got nervous at the bleak prospect of the International Press. But Gandhiji cheered him and wrote : " I have already shown you conclusively as in a mathematical problem, that the press wont break down. You had agreed with me in that, and now you write that the circumstances are unbearable and precarious. This is exactly what I consider a sign of weakness."

Without his advice nothing could be done. In his letter to Shri Chhaganlal, dated September 30, 1905, he wrote : " Anandlal writes that it has been decided to hire an office in Mercury Lane. If this is so, it should not be done. I feel it essential that I should be consulted before such changes are introduced . . . . "

He would also take him to task for failing to carefully scan through the paper. In his letter dated October 5, 1905, to Shri Chhaganlal he wrote : " You still do not publish all the notices from the *Gazette*. There are many notices from page 1705 onwards in the current issue of the *Gazette* . . . I have found these from a casual glance at the paper . . . carefully scrutinise the *Gazette* henceforth . . . ."

On January 5, 1906, he wrote to Shri Mansukhlal Hiralal Nazar: " I have been discussing with Chhaganlal the question of Tamil and Hindi editing . . . . The more I think, the more I feel that we ought for the present to do away both with Tamil and Hindi . . . ."

But above all, was his meticulous care for proper accounting. He was aware of the trust the public had in him in dealing with their matter and also the responsibility that this trust entailed. In his letter to Shri Chhaganlal dated February 13, 1906, Gandhiji wrote : " I sent you sometime ago Miss Neufliess' name as a paid subscriber . . . . Manji N. Ghelani writes to me saying that he has not received for the current year numbers two and three . . . . Please change Mr. Ritch's address at London . . . . Your immediate mainwork is to put the books straight as soon as possible, prepare the balance-sheet . . . . "

In his letter of April 7, 1906, to Shri Chhaganlal he gave priority to book keeping—" Books must be kept up to date." In the same letter he gave indication of recruiting new hands for the press :

" There are so many details to be attended to by me which I cannot without information from you. Motilal writes to me saying that there is a new arrival from Bombay. His name is Dhoribhai. He says he knows the press work well. He offers his services at £4 per month and free lodgings. It is worthwhile knowing him . . . . "

Gandhiji was also advising on arrangement of news, etc. and typographical setting. He developed such fastidiousness in printing that, in later years, he could not stand bad or careless printing. An artist in him would revolt : the politician in him would call that an ' outrage ' and " perpetration of ' Himsa ' or violence." Like Mr. Aldous Huxley he could say that " good printing can create a valuable spiritual state in the reader."

In his letter dated February 17, 1906, he wrote to Shri Chhaganlal : " You should divide the Gujarati pages into sections and see that, as far as possible, a particular type of material always appear in the same place."

And again on March 4, the same year : " You should have the same arrangement in the Gujarati section as you have in the English. The leading article should come first, followed by the smaller leaders. After that should come the translation of articles on important subjects etc. followed by letters like the ' Johannesburg Letter ' and last of all, Reuter's Telegram."

Gandhiji also gave detailed instructions regarding advertisements. To Shri Chhaganlal he wrote on March 4, 1906 : " Discontinue the advertisement from Haji Suleman Shah Mahomed as we are not going to get it. Reduce Mr. Gool's to half. He has made a special request about it as his condition is not sound at present. I see that many advertisements from Cape Town will be discontinued. But I am not worried in the least by that. We shall get others. I am persevering in my efforts."

Gandhiji was harping on the same tune. In his letter of April 6, 1906, he wrote to Shri Chhaganlal : " Why should there be any difficulty in giving quotation for full page, half page and quarter-page advertisements ? I do not think the rate depends upon the quantity of type to be used. When a man hires so much of space, we are bound to give him all he can acquire within that space, so long as we can put it in reasonably, so that it should not be difficult to give quotation for space. As soon as you give the quotation, it is possible to get a very good advertisement from Cape Town. Please therefore do not delay the matter."

Later on, as we have seen, he discontinued taking advertisements for his papers.

Even in England, where he went as a deputationist, the *Indian Opinion* was always in his mind. On October 26, 1906, he wrote to Mr. H. S. L. Polak : " I am sending you all the cuttings that I consider to be useful. If I can find the time, I shall translate the substance of the fight of the women suffragists for the Gujarati columns, but if I do not, let Chhaganlal translate them, and make an effective use of these valuable cuttings. I have asked Mr. Mukerji to deal with the matter in his London letter."

He would go into sorts of details. On January 5, 1907, he wrote to Shri Chhaganlal : " . . . . Kalyandas is now busy recovering the dues here. Many subscribers complain that they do not get *Indian Opinion* regularly . . . . Kalyandas believes that some of the people there pack the copies and stick the wrappers carelessly, and they therefore, fall apart and the papers get lost. I am writing to Mr. West also about this. We ought to be very careful. I think it necessary for someone to supervise the work of wrapping . . . ."

Earlier on April 6, 1906, he wrote : " . . . . Am I to understand from your letter that you received the Gujarati matter from me only on Wednesday ? If so, there must be something terribly wrong, for I took special precautions that the matter written on Sunday was posted before four o'clock. The matter written on Saturday was posted in due time. I have asked you to send me the envelopes bearing the dates so that I may have the matter investigated here . . . ."

To Mr. J. C. Mukerji, London, he wrote on October 27, 1906 : " . . . . Although you may send your correspondence on Friday nights, I think you should send from the *Times* the latest news and Parliamentary reports on Saturdays and post them, if necessary, up to the last moment at the General Post Office. That is the only way, I think, you will be able to make your correspondence effective and up to date."

Again he reverted to accounts and wrote to Shri Chhaganlal on January 28, 1907 : " This is the time for you to give your fullest attention to realising the dues and to the account books.

We must on any account satisfy our customers. If they do not get satisfaction just when they have begun to be interested in what we write, we shalln't be able to keep them on the register . . . . "

In the same letter he planned for the future of the Press. Wrote he : " . . . . I have therefore decided to send a person to England, whom I consider the most steadfast of all. He should go there with the firm resolve that he should not make a single pie for himself from the education he receives but would pass on all the benefit of that education to the Press and would accept and live on what the Press gave him. You appear to me to be the only Indian who has attained to this degree of fitness. . . . Our ultimate capital is not the money we have, but our courage, our faith, our truthfulness and our ability. If therefore you go to England, your intellect remains unspoiled and you return with your physical and mental powers strengthened, our capital will have appreciated to that extent."

How would Gandhiji react to a new feature in the paper ? He had an open mind, but would like to move cautiously. Some one suggested as part of sales promotion, riddle for the solution of which prizes were also provided. Shri Chhaganlal wanted his advice and got it (February 7, 1907) : " I did understand your suggestion about the riddles. I do not think it proper to introduce the riddles feature so long as we are not in a position to have it regularly and offer prizes ourselves. What can be the object of the man who wants to spend money on this ? How long can he be expected to do so ? Moreover, we can hardly expect many to take part in the competition. However, you may inquire of your correspondent if he intends paying for the prizes indefinitely. It would be very strange indeed if he wanted to do so. On the other hand, it would not be proper for us to start this feature if he agrees to give prizes once in a while. You may, however, write to me if you have more to say."

It may be of interest to know the various methods adopted by publishers to boost the sale of papers. " An example of circulation building by high-pressure methods, including premiums, that exceeded all bounds was the contest in which London, England, newspapers engaged some years ago. Lord Beaverbrook, in a page one announcement, admitted that between March 1st and June 30 his London *Daily Express* spent more than $1,000,000 in gifts

105

and prizes to get new readers or about $2 per new subscriber."[1]

Gandhiji was resorting to unorthodox ways to promote sale for the *Indian Opinion*. Addressing the readers under the caption—'Suggestion to Readers'—he wrote in the Gujarati section of the paper on August 24, 1907 :

" In our opinion, the Gujarati section of *Indian Opinion* is at present rendering invaluable service. This claim will probably appear exaggerated. However, the statement is justified. The Transvaal Indians are at present carrying on a heroic struggle and this paper is engaged in furthering that struggle in every possible manner. We therefore deem it to be the duty of every Indian to read every line of it pertaining to the struggle. Whatever is read is afterwards to be acted upon, and the issue, after being read, is to be preserved and not thrown away. We recommend that certain articles and translations should be read and re-read. Moreover, our cause needs to be discussed in every home in the required number of copies of *Indian Opinion* to their friends and, advising them to read them, seek all possible help from them. The present issue includes a letter addressed by the Hamidia Islamic Society to Indian Muslims. We think it necessary that hundreds of copies of this number should be sent out to India."

Gandhiji made the following appeal on behalf of the management, to the readers of the *Indian Opinion* (Gujarati), in its issue of October 12, 1907 :

" Our readers must have noticed that originally we gave four pages to the Gujarati section, but later increased them to 8 and then again to 12. For some weeks past the number has gone up to 13, 14 and even 15. Now we intend to give 16 pages every time. Owing to several difficulties, it may occasionally happen that we cannot give so many pages. Such an increase involves additional expenditure to us, though that will not deter us, for our aim is to earn our bread through public service. Service is the principal object. Earning a livelihood takes the second place. From the time that *Indian Opinion* was founded till today, no one has thought of making money out of it, and no one will ever think of it in future. Hence we intend to give to the reader greater benefits in proportion to the rise in income. If and when there remains any balance after the salaries of those connected with the journal reach a certain level, all of it will be spent on public work.

" We are convinced that an increased circulation of *Indian Opinion* will mean growth of education and patriotism among us. The journal has at present only 1,100 subscribers, though the number of readers is much larger. If all readers buy their copies, *Indian Opinion* can render three times better service than it does today. We hope it will not be considered unreasonable of us if we expect encouragement in proportion to the increase in the number of pages. If those who fully realise the value of the service rendered by this paper secure even one additional subscriber each, we shall feel heartened thereby and get some help

[1] J. E. Pollard : *Principles of Newspaper Management* (McGraw-Hill Book Company, New York, 1937), p. 91.

in meeting the increased expenditure consequent upon the increase in the number of pages."

In India, through the *Navajivan* Gandhiji proved, that a paper could pay its way through and need not depend on advertisement or external monetary help. The proprietors of the *Young India* also came round to his views.

The *Young India* soon started selling in thousands. The press was making profit. A correspondent suggested that because of the profit made, the price of the *Young India* and the *Navajivan* should be reduced simultaneously. It could be printed on cheap paper as well. But Gandhiji disagreed and said : "It is a bad policy to print cheap newspaper by making profits from other work. I want the readers to be just as much interested in the upkeep of the papers as the manager and the editor are."

Was he allowing profit at the cost of the poor people ? No. He knew that only those who could well afford it were paying for his papers. And why should they not pay ? If there is any profit made by the papers, that could be utilized for some other purpose—for the service of the community. In fact, earlier, i.e. on April 3, 1924, he said the profits of the paper run by him would be distributed for all India work and to the propagation of Hindi.

He would never agree to spend money unnecessarily. He would see that money was always spent on a worthy cause. He would not, as he said in a message, spend an anna if it was not necessary ; but if it was, he would not hesitate to spend a crore of rupees.

After 1920, Gandhiji was the undisputed leader of the Congress. As an organization, Congress was expanding fast. The message of the Congress was publicized through the cloumns of the papers in the country. But what about outside publicity ? Some suggested special bulletins or papers to be published at Congress expense, from abroad, for educating the outside world. That was quite an expensive affair. But something had to be done.

Gandhiji came out with a solution. He gave an alternative suggestion to the Congress which not only showed his interest in publicity, particularly external publicity, but his consideration for public money and the best way of utilizing that. Special bulletins, he thought, could be brought out and attached to the *Young India* whose circulation was then 25,000. A nominal charge would be made for this extra supplement to cover part of whole of the expenditure on the bulletin. His idea was to send such bulletins mainly " to the chief news agencies of the world ". By this method maximum result with minimum expenditure could be achieved.

In this context, it might be of interest to note that Gandhiji, a former " Durban, Johannesburg and South African correspondent " of the *India* in England, recommended the winding up of the paper as the return did not commensurate with the expenditure made. In the 20 October, 1921 issue of the *Young India* he wrote : " For the maintenance of *India* we pay—i.e., the poor people of India pay—£1,800 a year . . . the paper had a chequered career but was never a success from the propagandist point of view. It has never had a constructive policy. To squander £ 1,800 on a 3 d. weekly with a circulation of 500, and to spend another £ 1,500 on establishment charges, £ 3,000 in all, looks like reckless extravagance."

Gandhiji would plan weeks, if not months, ahead for the arrangement of the matters for the *Young India* or the *Navajivan*. Entries in his diary of January 18, 1925 indicated his plan for the *Young India* of 30 July 1925.

Here are the entries :

Young India 30th July

Congress and Political parties	17
An insult and Charkha	1
Too costly	7
Deshbandhu and spinning (not clear)	5
Congress corruption	3
China's plight	3
The Crisis in China	8
Misunderstanding	4
All-India Spinning Association	2
G.B.M. Centenary	3
Varnashram & Untouchability	9
Congress unemployed	10
Currency and cotton	16
Agriculture and Khaddar	17

Earlier, on March 12, 1922, he was giving instructions to Shri Krishnadas : " The correspondence, reports etc. should come to you for disposal. Unless it is too much for you, all articles must finally pass through your hands. I have several names as Satis

Babu, Rajagopalachari, you, Swaih Kaka, Devdas. It would be better now if Satis Babu gave you the permission to sign articles. The room should be entirely at your disposal. You should lock the verandah door from inside. Fix up the whole office there. Hordikar and the bulletin staff should be there for work but under your permission."

Gandhiji was very methodical in whatever subject he laid his hands on. He knew that mere good writing was not enough. He must see that the paper was published and despatched in time, and that proper account was maintained. He used to take the best out of his associates in running the paper.

The *Swarajya*, incidentally, was not accepting, like the *Young India* any advertisement. It gained support from the people from the beginning. It had a group of brilliant writers. But after twelve years it closed down for financial reasons. It had no solid financial ground to stand the stress and strain of the time. Moreover, it subordinated journalism to politics. " They recruited staff, somewhat in the manner of the Congress collecting volunteers ; and they utilised the national enthusiasm for securing low-paid staff."[2]

The *Harijan* started its publication. On January 25, 1933, Gandhiji wrote to Shri G. D. Birla : " Here is the estimate for the proposed English edition of *Harijan Sevak*. As you can see, it is a very moderate sum. I proposed to bring out, to start with, 10,000 copies. Then if there is not that demand, we might slow down. My policy, as you know, is that I shall not handle the paper except to make it self-supporting. If it does not become self-supporting, I should conclude that there is inefficient management or editing, or that there is no public demand for such a paper."[3]

And again on March 9, 1933, he wrote to Shri Birla: " The English *Harijan* has become self-supporting already. The subscription received to date from street sales and annual subscribers leave a balance without the aid of the Rs. 1,044 from the Central Board. This money, can, therefore, be refunded. . . . My enquiry is merely with a view to saving commission on money order, draft or cheque."

[2] S. Natarajan : *A History of the Press in India* (Asia Publishing House, Bombay, 1962), p. 188.

[3] G. D. Birla : *In the Shadow of the Mahatma* (Orient Longmans, Bombay, 1953), p. 97.

He would, as well, plan for the refund of money to the subscribers of the paper who paid in advance. In the *Harijan* of November 10, 1940, he wrote : ". . . . One word as to the practical question. You are a subscriber to one of the weeklies. I do not know when, if ever, they will be resumed. You are entitled to the return of the unused balance of your subscription. On receipt of a post card from you to the Manager, *Harijan*, Poona, for a refund, a money order for it will be sent to you. Those who do not ask for a refund will have their paper sent to them if it is resumed. If it is not, the unused balance will be spent in covering any loss that may be caused in winding up. And then the balance, if any, will be sent to the Harijan Sevak Sangh for use in the service of Harijans. If *Harijan* is not resumed within six months, it will be deemed to have been finally wound up. Meanwhile good-bye."

His punctuality in bringing out the journal regularly in time has been referred to. He succeeded in doing so throughout his life because of his meticulous care for details. He took particular pains to see that materials for the press are sent in time. He used to keep an exact time table of the working of the Post Office or the Railways.

Shri Pyarelal wrote :

"Despatching of matter for the *Harijan* weeklies always used to be a bit of an exciting adventure, when Gandhiji used to be constantly on the move. It involved poring over railway maps and columns of Bradshaw and Indian Post and Telegraph Guide, checking up of train timings and train connection not to mention the exigencies of late arrivals and erratic habits of certain trains. It made some of Gandhiji's staff fair experts in the arcana of India Postal world. For instance, Gandhiji could tell with exact precision the time the post would take to be delivered at particular place by the various alternative routes. Once in the course of Gandhi-Irwin negotiations a question arose as to whether a particular letter which Lord Irwin had sent to Gandhiji had been despatched in time. Lord Irwin maintained that it must have been. ' Then it ought to have reached me before I left Bardoli ' replied Gandhiji. ' You better make an enquiry in your office. There is bound to have been some despatching delay '. And so in the end it proved to be."[4]

It was a special pride of Gandhiji that the papers he was associated with—for about half a century—never got delayed. The publication date was always kept up even though he was constantly on tour in India. He even went abroad to Burma, Ceylon and

---

[4] Pyarelal: *Mahatma Gandhi: The Last Phase* (Navajivan Publishing House, Ahmedabad).

England. But his papers were coming out in time. The way the first issue of the *Harijan* was brought out after his release from jail as recorded by Shri Pyarelal has already been narrated.

Gandhiji was punctual in everything and demanded the same sternly from his associates. Kaka Saheb Kalelkar recalled an interesting incident of the Swami, who was requested by Gandhiji to set right the Navajivan Press. He failed to turn up at the appointed date. Gandhiji coolly remarked : " Either he is dead or has fallen ill. No one can promise to come on a certain day and then fail to come if he can possibly help it." Gandhiji was correct in studying the nature of his colleagues whom he selected for particular jobs. Swami got sick in the train and had to detrain at Surat for medical aid.

"One day I went to the Press. There was Swami, plunged in work as usual, a glass of milk beside him, some ripe and luscious bananas lying before him and, proof after proof coming into his hands from the press. He would break off a bit of banana with his left hand, and correct proofs with his right. The proof dealt with, he would take a hasty sip of the milk. The sip taken, back to his proof again. This kind of thing used to go on for three or four days at a stretch. No time to bathe. No time for anything at all—sleeping where he worked.

"This was the way he was working when he received a card from Bapu (Gandhiji), despatched from some place in North India. It ran like this : ' You are looking after Navajivan so well, that I have no cause to worry. I hope your work progresses satisfactorily.' Swami was greatly puzzled. Why had Bapu sent him such a card ? ' I have complained of no difficulties, nor is it likely that any one has complained about me.' He wondered and pondered, and then he suddenly remembered. ' Oh,' he said, ' of course, that is what it is : I promised to work for the Navajivan Press for six months, and the six months are up to-day. Oh ! the clever old ' bania ! ' This is the way of getting that promise renewed. I had completely forgotten that I came here for six months only. But that old man never forgets such things. Look at the way he is binding me over for a further period ! Jivatram (Kripalani) is quite right when he says that that old man is the wiliest bird you could come across in a day's journey!"[5]

Such was the atmosphere in which co-workers of Gandhiji for the paper worked. This was their relationship.

Any editor could reproduce his articles. He insisted on their being ' common property.' He was against copyright. In the *Harijan* of February 25, 1933, he wrote : " . . . . I do not believe in presenting the public with *free* literature on any subject. It may be ever so cheap, but never free. I believe in the old Sanskrit

[5] Kaka Kalelkar : *Stray Glimpses of Bapu* (Navajivan Publishing House, Ahmedabad, 1950), pp. 93-95.

proverb ' *Knowledge* is for those who would know '. But these are my personal views. I can only tender my advice to the organisations and organisers. There is no *copyright* in *Harijan*. Enterprising vernacular newspapers will publish their own editions of *Harijan*. Some have already written to me of their intention to do so. I can prevent no one. I can only plead with every one to follow the advice which I have tendered and which is based on considerable experience."

He published a letter from Shri Satish Kalelkar in the *Harijan* of June 15, 1940 and gave his own views on copyright :

" Being modern in my views and rather materialistic in temperament ", thus wrote Satish Babu, " I have always been sceptical about your views on the question of copyright. If I remember right, you needed some persuasion from friends before you consented to hold the copyright and save the profits on your Autobiography for the sake of the A.I.S.A. I agree that a seeker of truth should welcome its spread, and not put obstacles by insisting on the copyright. But surely there is a limit to this liberality, and an unscrupulous exploitation of it ought to be prevented.

" Perhaps you are aware that *Harijan* comes in very handy to the evening papers on Saturday and morning papers on Sunday. Some editors, not content with the ' whole week-end off ', draw liberally on *Harijan* even on Monday morning.

" I am not discussing here the possibility of raising the already excellent sales of *Harijan* by stopping the reproduction of articles in other papers, nor am I opposed to your views that truth should be spread widely. There are other results, however, which must not be ignored. Some Anglo-Indian papers, which are not exactly in love with the nationalist movement, sometimes reproduce convenient excerpts, and sometimes one side only, of the issues discussed in a series of articles in *Harijan*. Take for example the Ajmer case. The Anglo-Indian papers, that published an account of the incident and your cautious advice to the Ajmer workers to restrain themselves, took care to publish the Commissioner's ' explanation ' in that connection ; but they did not consider it a part of the ' gentleman's agreement ' with regard to the free reproduction of articles from *Harijan*, to publish the final and irrefutable reply from your pen. Your unwillingness in accusing before all facts are known, and your deliberate moderation and openness are interpreted as ' Gandhi's admission '. The ' awkward ' articles that appear later in *Harijan* are safely ignored !

" Perhaps you would argue that truth needs no tomtomming, and that it can never be suppressed in spite of a conspiracy of silence in papers. But surely one may not be a party to the spread of untruth by indirectly consenting to the publication of half-truths. Don't you agree that you should qualify your free permission so as to stop misleading excerpts and only a few of a series of articles being reproduced in other papers ? "

" There is much force in what young Kalelkar says," wrote Gandhiji,

" I own that often my articles suffer from consideration. They are made to yield a meaning I had never intended. The Ajmer illustration quoted by my correspondent is clinching. This matter of copyright has been often brought before me. But I have not the heart to copyright my articles. I know that there is a financial loss. But as *Harijan* is not published for profit I am content so long as there is no deficit. I must believe that in the end my self-denial must serve the cause of truth."

And again on July 13, 1940, in the *Harijan* under the caption ' Copyright ' he wrote :

" It is strange that what I would not do in response to the advice of a correspondent I have to do almost immediately after the refusal though, I feel, for a very cogent reason. Since my main article will henceforth be written in Gujarati, I would not like their unauthorised translations appearing in the Press. I have suffered much from mistranslations when I used to write profusely in Gujarati and had no time myself to produce simultaneous English translations. 1 have arranged this time for such translation in English and Hindustani. I would therefore ask editors and publishers kindly to regard English and Hindustani translation rights as reserved. I have no doubt that my request will be respected."

There had been comments on Gandhiji's attitude towards machines. The popular belief is that Gandhiji was against all types of machines. But it was not correct. He used a watch to keep time. A thermometer, to measure temperature, was also handy with him. Similar useful things, which do not harm Indian village industries, were used by him. He talked over the telephone as and when necessary. There were early pictures of Gandhiji showing him riding a bicycle. There were similar pictures showing him using a microscope.

The following note published in the *Harijan* of June 22, 1935, by Shri Mahadev Desai, Secretary to Gandhiji, would give an idea of his attitude towards machinery.

" A socialist holding a brief for machinery asked Gandhiji if the village industries movement was not meant to oust all machinery."

" 'Is not this wheel a machine ? ' was the counter-question that Gandhiji, who was then spinning, gave in reply. "

" ' I do not mean this machine, but I mean bigger machinery.'

" ' Do you mean Singer's Sewing machine ? That, too, is protected by the village industries movement, and for that matter any machinery which does not deprive masses of men of the opportunity to labour, but which helps the individual and adds to his efficiency, and which a man can handle at will without being its slave.'

" ' But what about the great inventions ? You would have nothing to do with electricity? '

" ' Who said so ? If we could have electricity in every home, I should not

113

mind villagers plying their implements and tools with the help of electricity. But then the village communities or the State would own power houses, just as they have their grazing pastures. But where there is no electricity and no machinery, what are idle hands to do ? Will you give them work, or would you have their owners cut them down for want of work ?'

" 'I would prize every invention of science made for the benefit of all. I should not care for the asphyxating gases capable of killing masses of men at a time. The heavy machinery for work of public utility which cannot be undertaken by human labour has its inevitable place, but all that would be owned by the State and used entirely for the benefit of the people. I can have no consideration for machinery which is meant either to enrich the few at the expense of the many, or without cause to displace the useful labour of many.'

" 'But even you as a socialist would not be in favour of an indiscriminate use of machinery. Take printing presses. They will go on. Take surgical instruments. How can one make them with one's hands ? Heavy machinery would be needed for them. But there is no machinery for the cure of idleness, but this,' said Gandhiji, pointing to his spinning wheel. 'I can work it whilst I am carrying on this conversation with you, and am adding a little to the wealth of the country. This machine no one can oust !'. "

As a journalist and publicist, he was in early years taking help of the typewriter. In his letter to Messrs. Nazar and Khan (June 3, 1902) he wrote : " Soon after reaching Bombay, I invested, in a typewriter, Rs. 200. The machine has been wholly used for public work."

On November 17, 1908, from London, he wrote to the Manager of the Empire Typewriting Company : " With reference to the ' Empire ' hired by me, I shall keep it for a month as from the 12th instant. I understand that the monthly terms are 15. You have already received 7/6 and I now enclose cheque for the balance. I shall thank you to let me have the receipt."

It appears that in the later period he was averse to typewriters. In his letter to Mr. Richard Gregg from Nandi Hill, dated May 29, 1927, he wrote : " . . . because of my dislike of typewriters, if I could possibly write with my own hand, I would inflict an illegible hand in preference to having my letters typed or typing them myself. . . . The typewriter is a cover for indifference and laziness. . . . And the inroads that the typewriter is making have all but to destroy magnificent art of calligraphy. I wonder if you have seen old handwritten manuscript when people used to pour forth their very soul into their work."[6]

[6] *Gandhi Marg* (Gandhi Smarak Nidhi, Rajghat, New Delhi, October, 1959), Vol. III, No. 4, p. 279.

Gandhiji would not stand wastage in whatever form it might be. He would like to utilize even the used envelopes, unused portions of letters, wrappers on packets or any piece of torn paper that was handy. He would keep notes, dictate instructions, or keep accounts on such scraps. Each one of these, addressed to his numerous colleagues and followers, were of great importance, as they indicated his thinking. Unfortunately, because of their very nature, many of these scraps were lost. But those which have been preserved would show his mastery of details and his clear instructions on writing, editing, printing and despatching of paper. On Mondays —days for silence—these scraps would be much more voluminous.

" Entering Mahatmaji's room at mid-day, I found him smiling all by himself in a gleeful mood. As soon as I entered, he said, 'Krishnadas, so many telegrams come to me daily, and yet not knowing what to do with the forms, I used to tear them. It gave me pain, and I was thinking on what use they could be put to. At last I have hit upon a plan.' He then took up a form and showed me how to make a cover out of it. He then directed me to prepare envelopes from the telegraph forms received by us every day. I have begun to make those covers, and he has been using them for the purpose of his letters. He has given them the name of ' Patent Envelope '. He finds so much genuine pleasure in using such covers that he would not touch envelopes of far superior quality even when they would be placed before him."[7]

Shri K. G. Mashruwala mentioned ' small things ' that he learnt from Gandhiji.

" This was perhaps when I met him for the first time in Champaran in 1917. He asked me to copy out a passage from the *Indian Year Book* on a sheet of foolscap paper. As the paper was larger than I needed I folded it up, made a crease by passing my fingers over it, and began to tear it along the crease. Gandhiji stopped me, and asked me to cut it with a knife. ' When you tear along a crease with your hands,' he said, ' fibres appear along the edges. They jar upon the eye. You should make it a rule always to divide the paper with a paper-cutter or an ordinary knife.'

" Once he showed me how to open up the flap of an envelope, the gum of which had got stuck. He introduced a fountain pen into a slight opening under the flap, and quickly rolled it round the edge. He said : ' Do you see how it opens up without injuring the paper ? This is a method which everyone should know.'

" He was displeased if he saw a letter placed in an envelope with irregular foldings. He said : ' When you fold your letter you must see that the edges coincide properly and the fold is regular. An irregular folding creates a bad impression upon the receiver about you. It looks slovenly.' "[8]

[7] Krishnadas : *Seven Months with Mahatma Gandhi* (S. Ganesan & Co., Madras, 1928), p. 117.

[8] K. G. Mashruwala : *Reminiscences of Gandhiji*, Ed. by Chandrashankar Shukla (Vora & Co., Bombay, 1949), p. 173.

6 / Curse of Advertisement

ADDRESSING a meeting of the ' Friends of India ' Club, at Dundee, on October 7, 1953, Mr. B. G. Kher, the then Indian High Commissioner in the United Kingdom, spoke about the weeklies edited by Gandhiji, and remarked : " They were unique in that they were entirely without a single advertisement and thus free from reliance on external commercial support for their circulation."[1]

But Gandhiji had to secure external commercial support at the early stage of his journalistic career. The *Indian Opinion*, in the beginning, was making all-out effort to secure advertisements. It announced, in the first issue : " To *Europeans* and *Indians* alike it would serve as the best advertising medium. . . . "

Advertisements were mostly from resident merchants, for sale of their products. The advertising rates were : Single Column 2s 6d per inch ; Double Column 5s per inch ; repeat half charges. One inch single column, for one year, would cost £ 2 10s. The *Indian Opinion* further intimated : " Liberal discount for standing advertisements for long periods. For further particulars : write to the Manager."

Reproduced below is a sample of an advertisement of the press from where the *Indian Opinion* was published :

> " FOR ARTISTIC PRINTING
> TRY THE
> INTERNATIONAL PRINTING PRESS "

Advertisements were miscellaneous in character, from dried

[1] *Gandhi Marg* (Gandhi Smarak Nidhi, Rajghat, New Delhi, October, 1957), Vol. I, No. 4, p. 276.

fish to cheap washing soap. Sometimes advertisements were secured from parties in India keen on selling goods in South Africa.

But slowly Gandhiji was changing his mind regarding acceptance of advertisements in the paper from practical and ideological points of view. In his book *Satyagraha in South Africa* Gandhiji spoke about his departure in policy. He found that some of the best men, his co-workers, were tied down only for securing advertisements. Their services to the community, which could otherwise have been even more substantial, were thus restricted. Then there was the problem of deciding as to which advertisements should be accepted or rejected. Sometimes an advertisement could not be refused, even if the management so desired, as the advertiser, an important person, had to be obliged. Years later, in 1916, when he, from India, sent his son Shri Manilal to edit the Gujarati edition of the *Indian Opinion*, Gandhiji wrote : " I have never desired to take advertisements."[2]

Realizing outstanding payments for advertisements published, involved much wastage of time and energy. Last but not the least of all was the spirit of service which dominated his entire activities in running the paper. If the Indian community in South Africa did not feel the necessity for the paper, better close it. The paper was for them—to voice their grievances against discriminating laws. It was by no means a commercial venture to make money. If there were adequate subscribers, there was no necessity of advertisement at all.

Gradually Gandhiji was limiting the space and scope for advertisements. Those of luxury goods or concerning entertainment were stopped long before the Satyagraha movement started. At the time of the movement the number of active workers for the paper dwindled and so, perforce, advertisements were stopped altogether. Gandhiji explained that the additional columns thus saved would be devoted for better coverage of the Satyagraha movement. He appealed to the readers to patronize the journal liberally and see that it continued for the service of the community.

Mr. Henry Polak narrated the decision to stop all advertisements in the following dramatic manner :

" It was about this time that Gandhiji amazed me by informing me one day

---

[2] *Indian Opinion—Mahatma Gandhi Memorial Number* (March, 1948), p. 22.

that he had come to the conclusion that *Indian Opinion* should no longer depend upon advertisements for its support. It seemed to me the death-knell of the paper, and I asked him whether that meant that he intended to close it down. ' By no means,' was his reply. ' Let us try to get a substantial increase in the number of subscribers to make up for what we shall lose by dropping the advertisements.' ' But ', I said, ' how are we to do this ? ' ' Well,' he replied, ' you can yourself travel around the country and get to know the Indian people better. You can bring the paper to the notice of many who are not already subscribers, and if you can convince them that they ought, they will certainly persuade others to subscribe. Explain that this is a non-profit venture for the community's service, and that all the workers responsible for it are performing a labour of love.' . . . . This was, indeed, the fact. I set out on a most interesting series of journeys . . . which gained for the paper considerable number of new and enthusiastic subscribers at what proved a critical period of the community's history." [3]

If exigency primarily compelled Gandhiji to stop securing advertisements for the *Indian Opinion*, it was, in the case of the *Young India*, a calculated move. He had now come to a definite view in respect of advertisements after weighing the good and bad points. Bad points far out-weighed the good ones. In the first issue of the *Young India* October 8, 1919, Gandhiji wrote: ".... The proprietors of the *Young India* have decided to give up advertisements. I know that they have not been, entirely, if at all, converted to my view that a newspaper ought to be conducted without advertisements. But they are willing to let me make the experiment."

It was an experiment for the proprietors. But so far as Gandhiji was concerned, it was a decision which he arrived at after years of work in the field of journalism. He appealed to his readers to make the venture a success and make the *Young India* free from the *curse* of advertisements. He continued: " The Gujarati *Navajivan* has already demonstrated the possibility of conducting a newspaper without advertisements soiling its pages."

Why was Gandhiji against advertisement? First and foremost was his consideration for social service. If a product is good, why should the producer spend money to advertise that product ? All journals should advocate the utility of such product for the benefit of the community. Was not the aim of journalism service ? Kaka Saheb Kalelkar mentioned about giving publicity to, through the columns of his paper, a pumping set which Gandhiji was convinced

[3] H. S. L. Polak : *Incidents of Gandhiji's Life*, Ed. by Chandrashankar Shukla (Vora & Co., Bombay, 1949), pp. 237-238.

would bring about immense good to the rural people.[4]

If it was something which will help the farmers, who constitute the overwhelming majority in the country, he would publish special write-ups. He would advertise, on his own, the improved oil crusher which could crush more oil; he would talk about hand pounding machine for husking paddy which would give producer more vitaminous rice with less exertion. He and his co-workers would endlessly talk about hand spinning and hand weaving gadgets which could make quick turn over. Any improvement on any of the existing looms or spindle would get prominence in the paper. Any invention in this line would be heralded with fan-fare. A special prize of one lakh of rupees was announced—in the shape of regular advertisement on behalf of the All-India Spinners Association—for a spinning wheel which would revolutionize the quantity and quality of production. Incidentally, the *Young India* was also advertising Gandhiji's books, particularly his autobiography, Shri Mahadev Desai's book on Bardoli Satyagraha and similar useful works.

For Khadi, he would go all the way to propagate it. He would even recommend any media for publicizing its use etc. The following question and answer appearing in the *Harijan* of June 1, 1940, would demonstrate his attitude on the subject.

" Q. 'Do you approve of the policy that is being followed by the Charkha Sangh in some places, of pushing the sale of Khadi by the use, for instance, of loud speakers, popular gramophone records and the like ? Don't you think that advertising, apart from supplying the necessary information about the marketing of Khadi is undignified and incompatible with the Khadi spirit? "

" A. ' I see nothing wrong or undignified in making use of loud speakers, etc., to popularise khadi. Through these means, too, one does no more than give the prices and other information about khadi. It will be certainly undignified and worse if false information is given whether with or without the use of loud speakers and the like.' "

If it was a product which would ultimately help the people, why should the manufacturer spend money in advertising that ? If the paper could not bring that to the notice of its readers, what for was the paper there ?

" I would be no party to the advertisement of tooth-brushes, even when they are made in India. I should declare my preference for the tooth-stick "— he wrote in the *Harijan*. He was convinced

---

[4] *Mentioned in the course of his talk with the author.*

that ' neem ' and ' babul ' sticks, which nature provided in plenty, were more useful to India's teeming millions than costly brushes. It may be of interest, in this context, to recall the findings on advertisement by the Press Commission which published its report in 1954. It estimated the total advertisement revenue of the daily papers to Rs. 5 crores per year. The Commission could not for certain difficulties, find out the same for weeklies and other periodicals. On the basis of the reports of the Advertising Agencies, the Commission expected the total value of advertisements in the periodicals to be about Rs. 2 crores. Of this total Government advertisement would be round about 7 per cent.

Discussing the nature of advertisement, the Commission came to the following conclusion : " Taking the total volume of consumer advertising, it will be seen that quite a large proportion is of items which would appeal only to those who are comparatively well-to-do. The advertisements of automobiles and accessories, refrigerators, washing machines, etc., watches, clocks and jewellery, transport, airlines, come to nearly one-third of the total."[5]

These advertisements were mainly inserted in city papers and journals and meant for sophisticated people. Articles beneficial to the rural people hardly find, even now, much space.

Incidentally, advertisements in newspapers up to 'thirties were mostly on imported goods. Cigarettes were the main item, soap coming close to it. Newspaper representatives had to go round to secure advertisements from the parties. Since the Second World War, the parties, whether Government or non-government, became conscious of the importance of advertisement.

Gandhiji supported his contention by the economic theory that advertisements cost money, thus enhancing the price of the product. That was indirect taxation. India's poor people could not afford it.

Advertisement is a huge national waste when a sizeable portion of the national wealth is diverted for this doubtful rivalry among manufacturers. Mr. John Kenneth Galbraith, in his book *Affluent Society*, suggested that this wealth could be better utilized for poorer sections of the people. Competition between advertisers raises the price of the product and the general public suffer. It creates new demand by stimulating want, without correspondingly opening

[5] India Government : *Report of the Press Commission* (Manager of Publications, Delhi, 1954), Part I, p. 81.

avenues for people to earn more. Wrote Gandhiji in the *Young India* of August 10, 1919 : "What financial gain it would be to the country if there was for each province only one advertisement medium — not a newspaper containing innocent, unvarnished notices of things useful for the public. But for our criminal indifference, we would decline to pay the huge indirect taxation by way of mischievous advertisements."

It also, through psychological approach, coerces people to buy things which, otherwise, they would not. Probing and manipulating of consumers' desires for goods is helped by psychologists, called by American advertisement consultants as motivational analysis. They have found their expert advice profitable as it helps in boosting up sales. Psychologists have become oracles of American business as they are successfully probing the minds of buyers. They are trying to prove that sales of goods are governed by the libido.

Dr. Dichter, in his publication — *Motivation* — said in April, 1956 :

"We now are confronted with the problem of permitting the average American to feel moral even when he is flirting, even when he is spending, even when he is not saving, even when he is taking two vacations a year and buying a second or third car. One of the basic problems of this prosperity, then, is to give people the sanction and justification to enjoy it and to demonstrate that the hedonistic approach to his life is a moral, not an immoral, one. This permission given to the consumer to enjoy his life freely, the demonstration that he is right in surrounding himself with products that enrich his life and give him pleasure must be one of the central themes of every advertising display and sales promotion plan."

This playing up of the part of the tempter is an unhealthy sign in any society. The famous historian, Mr. Arnold Toynbee, put it rather forcefully and called the whole game of advertising as 'unchristian.' "A considerable part of our ability, energy, time and material resources is being spent today on inducing us to . . . find the money for buying material goods that we should never have dreamed of wanting had we been left to ourselves." Prof. Toynbee concluded by saying that Christ would have rejected "this skilfully engineered besetting temptation."[6]

Advertisement creates systematic dissatisfaction. Take the example of cosmetics. Advertisement promises that use of such

[6] *Time* (New York, September 22, 1961), p. 74.

and such product will make women more beautiful. Constant dinning of this idea into their ears make women critical and anxious about their appearance. They wistfully look for advertised goods and often switch on to new products. There is no end to this.

By playing upon weaknesses and frailities, house-wives are encouraged to be non-rational and impulsive in buying family food. Customers are treated as voters. It would be difficult to lend moral support to advertisements which exploit human beings of deepest sexual sensitiveness and yearning for commercial purposes.

But can advertisements create artificial desire and demand ? There is another school of thought which will argue that advertisements can only stimulate existing desires by telling people what goods can be had, what they are like or what satisfaction they are likely to bring. It helps in the mass demand for products which, in turn, employs people in thousands. Mass distribution and mass buying help in building up an affluent society and people should work hard to achieve it. People should not aspire for a bare subsistence and should not admit that poverty is an essential condition of human existence.

The Indian Society of Advertisers in one of its recent statements claimed that advertisements play a tremendous part in building up mass participation for mass benefit. The whole scheme of insurance which is the basis of security in industry, in commerce and in family life draws its immense strength and solidity, the society claims, from members on participation. The more people insure, the more is the risk divided, the greater is the individual benefit both in lowered premiums and maximum indemnities.

Gandhiji objected to advertisements more on moral and ethical grounds. It became difficult, as he experienced in South Africa, to draw a line between what is bad or beneficial advertisement. Once a newspaper agreed to take advertisements, there was no limit to that. In their quest for money, they published indecent and harmful advertisements. This was, according to him, not the objective of journalism. Rather than serving the community, such action would run to the detriment of its interest. As far as the *Young India* or the *Harijan* was concerned, he would come down with a heavy hand on indecent or obscene advertisement and all along crusaded against it.

In the editorial of the *Young India* of October 8, 1919, to which reference was made earlier, he said : "Some readers who are interested in the purity of the paper sent me a most interesting extract from a well known newspaper. I have refused to soil the pages of *Navajivan* by reproducing it. Anyone turning advertisement of leading magazines can verify the truth of my criticism."

The *Shorter Oxford English Dictionary* defines obscenity as "indecency or lewdness (especially of language)". Indecency and obscenity are more or less synonyms and are used for the same purpose. To quote the *Dictionary* : "Indecency" is a "quality savouring of obscenity".

The Geneva Conference of 1923 on the Suppression of the Circulation of, and Traffic in, Obscene Publications could not satisfactorily define the word 'obscene'. In India there is no statutory definition of the word though the Obscene Publication Act 1925 was enacted to give effect to the Geneva Convention recommendation of 1923. Gandhiji's agitation had some effect in the sense that Government's attention was drawn to this vital problem. The Act, among others, set down that whoever "advertise or makes known by any means whatsoever that any person is engaged or is ready to engage in any act which is an offence under this Section or that any such obscene object can be procured from or through any person . . . shall be punished with imprisonment . . . ."

But though the statutory provisions were made, no statutory definition, was given to the word 'obscene'. Even as late as 1940, in a case in Calcutta,[7] the observation was made that picture of a nude woman was not *per se* 'obscene', when it would shock or offend the taste of a decent man. If such a picture does not excite the sensuality or impure thoughts to an average person, they are outside the purview of the provisions of the Penal Code. It was observed : "For the purpose of deciding whether a picture is obscene or not, one has to consider to a great extent the surrounding circumstances, the pose, the posture, the suggestive element in the picture, the person into whose hands it is likely to fall etc."

Because of the conflict in attitude between the conservative

[7] Emperor *vs.* Sree Ram Saksena, *Indian Law Reporter* (Calcutta, 1940), Vol. I, p. 581.

outlook on sex prevalent in India and the influence of English judicial decisions in British Indian Courts, the offenders, even if they were brought to court, which was one in thousand on the most optimistic estimate, would go scot free. In some cases they could take shelter under the exception clause of the Act which laid down, " This Section does not extend to any book, pamphlet, writing, drawing or painting kept or used *bona fide* for religious purpose represented on or in any temple, or on any car used for the conveyance of idols, or kept or used for any religious purpose."

Under the heading ' Indecent Advertisements,' Gandhiji wrote, in the *Young India* of June 25, 1927 : " . . . . I glance upon advertisement sheets of newspapers. They are sometimes painfully instructive. I see often in respectable papers advertisements of lewd nature. The headlines are deceptive. In one case the heading was ' Book relating to Yoga.' Looking at the contents of the advertisement, I discovered hardly one book, out of ten, having any reference to yogas ; all the rest had reference to sex suggesting that young men and women may indulge in sexual pleasures without coming to grief, promising to divulge secret remedies. I came upon worse things which I do not propose to copy in these pages." He was pained to see the editors not averse "to derive an income from advertisements which are obviously intended to spread the evils which they should shun."

Under the heading ' Advertisement Lewdness,' in the *Young India* of October 31, 1929, he said that immoral advertising pictures were used by sellers of foreign clothes. He received a few specimens from a correspondent, and was told that more indecent pictures could also be made available. One such picture was marked ' Vilas Jivan.' Gandhiji commented : " The un-scrupulous ways adopted for enticing simple folk by foreign cloth ought to disgust decent men . . . . "

There are many types of advertisements which mislead simple folks. These are mostly in cases of medicines and drugs for ailments which would require the treatment of qualified doctors and not quacks. Doubtful drugs to cure venereal diseases, or to stop pregnancy, are freely advertised which are likely to prove harmful. Credulous public are also lured to make investments in non-existent concerns. Offers of jobs on some security to be made in advance are also made through certain advertisements. There are advertisements of drugs which are habit forming and most dangerous from health point of view. "A single issue of a weekly or a monthly journal has often been found to contain about 10-15 advertisements relating to drugs for bringing about abortion under the title Regulation of menses, rejuvenation, and lascivious literature."[8]

The Press Commission also reported, ". . . lapses from good taste are most noticeable in case of advertisements of drugs intended for use in connection with women's ailments, venereal diseases or sexual indulgence. Even a widely respected Hindi literary monthly carried a large number of such advertisements."[9] Magical cures were also suggested for all sorts of known and unknown, curable and incurable diseases.

There are advertisements which are fraudulent in nature. Some of these try to exploit the unemployment situation in the country and lure simple folk into snares for purposes of extortion of money. Services of astrologers making predictions for all kinds of things are also offered through the columns of advertisements. On the top of it there is the cheap way of drawing attention of the readers by exposing nude poses or near nude poses of females to which the text of the advertisement has no relevance whatsoever. Then there is large proportion of cinema advertisements, illustrations and texts of which are sometimes quite objectionable.

Lack of good taste is also found while composing the advertising text. Matrimonial advertisements are sometimes crudely worded. While these may be done unwittingly, advertisements of medicines to be used for women's ailments or so called advice to the married couple are deliberately written in the most offensive manner.

Advertisers did not even hesitate to play with the national flag and photos of national leaders to boost up their products, immediately after independence. The public and the press were equally thoughtless in taking things lightly which they adore most. The pictures of Hindu Gods and Goddesses on match-box, cigarette box, liquor bottles, prominent sign boards of shops and calendars were abundant. Writing in the *Harijan* of April 18, 1948, Shri K. G. Mashruwala lamented :

[8] K. G. Mashruwala : "False and Obscene Advertisements," in *Harijan*, (Ahmedabad), November 7, 1948.
[9] India Government : *Report of the Press Commission* (Manager of Publications, Delhi, 1954), Part I, p. 97.

" . . . On the one hand we worship them (Gods and Avatars) as divine beings and on the other display them on the stage and screen and name our business concerns after them. You will not see Jesus or Mohammad represented on the stage or displayed on advertisements and sign-boards or business houses, such as Jesus Christ Mills or Rasul Mohammad Pharmacy. Christian or Muslim public opinion would not tolerate it. When you attach a kind of divinity to a person, it should be considered bad manners—if not blasphemy—to reproduce his image or presume to play his part or name your concerns after his in a light manner."

It is an irony that Gandhiji who was fighting against indecent advertisements, became himself an object of exploitation by the advertisers. Acharya J. B. Kripalani, Secretary, Gandhi National Memorial Fund, had to come out with a statement (reproduced in the same editorial referred to above) wherein he said :

" I have been pained to read in the papers advertisements inserted by private firms invoking the name of Gandhiji, ostensibly to pay homage to his memory but really to help in advertisement of their particular wares. Often the wares advertised are such as Gandhiji would have considered harmful and unpatriotic to use. . . . Gandhiji, as is well known, was against advertisements in general and never accepted any for the journals with which he was connected . . . . I hope the business community will respond to my appeal and will refrain from the use of Mahatma Gandhi's name in their advertisements."

The Press Commission discussed the whole question of advertisements in detail, their nature, problems, and suggested certain remedies. Objectionable advertisements could be grouped under the following main heads : (*i*) Indecent Cinema Advertisements, (*ii*) Misleading advertisements including those on spurious drugs and (*iii*) advertisements regarding obscene literature.

Reference has been made regarding cinema advertisements. There are many whose illustrations or texts may be considered objectionable. As remedy to this, the Commission pointed out the system in vogue in the United States of America where film advertisements are approved by a central body for the industry. This committee ensures that the advertisement does not show or narrate anything which does not find a place in the film which has been censored.

The British Medical Association has recommended a procedure for advertisement and sale of medicine passed by the Council. One of the recommendations was against any advertisement which should claim to cure any ailments. It also banned any offer to diagnose by correspondence disease or symptoms of ill health.

Nor could it advertise treatment by correspondence. In addition the Association listed certain diseases for which medicines, treatments, etc. could not be advertised.

Article 19 (2) of the Indian Constitution allows legislative measures curtailing freedom of speech and expression, for maintaining decency and morality. This clause can be used for checking indecent advertisements. The Drugs and Magic Remedies (Objectionable Advertisements) Act of 1954 was designed to eliminate many indecent advertisements but it could not check it altogether because of certain exemptions. One such exemption was the permission given to doctors to advertise on sign boards or notices the treatment of diseases. The Act banned advertisements of Talisman, *Mantras* and *Kavachas* for curing diseases. But it did not ban Talisman claiming to win friends or make fortunes. Sexual tonics were outside its purview. But there was no mention of advertising love-philtres. Unlike the British Medical Association, no ban had been placed for diagnosing or curing diseases through correspondence.

Under the signed article ' Spurious Medicines ' published in the *Harijan*, dated December 12, 1948, Shri K. G. Mashruwala who took over the editorship of the paper after the death of Gandhiji, published the copy of the resolution passed by the Newspapers Proprietors' Association in Great Britain. This was sent by an Indian doctor. The resolution was as follows :

" 1. No advertisement will be accepted which is claimed to be effective in Bright's Disease, Cancer, Tuberculosis, Diabetes, Epilepsy, Fits, Locomotor ataxia, Disseminated sclerosis, Osteo-arthritis, Spinal, Cerebral and Venereal diseases, Luppus, Paralysis, or for the cure of Amenorrhoea, Hernia, Blindness, Rheumatoid arthritis and for procuring miscarriage, or for the treatment of habits associated with sexual indulgence or for any ailment connected with these habits.

" 2. No advertisement will be accepted from any advertiser, who by printed matter, orally or in his advertisement undertakes to diagnose any condition or to receive a statement of any person's symptoms, with a view to advising or providing treatments by correspondence.

" 3. No advertisement will be accepted by containing a testimonial, other than limited to the actual views of the writer or any testimonial given by a doctor other than a recognised British Medical Practitioner.

" 4. No advertisement will be accepted, containing illustrations which are distorted or exaggerated to convey false impressions.

" 5. No advertisement will be accepted which may lead persons to believe that the medicine emanated from any hospital or official source or is any other

127

than the proprietary medicine advertised by the manufacturer for the purpose specified, unless the advertising agent submitting the copy declares that the authority of such hospital or official source has been duly obtained."

The doctor who sent this copy was the Chief Medical Officer of a T. B. Hospital. He narrated his seven years' experience. According to him many T. B. patients bought costly medicines as advertised in the press. They not only spent their money, but much of their health before they go to the public hospital. Thousands of poor and ignorant people could be saved of millions of rupees which they waste by becoming victims of fraudulent advertisements.

There is much undesirable literature in the country resulting in the demoralization of the people, particularly on the young ones who are the future hopes of the country. The advertisement of such literature is couched in a language from which it is difficult to know the exact content of the book. Earlier we have seen how the *Young India* drew the attention of the readers to some books on ' Yoga.' After years of agitation the Young Persons (Harmful Publications) Act of 1956 sought preventing circulation of publications which are likely to have baneful effects on young persons. In this case young persons are those under the age of 20. The harmful publication, according to the Act, was : " Any book, magazine, pamphlet, leaflet, newspaper or other like publication which consist of stories told with the aid of pictures or without the aid of pictures or wholly in pictures, being stories portraying wholly or mainly (i) the commission of offences, (ii) acts of violence and cruelty or (iii) incidents of a repulsive or horrible nature, in such a way that the publication as a whole would tend to corrupt a young person into whose hands it might fall, whether by inciting or encouraging him to commit offences or acts of violence or cruelty or in any other manner whatsoever."

Not only persons distributing such materials, but advertising in harmful publications could be punished with imprisonment up to six months or fine or both. On conviction Court might order destruction of copies of such harmful publications. Any offence objectionable under this Act was declared cognizable offence or an offence for which a police officer could arrest without any warrant.

The reforms in advertisement advocated by Gandhiji were later on pursued, though half-heartedly, by the Indian and Eastern

Newspapers Society which adopted a code for the press. Unfortunately most of the papers interpreted this code by saying that it was recommendatory and not obligatory. There had been a few exceptions where some papers tried to honour this code but they also soon fell prey to the same. The Press Commission said : " The Association of Advertising Agencies and the Indian Society of Advertisers have both informed us that they are in favour of a code of advertising that would keep out advertisement of an objectionable or doubtful character and are taking steps for its adoption."[10]

In this matter they decided to follow the codes adopted by the International Chamber of Commerce and by the widely known paper — the *New York Times*. The Commission recommended that the Indian and Eastern Newspapers Society, and the Indian Language Papers Association, should adopt a strict code of advertisement conduct and appealed to all their members to follow that. This code would also be binding on the Association of Advertising Agencies and Indian Society of Advertisers through whom a major portion of advertisements were distributed. The Commission further recommended that these four bodies should join and form an advertisement council by laying down high standards of ethics. These might leave out small language papers and periodicals. For that the Commission recommended strong legal measures. Such a council is yet to be formed. Such strong legal measures are still to be taken by the Government, though West Bengal and Bihar enacted Undesirable Advertisement Control Act, 1948 and Bihar Drug Advertisement Control Act of 1946, respectively. There were many lacunae and they did not cover the wide range of subjects as they should. Moreover advertisers of objectionable advertisements would often go unpunished because of the reluctance of people to bring the matter to the notice of the Court. The Commission suggested that to stop this nuisance the Government and the press had joint responsibility. It suggested that the Government could make an enactment whereby it could declare publishing of objectionable advertisement as " an offence punishable with fine or imprisonment". It also recommended that the Government should investigate advertisement of books offered to ' adults only ', advertisement items of ' birth control

[10] Ibid., p. 98.

clinics' or 'massage establishments', furnishing 'nurses', etc. The Press Commission appealed : " We would also urge upon the publishers and editors the wisdom of passing on for investigation any advertisements which they receive and which in their judgement are of this nature."[11]

Gandhiji did not believe that newspapers were to be published at any cost. It was not money but service which was the motto. He asked : " Is it necessary to conduct newspapers at any cost ? Is the good that they do so great as to outweigh the evil that mischievous advertisements cost ?"

As in other fields Gandhiji had a constructive approach to this problem as well. He did not believe much in the theory of imposing something from above. He had faith in self-control and self-restraint. He fervently hoped for a code of conduct amongst journalists which could alone stop such mischievous advertisements. He queried : " We have a Journalists' Association. Is it not possible, through it, to cultivate the uniform code of morals among them and create public opinion that would make it impossible for a respectable journal not to follow the prescribed code?"

Under the heading : 'How to stop obscene advertisements', Gandhiji wrote in the *Harijan* of November 14, 1936 :

" A sister, sending me a cutting from a well known magazine containing the advertisement of a most objectionable book, writes :

" ' The enclosed came under my eye when glancing over the pages of . . . . I do not know if you get this magazine. I do not suppose you ever have time to glance at it even if it is sent to you. Once before I spoke to you about the obscene advertisements. I do wish you would write about them sometime. That books of the type advertised are flooding the market today is only too true, but should responsible journals like. . . encourage their sale ? My woman's modesty is so utterly repelled by these things that I cannot write to anyone but you. To think that what God has given to woman with intent for an express purpose, should be advertised for abuse is too degrading for words. . . . I wish you would write about the responsibility of leading Indian newspapers and journals in this respect. This is not the first by any means that I could have sent to you for criticism.'

" From the advertisement I do not propose to reproduce any portion except to tell the reader that it describes as obscenely as it can be suggestive contents of books advertised. Its title is ' Sexual Beauty of the Female Forms ' and the advertising firm tells the reader that it will give away free to the buyer two

[11] Ibid., p. 101.

more books called 'New Knowledge for the Bride' and 'The Sexual Embrace or How to Please your Partner'.

"I fear that in relying on me in any way to affect the course of the advertisers of such books or to move the editors or publishers from their purpose of making their productions yield profits, she relies on a broken reed. No amount of appealing by me to the publishers of the objectionable books or advertisements of them will be of any use. But what I would like to tell the writer of the letter and other learned sisters like her, is to come out in the open and to do the work that is peculiarly and specially theirs."

He obviously wanted to create a strong public opinion, with women as the vanguard, against such advertisements. Earlier, he appealed to fellow journalists to adopt a code of conduct and put a stop to these horrible advertisements. There was some response. In the same journal, on January 2, 1937, he wrote : " A correspondent who saw my article on obscene advertisements writes :

"You can do much in preventing obscene advertisements by exposing the names of the papers and magazines which advertise such shameless things as you have mentioned.

"I can't undertake the censorship my correspondent advises, but I can suggest a better way.

"If public conscience is alive, subscribers can write to their respective papers if they contain objectionable advertisements, drawing their attention to them and stopping their subscriptions if the offence is not cured.

"The reader will be glad to know that the sister who complained to me about the obscene advertisements wrote also to the editor of the offending magazine who expressed his regret for the inadvertent admission of the obnoxious advertisement and promised to remove it forthwith.

"I am glad also to say that my caution has found support from some other papers. Thus the editor of the *Nispruha* of Nagpur, writes :

" ' I have not only read with great care your article in the *Harijan* regarding obscene advertisements but have given a detailed translation of it in the *Nispruha*. I have also added a short editorial comment thereon.'

"I am enclosing a typical advertisement which though not obscene, is yet immoral in a sense. The advertisement is obviously bogus and it is generally the villager who falls a prey to it. I have always refused such advertisements and I am also writing to this party similarly. If an editor must supervise the reading matter that he will allow, it is as much his duty to supervise the advertisements, and no editor can permit his paper to be used by people desirous of duping the simple villagers."

Though Gandhiji believed in self-imposed restrictions by the editors in not giving publicity to such things, he would not, as we saw earlier, hesitate to recommend to the Government sterner actions. As a practical man, he knew that while big papers would take steps to ban indecent advertisements, smaller language papers and journals would ignore such decisions. There the imposition of law was necessary. The Press Commission, as we have seen, also recommended the same thing.

In a country like India where democracy has not yet stood on solid grounds, some sort of legal action may be necessary in the initial stages. When average people see that the State is not interested in controlling bad things, nor does it extol virtues, they are likely to infer that the law has only negative sides. In the last analysis we come to the people who should be educated and be able to distinguish between right and wrong and should put voluntary restraint on things. Gandhiji believed in raising the standard of the community and creation of a strong public opinion which would force people to do things in the correct way.

In his book *Essays On Education* Mr. Whitney Griswold wrote : " Books won't stay banned. They won't burn. Ideas won't go to jail. In the long run of history, the censor and the inquisitor have always lost. The only sure weapon against bad ideas is better ideas."

In the editorial—' False and Obscene Advertisements '—published in the *Harijan*, November 7, 1948, Shri K. G. Mashruwala wrote :

"Public libraries and reading rooms can also play a great part in controlling papers and advertisers. They can keep a black-box, in which readers should put in complaints about a journal not keeping to a proper standard either in its writing, pictures or advertisements. The managers of libraries should verify such complaints, and if satisfied draw the attention of the journal asking them to correct themselves, and if not heeded refuse to patronize it. This would, by the way, be a superior and more effective censorship than that exercised through Government Executive."

Was Gandhiji afraid of taking advertisement lest it influenced the policy of the paper ? It is difficult to believe that he would personally have cared for any such outside influence. But none the less it raises an interesting issue. Cannot advertiser exert influence on the paper through which he advertises his products ? The *Harijan* of October 18, 1948, published an editorial by Shri K. G. Mashruwala, wherein it stated :

" We have been talking of freedom of the Press ; it has been called the Fourth Estate and so on. But what about the sacred responsibility of the journalists ? They seek to corrupt the Government through the criticism, but they themselves are under the effective control of their advertisers or the industrialists who pay them. They accept any rubbish of an advertisement or afford any industrialist interest if they are paid their price. They write a leader to denounce drink and at another place give a full-page advertisement of some wine."

The Press Commission went through this question and came to the conclusion that a single advertiser could not bring about pressure on the policy of a paper. Their finding is as follows :

" It is difficult to envisage that a single advertiser can act as a source of pressure on the general policy of a paper. We have naturally been anxious to ascertain whether it would be possible, even of any group of advertisers, to hold a paper to ransom or to force it to change its general policy. We find that out of a total estimated revenue of Rs. 5 crores to the daily newspapers about 60% reaches them through the Advertising Agencies and the balance is placed directly by small individual advertisers in the form of local and classified advertisements, each of which, by itself, would be of very small value. Taking the big advertisers who generally operate through agencies, we do not consider it likely that pressure would be exercised through the agencies, since the interests of one group might differ from the interests of another group handled by the same agency."

There is another type of advertisement which, though not much in vogue in India in the time of Gandhiji, has now become quite a problem. This is political advertisement — buying of newspaper space to sponsor a political cause or advertise a particular condition in a country. Sometimes Governments spend huge amount to publicize their point of view on certain issues. The *Daily Express*, London, disclosed on December 20, 1962 that the Soviet Government paid it £20,000 to print the full text of Mr. Khruschev's address to the Supreme Soviet on December 12, the same year.[12] It is often difficult to decide as to what is desirable and what is undesirable in paid advertisements for 'wonder cures', etc. in standard newspapers. But how to check controversial political advertisements ? If a businessman is allowed to advertise the good points of his merchandise why should not a politician do the same for his party or for his country ? This has been the argument of many people now-a-days.

Recently, the Government of India wanted to regulate foreign governments attempting to advertise their views through the columns of newspapers in India. The Government was seeking the advice of Indian and Eastern Newspapers Society on this matter. The *Statesman* of January 6, 1962, in an editorial note said:

" Historically there is a case for anxiety. Before World War I, perhaps a

---

[12] The *Statesman* (New Delhi, December 21, 1962).

major part of the Parisian Press was not unjustly popularly supposed to be subsidized by foreign embassies, partially though not exclusively that of Russia. Between the wars, similar charges were alleged without effective contradiction against the regimes of Mussolini and Hitler.... Present argument, however, concerns paid advertising: at least a less devious approach than some. In the USA this is not merely prevalent but difficult to assail without violating constitutional guarantees. If the erstwhile Trujillo regime in the Dominican Republic spent money on full-page announcements in the New York papers, Americans, whatever they thought of the content, found it difficult in principle to object. A reader was expected to form his own opinion, as in Britain of equal recently extensive publicity for the Federation of Rhodesia and Nyasaland. There is also—still not eliminated here through shortage of newsprint— the allied question of foreign sponsored supplements. What is most necessary to ensure is that advertisement should be clearly recognizable as such and not masquerade as news or the newspaper's own comment."

But Gandhiji would raise the basic question — the duty of a journalist to the community. If the system was good and worth emulating, why should space be purchased to publicize it ? Why should a conscientious newspaper black out a useful news item ? Is not money, in such cases, trying to influence the policy of some papers ?

7 / *Liberty of the Press*

It was a coincidence that the year the *Indian Opinion* started publishing, an Amendment in Indian Official Secrets Act of 1889 was brought about by the Government of India. But Gandhiji was not remotely concerned with that. Though his contemporaries in India were facing various repressive measures under Press Acts, he was not, during his entire stay in South Africa, handicapped in running the paper ; nor did he publish anything to incur the local Government's displeasure.

Tolstoy's letter to Gandhiji — Letter to a Hindoo — was published in the *Indian Opinion*. It was reproduced in the journal *Gujarat Patra* of Nadiad, a town in Gujarat. A notice under the Indian Penal Code was served on the journal by the Government of India. In the Gujarati edition of the *Indian Opinion* of April 9, 1910, Gandhiji mentioned about this and said : " It is not a little surprising, though it does not contain a single sentence which can promote violence, the person who reproduced it is being prosecuted. This betrays sheer madness on the part of the officers. . . . Our only regret is that though ours is the primary responsibility for publishing this letter, nothing is done to us and it is the editor of *Gujarat* who is in danger. We hope that the editor and the manager of *Gujarat* will do their duty fearlessly and not retrace a single step."

Gandhiji also mentioned about the ' Repressive Laws ' in India for ' Suppression of writings ' and cautioned : " Indiscriminate suppression of newspapers by the Government will not ensure peace. . . . True, the letter gave a vivid account of the harm done by the British Rule. That thought cannot be erased by suppressing writings."

135

Gandhiji was not quite sure what to do under the circumstances. He said : " Will our readers be intimidated by these developments or will they do their duty ? That is what remains to be seen."

In the Gujarati edition of the *Indian Opinion* of April 23, 1919, Gandhiji wrote an article under the caption ' Journalist's Duty '. He referred to the case against *Gujarat Patra* and asked: " What should an editor do when something he has published displeases the Government or is held to violate some law but is none the less true ? Should he apologise ? We should say, certainly not. True, he is not bound to publish such matter, but once it has been published, the editor ought to accept responsibility for it."

But he qualifies his statement and says :

" This raises a very important issue. If the principle we have laid down is correct, it follows that if any provocative writing has been published unintentionally and no apology is offered for the same, the newspaper will in consequence be prevented from rendering other services as well and the community will go without that benefit. We would not therefore, apply this principle to matter published unintentionally, but it should apply to what is published after full deliberation. If a newspaper runs into difficulties for publishing any such matter, we think the closing down of the newspaper will be a better service to the public. The argument that in that case one may have to face the confiscation of all one's property and be reduced to poverty has no force. Such a contingency may certainly arise, and it was precisely for this reason that we said that the editor of a journal devoted to public service must be ever ready for death.

" Let us take one or two obvious illustrations. Suppose that in a certain region there obtains the cruel practice of *Kanya-Vikraya*. A reformer starts a newspaper there and writes strongly against this practice. Those who follow the practice are angry with him and decide to outcaste him if he does not apologise. We are sure the reformer ought to go on writing against offering girls in marriage for a price, even if he has to face total ruin or be outcaste for that, and, when he is left without a single pie, he should close down the newspaper, he must not apologise, whatever happens. It is only by such conduct that he can prepare the ground for rooting out the practice.

" Let us take another illustration. Suppose that Government has committed a gross injustice and robbed the poor. A progressive newspaper is being published in such a place. It writes against the oppressive measure and advises the people to disregard the unjust law of the Government. The Government takes offence and threatens confiscation of property if no apology is forthcoming. Should the reformer apologise? We think the reply is again the same, that he should stand the confiscation of his property and close down the newspaper but certainly not offer an apology. The people would then see that, if the reformer could lose his all for their sake, they should also in their own interest oppose the law. If the reformer should apologise the effect on the people would exactly be the reverse of this. They would know that the man would not be concerned over much even if their houses were on fire, that, from a safe distance, he would only indulge in meaningless declamations. When he himself ran into trouble (they would say), he meekly retired. And so they will think of doing likewise and resign themselves to the inevitable. They will thus argue themselves into greater weakness. It is, therefore, clear in this instance that the best service that the reformer can render will be to stop the newspaper."

Early twentieth century was a period of expansion in the newspaper world in India. It also saw the emergence of nationalist press. Slowly but surely, newspapers were being sharply divided into those which supported the alien Government and those which advocated its withdrawal. The Indian Official Secrets Act was first promulgated in 1889 with a view to restricting information of military importance being published in newspapers. The amendment also placed civil matters, of public interest, at par with military matters. This was applicable to anybody, who " without lawful authority or permission (the proof whereof shall be upon him) goes to a Government Office, and commits an offence under the Act ".[1] Thus the Government was empowered to prosecute any newspaper it chose. Among others, Shri Gopal Krishna Gokhale, whom Gandhiji had earlier accepted as his leader, criticized the amendment by saying : " It is dreadful to think of the abuse of authority which is almost certain to result from this placing of Indian editors, especially the smaller ones among them, completely at the mercy of those whom they constantly irritate or displease by their criticism ". And again : " . . . . From the standpoint of rulers, no less than that of the ruled, it will be most unfortunate if Indian papers were thus debarred from writing about matters which agitate the Indian community most."[2]

Shri Gokhale in his campaign against the Act pointed out the irony of the fact that while India was governed, of all the colonies, in the most strong handed manner and where, compared to other countries, press is weak, the Government tried to further restrict a weak press in their functioning. To him the press, like the Government, was a custodian of public interest. Any attempt to put

[1] Margarita Barns : *The Indian Press* (George Allen and Unwin Ltd., 1940), p. 318.
[2] Gopal Krishna Gokhale : *Collection of Speeches*, (G. A. Natesan & Co., Madras, 1916), pp. 214–216,

obstacles in its free work will detrimentally affect the interest of the people. He was also drawing a parallel with the liberty of the press enjoyed in England. There, he stated, even if the disclosures were of the most embarrassing nature to the Government such attempts would be looked upon as "journalistic enterprise ".[3]

Shri Gokhale's comparison with the British Press, though cogent, was not quite valid considering the condition in India. In England the cry for the liberty of press was given by the pioneers of democracy, and the middle class which, after the Industrial Revolution, was coming to power. They regarded monopoly, patronage or Government interference as obstacles to democracy. Free press was part of their political programme which also included unhindered elections, enlarged franchize and free trade. Free press was necessary to them to criticize the controlling feudal group in the Government responsible for mal-administration which hampered their policy. These champions could not then foresee that newspaper running would grow into a profitable business and would be converted into a vehicle for personal or class propaganda, with an altogether different connotation of liberty.

The Act of 1910 " to provide for the better control of the press " was later passed in India. In outlining the objective it was said that " the continued recurrence of murders and outrages has shown that the measures which have hitherto been taken to deal with anarchy and sedition require strengthening and that the root source of the evil has not been touched. Prosecutions have invariably proved successful, but have produced no permanent improvement in the tone of the press." The most objectionable clause in the Act was that the executive could take recourse to punitive action at its own will.

Again the champion of the press was Shri Gokhale who declared that the Indian press had been " a potent instrument of progress : it had quickened national conscience ; it had spread in the country ideas of justice and equality not only between man and man but also between class and class ; it has stimulated public spirit, it had set higher standards of public duty."

But the Government was not quite sure of that. Its repressive policy against the Press remained unabated. To uphold "the liberty of the Press and protest against the Press Act of 1910" a

[3] Ibid., pp. 222–223.

largely attended meeting of the citizens of Bombay, under the Chairmanship of Mr. B. G. Horniman, Editor, *Bombay Chronicle*, was convened on June 24, 1916. Gandhiji was invited to speak. He spoke in Gujarati against the Press Act and read the text of the resolution which ran as follows :

" That this meeting of loyal and law-abiding Indian subjects of His Majesty the King-Emperor, believing the existence of a free public Press to be one of the first essentials of a healthy and progressive State and necessary to the proper development, political and moral, of civilised peoples; and further that the extension and maintenance of freedom in all departments of public life is the surest guarantee of popular progress and contentment and of mutual trust between the Government and the people, asks that the Press in the country should enjoy the utmost liberty of expression, subject to the legal restraints of the ordinary law and of penalties inflicted only after proper trial and conviction."

He spoke of the " attack made by the Government against Mrs. Annie Besant," Editor, *New India*, and said : " It is simply a waste of time to hold these meetings and carry these resolutions. But what else can we do? There is no alternative for us — the subject people — to do aught but place on record our view on a given subject. And, therefore, I have come here in response to an invitation. I feel that something should be done in this matter — something done so that our complaint may reach the ears of the Government." He agreed that some restraint is necessarily to be exercised on newspapers. But he was against " unwarranted restraint ".

He had, till then, faith in British justice and appealed to the Government " to do everything that is just and righteous ; if that is done, there would be no necessity for these meetings ". As one who had edited a newspaper in South Africa, he made a special request to the Government " on behalf of the newspaper writers ". " Do not harass the respectable editors and proprietors .... Treat us as generously as you would the English people." To the Indian newspapers his advice was " Say openly whatever you have to say. That is our duty," and concluded by saying that at best the Government could take the bodies of the Editor. But souls will remain free.

In a Diwali message in November, 1917, to the Gujarati Daily of Bombay, *Hindustan*, he said :

" What is the duty of newspapers when laws like the Seditious Writings Act and the Defence of India Act are in force? We often find our papers

139

guilty of equivocation. Some have preferred this method into a science. But, in my opinion, this harms the country. People become weak and equivocation becomes a habit with them. This changes the form of language: instead of being a medium for the expression of one's thoughts, it becomes a mask for concealing them. I am convinced that this is not the way to develop strength in the people. The people, both collectively and individually, must cultivate the habit of speaking only what is in their minds. Newspapers are a good means of such education, for those who would evade these laws had better not bring out a paper at all ; the other course is to ignore the laws in question and state one's real views fearlessly but respectfully and bear the consequences. Mr Justice Stephen has said somewhere that a man who has no reason in his heart can speak no reason. If it is there in the heart, one should speak it out. If one does not have the courage for this, one should stop publishing a newspaper. This is in the best interests of all.''

During the war, 1914–1918, Indian press suffered heavily at Government hands. In its memorandum, the Press Association of India, which was formed in 1915 to protect the interests of the Press, pointed out that " up to 1917 twenty-two newspapers had been called on to furnish security and 18 of them had shut down rather than function under official tutelage. Between 1917 and 1919, some 963 newspapers and printing presses which had existed before the Press Act of 1910, had been proceeded against under the Act — in all 286 cases of warning which stifled the victims, and 705 cases of demand of heavy security and forfeitures by executive orders. There were 173 new printing presses too and 129 new newspapers that were killed at birth by security demands, and many more were deterred from coming into being by the very presence of the Act. The Association observed that the Government collected nearly Rs. 500,000 during the first five years of the Act by securities and forfeitures, and that later there were more accelerated receipts ; it was also stated that over 500 publications were proscribed under the Act."[4]

After the war discontent was rampant in India. Farmers were not getting price for their agricultural produce. Industries, expanded during the war, had to shrink resulting in unemployment. There were strikes by the labourers. Muslims were unhappy about the treatment given to the Caliph of Turkey. Those, and Gandhiji who came to India in 1915 was one of them, who relied on British

[4] S. Natarajan : *A History of the Press in India* (Asia Publishing House, Bombay, 1962), p. 172.

justice and helped the war efforts, were disillusioned. The extremists in the Congress wanted some sort of action against the Government.

While conducting the *Indian Opinion*, Gandhiji had not any occasion to discuss, participate or uphold freedom of expression or liberty of the press in South Africa. There was no restriction on his paper. But in India the situation was different. Here the freedom of expression and the liberty of the press were being suppressed by Government action. Gandhiji had not yet associated himself directly with the *Navajivan* and the *Young India*. As editor, he had not yet faced, as others did, the direct assault of censorship and other associated evils. Nationalist leaders who had their own papers to express views were, on the other hand, debarred from freely commenting on political matters. They felt aggrieved but were helpless before the might of the British Government. Shri Gokhale, the champion of the liberty of press, died in 1915. Who was to stand up against various Government gagging orders ?

Thus from political exigency Gandhiji emerged as the champion for the freedom of expression and for the liberty of the press. The moment the Rowlatt Committee's recommendations came to be known, Gandhiji drafted a pledge which was signed by many important people. It said :

" Being conscientiously of opinion that the Bills known as the Indian Criminal Law (Amendment) Bill No. I of 1919, and Criminal Law (Emergency Power) Bill No. II of 1919 are unjust, subversive of the principles of liberty and justice and destruction of elementary rights of individuals on which the safety of the community as a whole and the State itself is based, we solemnly affirm that in the event of these Bills becoming law and until they are withdrawn, we shall refuse civilly to obey these laws and such other laws as a committee, to be hereafter appointed, may think fit, and we further affirm that in this struggle, we will faithfully follow truth and refrain from violence to life, person or property."

The ' Satyagraha ' pledge was signed and it was agreed that private literature should be sold openly and that the registration of newspapers could be civilly disobeyed. In the list of the prohibited literature were Gandhiji's ' Hind Swaraj ' and ' Sarvodaya '. These were sold openly and in defiance of the law.

" Gandhiji and Mrs. Naidu went out in cars to sell the books. All the copies were soon sold out. People willingly paid more than the published price of the book which was four annas. As high as Rs. 50 were paid to Gandhi for one copy. The intending purchasers were told that they were liable to be arrested and imprisoned for possessing the proscribed literature. But they had shed all fear of jail-going. The proceeds of the sale were utilised for furthering the civil disobedience campaign."[5]

Mention has been made about the unregistered weekly — the *Satyagraha* — edited by Gandhiji. This was again in defiance of the law which required registration of newspapers. In the first issue, dated April 7, 1919, he wrote editorially : " . . . . A ' Satyagrahi' for whom punishments provided by law have lost all terror can give only in an unregistered newspaper his thoughts and opinion unhampered by any other consideration than that of his own conscience. His newspaper, therefore, if otherwise well edited, can become a most powerful vehicle for transmitting pure ideas in a concise manner."[6] The Government might confiscate all such newspapers. Gandhiji advised workers to copy out extracts for readers.

The *Navajivan* and the *Young India* first made their appearance, under Gandhiji's control, on October 7 and October 8, 1919, respectively. In the first issue of the *Young India* Gandhiji wrote a front page article under the heading ' No Security', wherein he informed readers that though the *Young India* could escape security the *Navajivan* had to pay Rs. 500. But he was not happy to publish the papers in the abnormal situation — at a time when the objectionable " features of the Press Act continue to disfigure it ".

He wanted fearless editors. He wanted to keep up their morale at a time when Government was waging, so to say, a war against them. Simultaneously with the suggestion for a defiant attitude, he was giving the press constructive ideas. He advised :

" We must devise methods of circulating our ideas unless and until the whole Press becomes fearless, defies consequences and publishes ideas, even when it is in disagreement with them, just for the purpose of securing that freedom. An editor with an original idea or an effective prescription for India's ills can easily write them out, a hundred hands can copy them, many more can read them out to thousands of listeners. I do hope, therefore, that Non-cooperation editors, at any rate, will not refrain from expressing their thoughts for fear of the Press Act. They should regard it as sinful to keep their thoughts secret— a waste of energy to conduct a newspaper that cramps their thoughts. It is negation of one's calling for an editor to have to suppress his best thoughts."[7]

[5] D. G. Tendulkar : *Mahatma* (V. K. Jhaveri and D. G. Tendulkar, Bombay, 1951), Vol. I, p. 302.

[6] *The Satyagraha* (Bombay, April 7, 1919).

[7] S. Natarajan : *A History of the Press in India* (Asia Publishing House, Bombay, 1962), p. 195.

Speaking about the 'Khilafat' agitation later on, he narrated the story of one of his friends asking him whether his speeches could not come under the sedition section of the Indian Penal Code. Gandhiji said that it would be difficult for him to plead not guilty if he was charged under it. He further elaborated by saying that his speeches were of such a nature so that people "might consider it a shame to assist or cooperate with the Government that had forfeited all title to confidence, respect or support". His stand was that when the Government forfeited its claim to rule, it was but right for the people to express their feelings openly. This would bring the rulers to senses so that they could behave according to civilized rules.

In the *Young India* of January 12, 1922 he wrote on the liberty of the press :

" Liberty of speech means that it is unassailed even when the speech hurts ; liberty of the press can be said to be truly respected only when the press can comment in the severest terms upon and even misrepresent matters ; broken against misrepresentation or violence being secured not by an administrative gagging order, not by closing down the press but by punishing the real offender, leaving the press itself unrestricted. Freedom of association is truly respected when assemblies of people can discuss even revolutionary projects, the state relying upon the force of public opinion and the civil policy, not the savage military at its disposal, to crush any actual outbreak of revolution that is designed to confound public opinion and the state representing it."

In his letter to the Viceroy, written from Bardoli on February 1, 1922, Gandhiji wrote :

". . . nor again can the administrative interference with the liberty of the Press under a Law that is under promise of repeal be regarded as anything but repression. The immediate task before the country, therefore, is to rescue from paralysis freedom of speech, freedom of association, and freedom of Press. . . . I would further urge you to free the Press from all administrative control and restore all the fines and forfeitures recently imposed. In thus urging, I am asking Your Excellency to do what is today being done in every country which is deemed to be under civilised government."[8]

Gandhiji was charged for writing seditious article and gaoled.

Soon after he was released ; but there was no peace in the country. In 1929 Labour Party formed Government in England. Gandhiji, the same year, started the Civil Disobedience movement by launching his famous march to Dandi, from Ahmedabad, to break the Salt Laws.

[8] B. Pattabhi Sitaramayya : *The History of the Indian National Congress* (Padma Publications, Bombay, 1946), Vol. I, pp. 233–234.

There was excitement throughout the country and the Government enacted the Indian Press Ordinance of 1930, aimed at controlling the press. Magistrates were given power to ask for securities from printing presses. The magistrate could also demand securities from publishers of papers. Such securities could any moment be forfeited.

In 1931, the Indian Press (Emergency Powers) Act was passed. The magistrates were empowered to ask for security along with the declaration under the Press and Registration of Books Act of 1867. The same could be done in case of publishers. It also empowered the magistrates to issue search warrant for property where copies of newspapers and books were suspected to be stored.

Under the relentless sweep of the Press Ordinance a toll of Rs. 2,40,000 from 131 newspapers during the first six months of the Civil Disobedience movement was exacted. The maximum demanded from a single newspaper was Rs. 30,000. About 450 newspapers failed to deposit the security. In 1936, action was taken against 72 newspapers and a total security of over a lakh was demanded. Only 15 did furnish it.[9]

Congress came to power, for the first time, in 1937, after elections were held under the Act of 1935. People started interpreting civil liberty very liberally. To many people it was a licence to do anything as one pleased. Gandhiji once asked them to defy law. Now, under changed circumstances, he wanted them to realize the meaning of civil liberty. He focused on the subject of responsibility which civil liberty presupposes. He wrote in the *Harijan* of October 23, 1937 :

" Civil liberty is not criminal liberty. When law and order are under popular control, the ministers in charge of the department cannot hold the portfolio for a day, if they act against the popular will. . . . In seven provinces, the Congress rules. It seems to be assumed by some persons that in these provinces at least, individuals can say and do what they like. But so far as I know the Congress mind, it will not tolerate any such licence. Civil liberty means the fullest liberty to say and to do what one likes within the ordinary law of the land. The word ' ordinary ' has been purposely used here. The Penal Code and the Criminal Procedure Code, not to speak of the Special Powers Legislation, contain provisions which the foreign rulers have enacted for their own safety. These provisions can be easily identified, and must be ruled out of operation. The real test, however, is the interpretation by the Working Committee of the power of the ministers of law and order. Subject, therefore, to the general instruc-

[9] Ibid., Vol. II, p. 3.

tions laid down by the Working Committee for the guidance of Congress ministers, the statutory powers limited in the manner indicated by me, must be exercised by the ministers against those who, in the name of civil liberty, preach lawlessness in the popular sense of the term."

His attitude on the question of liberty of expression and press was again stiffened when India, without her consent, was dragged to join the Second World War. The All-India Congress Committee, under his guidance, accepted a few resolutions on the subject. In a statement issued on August 13, 1940, Gandhiji said : " The All-India Congress Committee cannot submit to a policy which is a denial of India's national right to freedom, which suppresses the free expression of the public opinion and which would lead to the degradation of her people and to her continued enslavement." Gandhiji himself explained the resolution and concluded by saying : " Freedom of speech and pen is the foundation of Sawaraj. If the foundation stone is in danger, you have to exert the whole of your might in order to defend that single stone."[10]

Before the ' Quit India ' movement, in 1942, Gandhiji was preparing his fellow journalists for the coming struggle. He asked them to preserve the sacred liberty of the press at any cost. Said he : " The Press should discharge its obligations and duties freely and fearlessly and not allow itself to be cowed down or bribed by Government. Let the Press be ready to be closed down rather than allow itself to be misused by the authorities ; and then be prepared to sacrifice their buildings, machinery and big establishment."

The Press in India did not compromise where self-respect was involved. And it had to pay dearly to preserve its liberty. According to All-India Editors' Conference, in August 1942 alone, 96 journals were either suspended or suppressed. So that Gandhiji could say :

" I am proud of the way the Indian Press as a whole has reacted to the Congress resolutions. The acid test has yet to come. I hope the Press will then fearlessly represent the national cause. It is better not to issue newspapers than to issue them under a feeling of suppression. At the same time, I do not want them to be blind followers of Congress and to endorse what their reason or conscience rebels against. The national cause will never suffer by honest criticism of national institutions and national policies."

[10] D. G. Tendulkar : *Mahatma* (V. K. Jhaveri and D. G. Tendulkar, Bombay, 1952), Vol. V, p. 406.

G—10

While explaining the 'Quit India' resolution on August 8, 1942, he made a special appeal to the journalists :

" A word to the journalists. I congratulate you on the support you have hitherto given to the national demand. I know the restrictions and handicaps under which you have to labour. But I would now ask you to snap the chains that bind you. It should be the proud privilege of the newspapers to lead and set an example in laying one's own life for freedom. You have the pen which the Government cannot suppress."

The man who relied so heavily on the Press, demanded so much from them and, in response, got so much, was, as we had seen, advocating banning of newspapers at the fag-end of his life.

Before the transfer of power, there were communal tensions leading to, in some cases, mass killings. As in the 'twenties and 'thirties, he appealed to the press to publish such news very very carefully. He asked them to verify before printing any such item. He even demanded from Prime Minister Nehru, after transfer of power, publication of correct information and criticized for his ' hush hush ' policy. But papers, by and large, let him down. His was the lone sane voice amidst mass frenzy and hysteria.

There were also political kite-flying by the press creating only misunderstanding. Should they give correct news or their assumption to the readers, he asked ?

Free India's first Government under the leadership of Shri Jawaharlal Nehru, tried to strike a compromise between the concept of the liberty of press and its responsibility in a democratic set-up.

India adopted the Constitution in 1950 which, among other things, gave people, under Article 19 the freedom of speech. It said : " All citizens shall have the right — (a) to freedom of speech and expression." It was interpreted to have included the freedom of the press as well.

The Press Commission elaborated the point and said :

" This freedom is stated in wide terms and includes not only freedom of speech which manifests itself by oral utterance, but freedom of expression, whether such expression is communicated by written word or printed matter. Thus, freedom of the Press, particularly of newspapers and periodicals, is a species of which the freedom of expression is a genus. There can, therefore, be no doubt that freedom of the Press is included in the fundamental right of the freedom of expression guaranteed to the citizens under Article 19 (1) (a) of the Constitution."[11]

[11] India Government : *Report of the Press Commission* (Manager of Publications, Delhi, 1954), Part I, p. 357.

The Constitution adopted was democratic in character. It gave all adults the right to vote. That entailed responsibility not only to the Government, but to the press as well. Press, as is acknowledged, ought to play a very responsible part in the democratic country. It should educate the public — and this was Gandhiji's dream all along — about the happenings in the country and abroad — and their possible impact on the political, social and economic life in the country.

The Press Commission further said :

"In their memorandum to us, the All-India Newspaper Editors' Conference have said that journalism should strive to inform the people of current events and trends of opinion, to create and sustain an ever widening range of interest and to encourage discussion of current problems with due regard to all points of view, all of which involves accurate and impartial presentation of news and views and dispassionate evaluation of conflicting ideals. The Indian Federation of Working Journalists have emphasized the need for constant and conscious striving to distinguish between fact and comment, to present objectively and fully 'all the news that is fit to print,' to give impartially news of interest to all sections of the community, to maintain high standards of public taste and national culture, to support and promote public causes and to foster a due sense of the rights and responsibilities of citizenship."[12]

The Commission discussed in detail the various implications of the freedom of expression and liberty of press vis-a-vis the democratic society. It said :

"Democratic society lives and grows by accepting ideas, by experimenting with them, and where necessary, rejecting them. It is necessary, therefore, that as many as possible of these ideas which its members hold are freely put before the public. We would, however, emphasise that the right of free expression is derived from the responsibility for the common good. Acceptance of that responsibility is the only basis for this right which has been accepted as fundamental. Freedom of the Press does not mean freedom from responsibility for its exercise. Democratic freedom in India, and the freedom of the Press, can have meaning only if this background is properly understood. In any modern democratic society, freedom of the Press from political restrictions is as vital as before, and it is generally taken for granted. But there are other pressures, which we have discussed elsewhere, which have become more restrictive and inhibitive than political pressure, and which have also to be fought with vigilance and courage. We would emphasise further that the right of free expression is essentially as an appeal to reason, and its accent should, therefore, be tolerant and friendly. One cannot in the name of free speech give vent to malice or prejudice."

[12] Ibid., p. 339.

But papers were, as Gandhiji saw in 1947, or earlier in the 'thirties, giving vent to such malice and prejudices. They were publishing exaggerated news of communal disturbances without verifying them. That also increased tension leading to mob-violence. When his appeal to the press fell into deaf ears, he solicited the influence of the reading public not to patronize these papers. He earlier approached the editors "to see that false report or report likely to excite the public was not published in their newspapers."[13] But these requests were of no avail. In desperation he said : "The kind of stuff that was read out to him (from press) should never be allowed to be published. Such newspapers should be banned."[14]

As a journalist how could he recommend the banning of papers ? He had very definite views about freedom of Press which was, as we saw earlier, so dear to his heart. He was all for press liberty, excepting the liberty to commit a crime. Service and not irresponsibility, he expected, should be the motive behind papers. Mischievous papers, if these did disservice to the community and the country, should be banned. He had no compromise on that issue. It was no infringement of the liberty of Press. "It is my certain conviction that no man loses his freedom except through his own weakness," he said.

He was also criticizing those papers which were indulging in political kite-flying. They were publishing scoops giving so-called inside information of the impending political changes. Such unconfirmed reports, according to Gandhiji, created unnecessary misunderstanding with detrimental results. On May 3, 1947 at the prayer meeting, he criticized a newspaper report. The occasion was attempted disclosure in a leading newspaper in Delhi the decision of the Viceroy and the Congress Working Committee. He thought that to act in such a fashion was nothing but lowering the standard of journalism. The tendency of the journalists to pick up the bits from here and there and dish them up for the purpose of creating sensation was, according to him, back door journalism. That misled the public and harmed the cause. Calling them bad examples of foreign journalists, he requested the

[13] M. K. Gandhi : *Delhi Diary* (Navajivan Publishing House, Ahmedabad, 1948), p. 73.
[14] Ibid., pp. 104–105.

Indian counterparts to desist from such cheap performance.[15]

Gandhiji did not believe in any imposition from outside to curb this freedom from responsibility. But the Government of India, soon after the adoption of the Constitution, when freedom of expression was declared a Constitutional right, became involved in a number of problems leading to an amendment of the Constitution qualifying Article 19.

Government had to take certain action against some newspapers. But the High Courts and the Supreme Court overruled the action of the Government on the ground that they were *ultra vires* of Article 19(2) of the Constitution as it laid down that "nothing in sub-clause (a) of clause 1 of the Article (which guaranteed the right of freedom of speech and expression to all citizens) shall affect the operation of any existing law in so far as it related to or present the state from making any law relating to libel, slander, defamation, contempt of court or any matter which offends against decency or morality or which undermines the security of, or tends to overthrow, the State."

In the amendment introduced by the Government, it was said :

"(iii) Amendment of Article 19 and validation of certain laws : (1) in Article 19 of the Constitution (A) for clause (2), the following clause shall be substituted, and the said clause shall be deemed to have been originally enacted in the following form, namely : (2) Nothing in sub-clause (a) of clause (1) shall affect the operation of any existing law in so far as it imposes, or prevent the State from making any law imposing, in the interests of the security of the State, friendly relations with foreign States, public order, decency or morality, restrictions on the exercise of the right conferred by the said sub-clause, and in particular, nothing in the said sub-clause shall affect the operation of any existing law in so far as it imposes related to, or prevent the State from making any law relating to, contempt of court, defamation or incitement to an offence.

"No law in force in the territory of India immediately before the commencement of the Constitution, which is consistent with the provisions of Article 19 of the Constitution, as amended by sub-section (1) of this section, shall be deemed to be void, or ever to have become void, on the ground only that, being a law which takes away or abridges the right conferred by sub-clause (a) of clause (1) of the said Article, its operation was not saved by sub-clause (2) of that Article as originally enacted, and notwithstanding any judgment, decree or order of any court or tribunal to the contrary, every such law shall continue in force until altered or repealed by a competent legislature or other competent authority."

[15] D. G. Tendulkar : *Mahatma* (V. K. Jhaveri and D. G. Tendulkar, Bombay, 1953), Vol. VII, p. 457.

The Select Committee amended it by putting :

" 3. Amendment of Article 19 of the Constitution and validation of certain laws :

(1) in Article 19 of the Constitution :

(*a*) For clause (2), the following clause shall be substituted and the said clause shall be deemed always to have been enacted in the following form, namely :

(2) Nothing in sub-clause (a) of clause (1) shall affect the operation of any existing law, or prevent the State from making any law, in so far as such law imposes reasonable restrictions on the exercise of the right conferred by the said sub-clause in the interests of the security of the State, friendly relations with foreign States, public order, decency or morality, including, in particular, any existing or other law relating to contempt of court defamation or incitement to an offence."

All-India Newspapers Editors' Conference characterized the amendment as ' unwarranted and uncalled for.' They called it ' a threat to freedom of expression,' and declared : " Freedom of expression is our birthright and we shall not rest until it is fully guaranteed by the Constitution." The Indian Federation of Working Journalists also made similar protest.

In the same year the Press (Objectionable Matters) Act became a law which " made all actions by Government against the press subject to judicial sanction."

Government also agreed to create a Press Commission which was subsequently formed with, among others, representatives of All-India Newspapers Editors' Conference, ¦Indian Federation of Working Journalists and Indian Languages Newspapers Association, to investigate the entire field of journalism.

The amendment, as mentioned, qualified freedom of expression. No doubt the liberty of the press should be harmonious with individual's or group's duty to the community. But that implied some restrictions. M. Lopez in his report to United Nations cautioned by saying that " concept of freedom with responsibility can be pushed to a point where the emphasis on responsibility becomes in effect the negation of freedom itself. It should be the common concern of developed and undeveloped countries alike to seek a cure for the disease without killing the patient. The doctrine of absolute freedom of information has its dangers ; but they may be no more formidable than those which could arise from the irresponsible use of the concept of responsibility."

The American Press Commission was more emphatic. In the book *A Free and Responsible Press* it pointed out :

" Freedom of the Press is essential to political liberty. Where men cannot freely convey their thoughts to one another, no freedom is secure. Where freedom of expression exists, the beginnings of a free society and a means for every retention of liberty are already present. Free expression is therefore unique among liberties.

The right to freedom of expression is an expression of confidence in the ability of free men to learn the truth through the unhampered interplay of competing ideas. Where the right is generally exercised, the public benefits from the selective process of winnowing truth from falsehood, desirable ideas from evil ones. If the people are to govern themselves, their only hope of doing so wisely lies in the collective wisdom derived from the fullest possible information, and in the fair presentation of differing opinions. The right is also necessary to permit each man to find his way to the religious and political beliefs which suit his private needs."

More dangerous than the Government restrictions, there is the tendency now of baneful effect of other subtle but more vicious control of which Gandhiji could not much foresee. It was the emergence of big industrialists as newspaper proprietors. They controlled a number of papers and formed ' chain ' which would give people news and views designed to suit their own class or group interest, quite contrary to the Press Commission's concept when it said :

" Just as the public have a vital interest in the purity of their water supply so have they an equally vital interest in the accurate presentation of news and fair presentation of views. In other words the news and views which newspapers purvey carry with them a vital public interest."

The *Link* magazine, in its issue of September 2, 1962, gave a detailed account of the rising vested interest in the free flow of news and views and said :

" Alistair Hetherington, editor of the *Manchester Guardian*, interviewed by a group of Asian students over the BBC television system early last year, pointed out that in Britain ' the big newspaper proprietors are mainly concerned with newspapers and not with other things. Lord Rothermere, Lord Beaverbrook, Cecil King, Roy Thompson—these people are primarily in the newspaper business. They are not making soap. They are not selling soap. They are not making steel, or bananas, or whatever else it may be '.

He contrasted this with the situation in India :

" ' I well realise that in India. . . the ownership of newspapers is often much more concealed and that newspapers are frequently run as ancillaries to another business or part of a large trading empire. It may be that the newspaper will be used—it sometimes has been the case—to forward the interest of the particular empire. It can lead to a measure of political corruption '. "

This tendency in newspapers in India has indeed a danger in that news and views are handled to suit the big industrialists whose business policies are not always to help common people. They are utilizing newspapers to bring in pressure on the Government so that they toe their line. They know very well the power of the press which had formed public opinion in the country for years. Hence they purchased a number of them. To quote the *Link* magazine again :

"... In buying up newspapers the founders of Jute Press were in fact investing not so much in a source of direct profit as in a weapon with which the State could be made to protect and defend the profit motive. ...

" By the time the Press Commission submitted its report, the exploitation of the press by the most powerful section of the Indian Industrialists had become an established fact in Indian public life. The Press Commission said, for example : ' We have seen instructions given to the editor in the name of the proprietor, directing him to give special prominence to an interview on a subject of economic controversy and another which calls for full publicity to statements issued by the president of the Sugar Merchants' Association.' "

The Commission also mentioned a directive ' issued to every member of the editorial staff ' and referring to the criticism that the proprietor had chance to make regarding the news and articles published on princes. He (the proprietor) says, " however strongly one may dislike the princes, it is a hard fact that the rights of princes are popular in Rajasthan like anything. All friends should keep these things in view."

Shri Jawaharlal Nehru, speaking at the seminar, on February 17, 1963 on the subject, ' The Prospect for the Indian Press, 1963–73,' sponsored by the Press Institute of India, asked people to be cautious about the news and views dished out by the monopoly press. He said :

" Freedom of the press usually means non-interference by Government. There is such a thing as interference by private interests, by limited private interests, by the individual or the group that owns the Press. I am unable to understand how a small group represents the freedom of the press although he may not be interfered with by Government or anything. But surely the power of money itself is a very important element which interfered with the freedom and so many other things .... If one person owns all the major newspapers, well, naturally he will see to it that his views are expressed and contrary views are not expressed in a way that he dislikes. The man may be a good man—since there is no question of an individual—but it is obvious that freedom of the press cannot easily subsist where there is monopoly. Where there are chain newspapers, the same thing appears everywhere and gives the impression that large numbers of people, intelligent people, hold a certain opinion, while it may be the opinion of just the individual who writes, who does not represent anybody but himself. He may influence others, certainly, but it is a misleading phenomena brought about by concentration of money."[16]

Reaction of the chain papers to this speech of the Prime Minister was as expected. In the leading editorial of February 19, 1963 — ' What is a Free Press ' — The *Indian Express* wrote :

" The bogey of monopoly of the capitalism and of the menace of the private sector is a favourite war-cry to conceal the ineptitude and bungling of a great part of the public sector whose loss of public moneys would by now have created an outcry, if not an uproar, among the shareholders of any private company. But the public sector continues unabashed in its own sheltered inefficiency. Is the official protective umbrella now to be extended to the public sector of the Indian Press, represented by the anti-monopolist, anti-capitalist and anti-public sector patriots of the Communist press which we notice is spreading its tentacles beneath the benign gaze of the Government. If the much maligned private sector press is to be chastised day in and day out by the Government we seem to be on the threshold of a regimented press required to say and do as an omnipotent Government, using its emergency powers and decrees. This might be a press in the Government's image. It would not be a free press."

The *Hindustan Times*, in its leader of the same day — ' A Free Press ' — explained the circumstances leading to the growth of newspaper monopoly. It said :

" Not unexpectedly, Mr. Nehru used the opportunity to speak to an audience of journalists on Sunday to dwell on the threats to the freedom of the Press that are inherent in the manner the Press is organised in this country. Mr. Nehru deplored the fact that the big newspapers were controlled by industrial interests and he referred to the stranglehold of the power of money on the dissemination of news and the expression of views. A great deal of thought has been given to the countering of these dangers by, among other, the Press Commission. But one difficulty that anyone who has given any consideration to the subject has come up against is that the resources required to run a good modern newspaper are of a scale which have made newspapers themselves very big business. This cannot be changed. Quite apart from this, it may be pertinent to remind ourselves that newspapers were acquired by big industrial interests at a time when the Press was a business hazard. What those who had started newspapers in the days of the national struggle were looking for were rich men to pay the losses. Times have certainly changed for the newspaper industry and, by the standards of those early years of struggle, they may now be said to have entered a period of prosperity. But we may doubt that the prosperity is such as to attract public investment interest for new newspaper ventures."

In conclusion it said :

" On the whole, it must also be acknowledged that those who control big newspapers have not used them for anti-social ends though the outcry against ' monopoly ' has been made a fashionable one by a certain type of politician. But the dangers mentioned by Mr. Nehru are very real ones and it would be

[16] *Press Release* (Press Information Bureau, Government of India, New Delhi, February 17, 1963).

153

folly to entrust such vital issues as freedom of the Press to the continued good sense and enlightenment of the newspaper magnates. If a change in newspaper ownership in today's conditions is not practical, new thinking could more usefully turn to other methods of achieving the results mentioned by Mr. Nehru. In Great Britain, for instance, the separation of ownership and responsibility for editorial conduct has been adopted successfully in several newspapers. There is no reason why the pattern cannot be followed here by creating trusts charged with the special function of keeping an eye on editorial policy and insulating the editor and the editorial staff from the influence of the proprietors."

The colossus of newspaper trade, in this context, was nicely put in by Mr. Kingsley Martin. He said :

" Before Lord Northcliffe died, the owner of some seventy papers of various types, he declared that no one could in future start a daily paper with less than £ 2,000,000 capital. In 1947 the figure would be much higher, even if supplies of newsprint could be obtained. Thus the freedom of the press, still immensely important in the sense of the freedom freely to inform, comment and criticise, has become, in the sense of the right to start and run a daily newspaper, as meaningless as the slum-dweller's legal freedom to live in the Ritz or to spend his unemployment pay in touring the Riviera in a Rolls-Royce. The position is much worse now." [17]

Considering all these obstacles in a country when democracy is in its infancy, the Press Commission, while dealing with the subject of liberty of press suggested some course which is worth reproducing in details : [18]

" The tender plant of democracy can flourish only in an atmosphere where there is a free interchange of views and ideas which one not only has a moral right, but a moral duty, to express. As Mahatma Gandhi has stated in words which have been inscribed in the portals of All India Radio at Delhi, ' I do not want my house to be walled in on all sides and my windows to be stuffed. I want the culture of all lands to be blown about my house as freely as possible. But I refuse to be blown off my feet by any of them. Mine is not a religion of the prison house. It has room for the least among God's creation. But it is proof against insolence, pride of race, religion or colour.'

"Democracy can thrive not only under the vigilant eye of its legislature, but also under the care and guidance of public opinion, and the Press is, par excellence, the vehicle through which opinion can become articulate. Its role consists not only in reflecting public opinion, but in instructing it and giving it proper orientation and guidance. For this, the Press has not only a moral right to free expression, but is subject to certain responsibilities also. ' In the absence of accepted moral duties, there can be no moral rights. From the moral point

[17] Kingsley Martin : *The Press the Public Wants* (The Hogarth Press, London, 1947), p. 32.

[18] India Government : *Report of the Press Commission* (Manager of Publications, Delhi, 1954), Part I, pp. 359-360.

of view, freedom of expression does not include the right to lie as a deliberate instrument of policy. The moral right does not cover the right to be deliberately or irresponsibly in error.' But the terrain of moral restrictions is not always co-extensive with the legal restrictions which may be imposed upon the right. Upto a point the restrictions must come from within. The legal protection may continue to remain even though the moral right to it has been forfeited. To quote again from the American Commission's Report, ' Many a lying venal, and scoundrelly public expression must continue to find shelter under a ' Freedom of the Press ' built for widely different purposes, for to impair the legal right even when the moral right is gone may easily be a cure worse than the disease. Each definition of an abuse invites abuse of definition. If the courts had to determine the inner corruptions of personal intention, honest and necessary criticism would proceed under an added peril. Though the presumption is against resort to legal action to curb abuses of the Press, there are limits to legal toleration.' Within the limits of this legal tolerance, the control over the Press must be subjective or professional. The ethical sense of the individual, the consciousness that abuse of freedom of expression, though not legally punishable, must tarnish the fair name of the Press and the censure of fellow journalists, should all operate as powerful factors towards the maintenance of the freedom even without any legal restrictions being placed on that freedom.''

By suggesting this, the Commission, more or less, voiced the feelings of Gandhiji who did not believe in Government measures to protect the liberty of press. Besides suggesting control of pen while writing for papers, he gave, long back, a solution to check irresponsibility. He said :

"The real remedy is healthy public opinion that will refuse to patronise poisonous journals. We have our journalists' association. Why should it not create a department whose business it would be to study the various journals and find objectionable articles and bring them to the notice of the respective editors ? The function of the department will be confined to the establishment of contact with the offending journals and public criticism of offending articles where the contact fails to bring about the desired reform. Freedom of the press is a precious privilege that no country can forego.''

But are the journalists listening ?

8 / *In Retrospect and Prospect*

GANDHIJI breathed his last on January 30, 1948. On March 29, 1949, the *Harijan*, which Gandhiji had been editing for a long time issued the following :

"All work in whatsoever sphere, was a means primarily of service in Gandhiji's eyes. Newspapers and journals can build up a fitting memorial to him in this matter by conforming or trying to conform to the unimpeachable standards of journalism practised by our revered and beloved leader."

Since 1903, Gandhiji, through his journals the *Indian Opinion*, the *Young India*, the *Navajivan* and the *Harijan*, not only did propagate his views, but, in the process, laid down a standard for journalists to emulate. While running the papers, his idea was to educate the people so that they could understand not only the significance of independence — political, economic and social — but also participate actively in freeing humanity from the bondage it was in. His motto, as a journalist, was service. He declared earlier : " One of the objects of a newspaper is to understand the popular feeling and give expression to it ; another is to arouse among the people certain desirable sentiments and the third is fearlessly to expose popular defects."

All through his life Gandhiji tried to uphold these tenets of faith. He did not take a short-term view on anything. He would not care for quick or spectacular success. His was a steady and sure process with a clear-cut objective. To him means were as important as ends. Moreover, truth with him was God. He could not barter away truth for anything.

The Press Commission also felt the absolute necessity of truthful and objective presentation of news and views and said :

" The need for truthful, objective and comprehensive presentation of news from all corners of the world was never more urgent. Hundreds of millions of our people have been enfranchised. A large number of them may yet be illiterate. But they have also shown considerable shrewdness and understanding of political events. The man behind the plough is eager to understand the world community of which he has become a part. He wants to know all that is happening around him, and he reads the newspapers eagerly or listens to it being read out. The future of the country depends on him, and it is his choice that is going to decide questions of peace or war. He wants facts, but also expects his newspaper to give him the truth about the facts."[1]

Mr. Henry Polak, as mentioned earlier, recalled stories when Gandhiji would insist on high standard of responsibility while editing the *Indian Opinion*. *The Times*, London, was his model in those days. Like the famous John Thaddous Delane, editor of *The Times*, Gandhiji could say : " . . . . The duty of the journalists is the same as that of the historian — to seek out the truth, above all things, and to present to his readers not such things as statecraft would wish them to know but the truth as near as he can attain it."

With Mr. Henry Polak he was insistent that objectivity must be maintained — ' Keep your standards right.' To his son Shri Manilal, in South Africa, Gandhiji wrote : " You should write what is the truth in the *Indian Opinion*. If you err do not hesitate to confess it."

And again in 1919, he reiterated in the unauthorized paper the *Satyagraha* : " There can be no room for untruth in my writings."

Gandhiji will correct any mistakes found in his writings. Instances of these have been given earlier. He had his own concept of newspaper running which was not only unconventional, but diametrically opposite to the usual norm. Gandhiji did not like the idea of building up the sales of his paper on the theory of ' what the readers want.' He would never, for that, publish sensational stories with breath-taking headlines.

He believed that the readers should support the paper for whom it was published. If they did not want it, Gandhiji would not run it on advertisement or adopt any and every means to promote sales. He would never be a party to exploit the base elements in human beings. He believed in the nobler traits in them and would feed his eternal craving — the quest for truth.

He tried, as we saw, to understand peoples' feelings and give

---

[1] India Government : *Report of the Press Commission* (Manager of Publications, Delhi, 1954), Part I, p. 340.

expression to these. He identified himself with the common man.
He tried and was successful to a very great extent, in feeling the
pulse of the mute millions, so that he would know what exactly
they wanted.

He would communicate with his readers. He would talk to
them, not talk at them, as Mr. Louis Fischer said. His was not a
sermon from the hill top. It was a communion with people. He
broke the convention of Town Hall speeches and pulled down the
decorated rostrums set up for brilliant speeches. He walked
straight down to the field where millions were slogging. He would
sit with them and speak about things which affect their lives,
in a language understood by them. This was a big departure from
the technique of Indian journalism of the 'twenties and
'thirties. He was an editor leading his readers to the righteous
path. He was ' Bapu ' or father to all. He did not like to be called
Mahatma, and with his frank sincerity declared the mission of his
life. He said :

" To describe truth, as it has appeared to me, and in the exact manner
in which I have arrived at it, has been my ceaseless effort. The exercise has
given me ineffable mental peace . . . .

" But the path of self-purification is hard and steep. To attain to perfect
purity one has to become absolutely passion free in thought, speech and action ;
to rise above the opposing currents of love and hatred, attachment and
repulsion. I know that I have not in me as yet that triple purity, in spite of
constant ceaseless striving for it. That is why the world's praise fails to move
me, indeed it often stings me . . . . "

Journalists began to imitate him. They went to the field and
collected stories about the common man — his thought and feeling,
his desire and ambition. Whether it was a political, economic or
social article, it invariably centred round the masses.

Gandhiji's editing of the *Navajivan*, in Gujarati, gave language
papers a prestige, they had hitherto lacked. In practically all the
provinces language papers began to be published. In a few cases
they showed the largest circulation in the country. This circulation
was not only confined to towns ; it travelled down to remote
corners. Newspapers appointed correspondents in many far away
places to get news from the villages.

" Many of his followers were moved to write and publish in the Indian
languages, in imitation of his own direct style. They wrote a simple prose.
Regional journalism began to acquire an importance and there was hardly any

area of the country which did not have its newspaper. These did not displace the English Press which provided all-India media."[2]

Among the regional papers the *Nayak*, the *Basumati*, the *Nabashakti*, the *Sanjibani* in Bengali, the *Sandesh*, the *Lokmanya* in Marathi, the *Bharat Mitra*, the *Vishwamitra* in Hindi became quite well known. Pandit Madan Mohan Malaviya himself started the *Abhyudaya*. Similarly, the Urdu papers, particularly Abul Kalam Azad's the *Al Hilal*, Mohammed Ali's the *Hamdard*, and others published from Lucknow and Lahore became quite popular.

In Kerala the *Malayala Manorama*, the *Kerala*, the *Malayalam*, etc., are worth mentioning in this connection. In Tamil the *Swadeshamitran*, the *Desabakhtan*, among others, soon made their mark.

This growth of Indian journalism was not without problems. Newspapers had to appoint many people as correspondents, reporters, sub-editors, etc. They were mostly new in the field. The reports coming from them were in many cases faulty. Editors or proprietors could not check all that was coming in as news and being printed. In many cases, they willy-nilly, were party to the printing of such incorrect news.

The Press Commission, much later, opined :

"The analysis shown in inaccuracies, mistakes and slips are more numerous in the Indian language newspapers than in those published in English. Instances are not many of the essential facts being deliberately omitted or suppressed to suit the editorial policy of the newspapers. In most cases, the mistakes are unintentional and can be attributed to many causes."[3]

In 1946–47, before partition of the country, the situation was very bad. Rather than stopping rumours newspapers were adding to these. Gandhiji in desparation said :

"The newspaperman has become a walking plague. In the East as in the West, newspapers are fast becoming the people's Bible, the Koran, Zend-Avesta and the Gita, rolled into one. All that appears in the papers is looked upon as God's truth. For instance, a newspaper predicts that riots are coming, that all the sticks and knives in Delhi have been sold out, and the news throws everybody into a panic. That is bad. Another newspaper reports the occurrence of riots here and there, and blames the police with taking sides with the Hindus in one place and the Muslims in another. Again the man in the street is upset. I want you all to shed this craven fear. It is not becoming of

[2] S. Natarajan : *A History of the Press in India* (Asia Publishing House, Bombay, 1962), p. 190.
[3] India Government : *Report of the Press Commission* (Manager of Publications, Delhi, 1954), Part I, pp. 341–342.

men and women, who believe in God and take part in the prayers, to be afraid of anyone."

On another occasion, he advised the pressmen as to their duties. He said, " There are occasions, when a journalist serves his profession best by his silence."

" But it is a journalist's job to purvey the facts and let the public judge for itself," the journalist argued. Did not Gandhiji believe in the capacity of the average man to judge correctly, provided he had enough knowledge of facts ? But Gandhiji demurred : " Not knowledge of facts. What passes for fact is only impressions or estimates of things, and estimates vary. Hence, one gets different versions of the same event." As an illustration, he mentioned the parable of seven blind men of Hindustan, each one describing the elephant differently and each one believing himself to be right.

"What is really needed to make democracy to function is not the knowledge of facts, but right education. And the true function of journalism is to educate the public mind, not to stock the public mind with wanted and unwanted impressions. A journalist has, therefore, to use his discretion, as to what to report and when. As it is, the journalists are not content to stick to the facts alone. Journalism has become the art of ' intelligent anticipation of events'."[4]

Gandhiji differentiated between news and journalists' impression of coming events. He would not like interpretative news, which to him, was journalistic kite-flying. He would advise journalists to print authentic news with no fear of contradiction. He would ask them to withhold news as long as it could not be verified. But, for the journalists it was not easy to listen to his advice. Not that they differed theoretically from him on the question of authenticity, but because of the keen competition amongst newspapers in coming out with the news first. What could be true with Gandhiji and his weekly paper, could not be true with a daily newspaper with all the competition involved in running it.

Interpretative news was a recent phenomenon of which Gandhiji, apart from his basic disagreement, was not very well aware. The readers in the West were not only getting the news but speculative news with particular slant or with different interpretations so as to create a public opinion the paper desired. Gandhiji would on the other hand educate them as intelligent fellow beings. He would

⁴ D. G. Tendulkar : *Mahatma* (V. K. Jhaveri and D. G. Tendulkar, Bombay, 1953), p. 247.

not lead them by the noose as a politician leads the masses.

To a Director of an influential British paper, Gandhiji said : " We are today suffering from a double evil — the suppression of the facts and concoction."[5]

In another of his prayer speeches, he said : " The press was called the Fourth Estate. It was definitely a power but to misuse that power was criminal. He was a journalist himself and he would appeal to fellow journalists to realize their responsibility and to carry on their work with no idea other than that of upholding the truth . . . ."[6]

But as mentioned earlier, it is difficult to maintain truth all the time. Besides the lack of trained workers in the field of journalism, there are other impediments in the way. The Press Commission, in the course of its investigation, did come across instances where news items were suppressed in order to please advertisers. In one case an advertiser, involved in a criminal case would influence that papers did not print the news which were earlier supplied by news agencies. In one case a business magnate of Ahmedabad was stated to have been arrested in a prohibition case in Bombay. But the Ahmedabad papers, obviously, because of pressure, did not publish the news. The Commission also pointed out how managing editors or influential editors ' accommodate ' their friends by suppressing news which otherwise could embarrass them. In conclusion, the report says : " Our view is that, once the editor feels that there is a conflict between the loyalty to his friends (including advertisers) and his duty with the public, there is a risk of his falling short of the high standard of his profession."[7]

There can be pressure through other means. The All-India Newspapers Editors' Conference alleged that papers were put to pressure to support the policy of political and communal organizations.

Then there is pressure from foreign Governments. The General Manager of a prominent Bengali paper, which has since discontinued publication, said that nearly 75 per cent of its circulation was in East Pakistan was due to the fact that other papers had been

---

[5] Ibid., Vol. VII, p. 282.   [6] Ibid., Vol. VII, p. 115.

[7] India Government : *Report of the Press Commission* (Manager of Publications, Delhi, 1954), Part I, pp. 323-324.

G—11

banned. Asked whether the authorities there had no objection to the policy of his paper, he answered that it had always maintained an independent editorial policy " which might have suited the East Pakistan Government."[8]

Bias in news presentation may also be due to the fact that a person or a group of persons, controlling a paper, belonged to a particular class which subscribed to a particular faith. They may believe in the institution of private property and hence black out any news to control them.

Gandhiji was against premature disclosure of news. He did not entirely agree with the dictum that the ' Press live by disclosures.' He had, as mentioned earlier, disclosed top secret matters. But he did that after ascertaining the correctness of the fact. Like the famous Delane he would agree that the duty of newspaper is " to obtain the earliest and most correct intelligence of the events of the time and instantly, by disclosing them, to make them common property of the nation."

In another prayer speech, Gandhiji criticized as already referred to the attempted disclosures of the so-called agreement reached between the Viceroy and the Congress Working Committee.

But could the Indian journalists get away from this influence ?

There was, and still is, to some extent, some sensation-mongering in the Indian press. In 1954, the Press Commission did not notice that rise in an alarming manner, whether in headlines or in news presentation. It said, " . . . . The well established newspapers have on the whole maintained a high standard of journalism. We are glad to state that they have avoided cheap sensationalism and unwarranted intrusion into private lives. They represent a decisive majority of the total circulation in India. Objectionable features have been noticed in a small section of the Press."

But Shri J. Natarajan, in his book, *History of Indian Journalism*, did not agree with this. He said :

"The press developed in those early years of freedom the sensational side of journalism which has now become a permanent factor in Indian journalism. The bulk of the newspapers was politically minded. A Bengal editor-proprietor unblushingly avowed that he had to adopt a communal policy

---

[8] Ibid., p. 352.

because playing down riots and disturbances curbed his sales. 'Even the newsboys refuse to touch my paper if my rivals report a large number of deaths than I do,' he remarked, adding eloquently that he had taken the hint and been justified by results."

Yellow journalism is not easy to define. Normally, it should be malicious and wilful publication of reports known to be false. It may also be building up of a cock and bull story on an insignificant matter. It may also include a lurid exposure of personal lives of individuals. Also included in it is abusive or suggestive language to debase public tastes.

"Yellow journalism of one type or another is increasing in this country. It is confined not to any particular area or language but is perhaps more discernible in some than others. It was a matter of great concern to us to find, instances of such yellow journalism are to be found, everywhere the majority of the journalists, who appeared before us, had little to say about it except of course, to condemn in general terms." [9]

The Press Commission further said,

"We must mention with regret that a great deal of the objectionable writings scurrilous, obscene, indecent and personal does exist in the Indian Press though it is convenient to the periodical Press, and the daily newspapers have been comparatively free from these evils." [10]

Though, more or less, the Indian Press has maintained their position till now, its counterpart in the West was going from bad to worse.

More than thirty years after Gandhiji commented on such catchy or misleading displays, we find President Kennedy worried about the same. It concerned relationship of Mrs. Kennedy with the press ; the danger of twisted and out of context captions, is nonetheless of concern to all. The so-called confidential type of magazines were continuously publishing Mrs. Kennedy's photograph on covers with headlines calculated to draw the immediate attention of the readers in thinking that "they will learn about the most intimate recesses of Jackie's life." A few samples were : "How long can they hide the truth from Caroline Kennedy ? " Though the headline was breath-taking, the story was in the form of an advice that Caroline must be protected from over exposure to public. Another sample : "Told for the first time. The illness that's breaking Jackie's heart." Inside material revealed that it was a story about the illness of the President's father. Another

---

[9] Ibid., p. 346,   [10] Ibid., p. 39.

headline : " The hidden life of Jackie Kennedy." The story is about Mrs. Kennedy's love for her husband and their quiet life. The President, it was reported, called these articles " Chessy " and was considering whether steps could be taken against such things.[11]

Lord Shawcross, ex-chairman of the British Royal Commission on the press, while addressing the annual conference of the Commonwealth Press Union, inaugurated on June 17, 1963, by Prime Minister Harold Macmillan, said :

" Although in many respects we have the best Press in the world, I should lack courage if I did not say it is open to criticism here. It may be that the Press has less influence now a days on political opinion ; it certainly has great influence on the manners and morals of the community.... Evil communications corrupt good manners. I think we should all ask ourselves whether the publicising of pimps, prostitutes or perverts in highly paid interviews of feature articles is really a good thing. Is it useful to pay large sums for the so-called memoirs — usually written by a ghost — of criminals convicted of crimes, however sensational, of prostitutes, however degraded, or adulteresses, however notorious in cafe society ? ....

" When young women through some glandular malfunction develop unduly large busts, whilst they may be suitable exhibits in a medical museum, is it helpful to publish their photographs in the popular Press ? Is it wise constantly to advertise the fact (without which advertisement it would often not be the fact) that the wages of sin are sometimes great, as for instance, when some trollop is offered six times the salary of a Prime Minister to appear in a night club ? I put these problems as questions....

" I have heard newspapermen say that the public has to be given what it wants. Any prostitute could say the same. But there is some truth in it. The fact is that we get the papers, and for that matter the politicians we deserve."

He voiced the same feelings as did Gandhiji throughout his life, however, much Mr. Ed Mowrer, as narrated earlier, might differ that paper was not a school to educate the readers, and said :

" We ordinary people, weak, untutored, open to all sorts of temptations and influences are entitled to look to the Press for a beneficient influence. There is much that is beastly and squalid in the world. But there remains far more that is beautiful and splendid. Let us hear more about the beautiful and splendid and give less advertisement to the beastly and the squalid."

So far, about news, what about views ? Are the editors upholding the standards as Gandhiji preached and practised ? By and large, these have not fallen short of the usual standard — though not the standards of Gandhiji. But there are persons who do not think high of the editorials. Shri Chalapathi Rao of the *National Herald*,

[11] *Time* (New York, December 14, 1962), p. 54.

In Retrospect and Prospect

speaking on the seminar on Indian Press, 1963–73, organized by the International Press Institute, said :

"Much of the editorial writing lacks force, conviction of style. Fear and timidity, collective and individual, are inhibiting factors and they are often the result of lack of freedom. If most newspaper editorials in India sound as though they had been ground out of a machine that manufactures manifestoes, it is partly because of cowardice, of a certain fear of offending important interests, of lack of conscience, and even of a sense of duty. The editorial writer, who is not usually the editor, has his problems of conformity and conscience. This is not so difficult of adjustment. But as long as the editorial writer is merely told what to write on or is asked to write on whatever he likes, there can be no authentic articulation and no circulation of policy. The editorial writer is being pushed aside, if not quite displaced, by the columnists, and while the columnists were originally employed in America because it was thought editorial writers lacked guts and personality, publishers now seek to buy columnists who echo their views."

If Gandhiji, as an editor, was able to focus the attention of the journalists to the villages of India, he was much more successful, as a writer, in influencing authors to write on the same subject. Presiding over the Gujarati Literary Conference on November 2, 1936, reference of which was made earlier, Gandhiji posed the question : Whom should the author write for ? For the few intellectuals or for the general masses ?

Not only in style which from the Johnsonian or Macaulayan verbosity gave place to the Gandhian simplicity but in the content as well, Gandhiji revolutionized the thinking of his contemporaries. We discussed earlier Gandhiji's contribution to Gujarati literature. He reformed it and helped in its all round growth. Quite a number of Gujarati authors not only followed his style but wrote on subjects dear to Gandhiji's heart.

In other languages also, the impact of Gandhiji was great. To take a few examples, Shri Sankarram wrote about the ' Children of the Kaveri.' Shri Humayun Kabir in *Man and Rivers* portrayed the picture of rural life in Bengal. It was the day-to-day life of common people. Land to the cultivators, as portrayed, was no longer a piece of earth. It was part of ' Bharat Mata ' — Mother India — which nourished them. Similar was the theme of the writings of Shri K. S. Venkataraman. His *Murugan the Tiller* or *Kandan the Patriot* created quite a sensation, in Tamilnad in the 'twenties and 'thirties. The fortitude and trials of the forties were ably portrayed by Smt. Kamala Markandaya (*Some Inner*

Fury), Shri R. K. Narayan ('*Waiting for the Mahatma*), Shri Mulk Raj Anand (*Untouchable*), Shri Khwaja Ahmed Abbas (*Inquilab*), Shri Bhabani Bhattacharyya (*So Many Hungers*), to mention a few of the literatures produced during the period. Gandhiji's political movements, as they nourished and built up editors, so did they provide ample scope to authors to wield their pen upon.

As we had seen, Gandhiji was very cautious about the freedom of expression and liberty of the press during the political movement in South Africa. In India, when the Government, with a heavy hand, was curtailing the same, he started writing vehemently against Government action. According to him, the duty of the press was to expose fearlessly the defects.

Gandhiji used to say that the press lost freedom through its own weakness. If the press behaved properly, i.e., if it was correct in its presentation of news and views, nobody could restrict its freedom ; but, if, on the other hand, it could not check its pen, it might invite restrictions through its own columns. He was constantly reminding his fellow journalists of this, all the time, particularly during the communal tension. Under the sub-head ' Poisonous Journalism,' in the *Young India* of May 28, 1931, Gandhiji wrote :

"I have before me extracts from journals containing some gruesome things. There is communal incitement, gross misrepresentation and incitement to political violence bordering on murder. It is of course easy enough for the Government to launch out prosecutions or to pass repressive ordinances. These fail to serve the purpose intended except very temporarily, and in no case they convert the writers, who often take the secret propaganda, when the open forum of the press is denied to them."

But, as we saw, not many people were listening to his advice. It was much worse in 1946–47, immediately before and after partition of the country. He got so much fed up with the press that he himself suggested the banning of the papers.

During the Second World War, when Gandhiji was hardening his attitude towards the British Government which committed India into the war without consulting her, he was, even then, careful about publishing war news in his own paper. He would not write anything which would embarrass the Government and help the enemies. In the July 19, 1942, issue of the *Harijan*, he wrote :

"Let me add too that without needing any pressure from outside, I am using the greatest restraint in the choice of printing matter. Nothing is being consciously published that would give any clue to the ' enemy ' as to military objectives or dispositions. Care is being exercised to avoid all exaggeration or sensational matter. Adjectives and adverbs are well weighed before being used. And they know that I am ever ready to acknowledge errors and mend them."

Gandhiji, thus, believed in self-control. As we saw earlier, he was exhorting journalists to have control on pen. He knew the power of the press and that is why he was cautious about self-discipline.

But his advice was not much heeded by the journalists. Though in the Constitution adopted in 1950, freedom of expression and liberty of the press were guaranteed, the Government of India had to amend it. This was because of the exigency of the situation. People were stretching this concept of freedom of expression to the utmost length. The judicial courts, in a few cases, exempted people from punishment under the constitutional safeguard. Thus, the press lost its liberty to a certain extent through its own weakness — weakness in not controlling itself in time.

What was the impact of Gandhiji on fellow journalists so far as advertisements were concerned ? Gandhiji would not soil his papers with advertisements. Only one paper of importance — the *Swarajya* — founded by T. Prakasam followed Gandhiji's example.

As early as 1919, Gandhiji suggested that there should be, in each province, only one advertising medium which could display advertisements of things useful to the public. But it was not accepted by any party — advertiser, advertising agency or the Government.

Gandhiji had all along been crusading against immoral and obscene advertisements. Lengthy excerpts had earlier been reproduced on this. He was pained to see editors not averse " to derive an income from advertisements which are obviously intended to spread the evils which they should shun." Press Commission also in 1954 noticed many lewd and obscene advertisements in the paper.

To stop them, Gandhiji suggested the following courses :
(1) Readers' control. He asked the readers to stop their patronage for the paper when they find them displaying indecent advertisements. Gandhiji desired an enlightened public opinion which could bring a pressure on the newspapers. He wanted women, as they were shamelessly exploited for this

purpose, to be the vanguard in creating public opinion. But readers, unfortunately, could not, as desired by Gandhiji, put any pressure on the newspapers.

(2) Editors' or proprietors' control. He requested editors or the proprietors of papers to stop publishing questionable advertisements. Mention has been made of Gandhiji's article, dated November 14, 1936 in the *Harijan* where he quoted a letter from a ' sister ' requesting journalists to stop such horrible advertisements. At least one editor, that of the *Nispruha* of Nagpur, as recorded by Gandhiji, agreed with his views and forthwith stopped such advertisements.

Has the press, by and large, kept up the standard practised and preached by Gandhiji ? To this an alternative question may be asked : Did those who lived with or believed in Gandhiji's way of life uphold his standard in their day-to-day life ? Did the people of the country, for whom Gandhiji did so much and ultimately gave his life, practise truth ? Or in other words, why should we expect something special from the journalists, if we do not expect the same from other segments of the community.

In summing up, it may be said that though the journalists did not rise up to the expectation of Gandhiji, the Press, by and large is not worse than it was in 1948. Rather, it is showing signs of progress, adjustment and much vigour.

Press, despite stray pulls here and there, by and large, is performing a special service. It is, within its limitations, educating the readers. While talking about its responsibility and duty, we should not forget the handicap it faces. For foreign news it has to depend mostly on foreign sources and news agencies. The news etc., are to be speedily translated for language papers and edited properly. And who does all these ? Half trained or ill trained and lowly paid journalists ? As in case of agriculture where we have to look to the man behind the plough, more so the journalists in newspaper who are to be trained properly before we can expect presentation of balanced news and views by them. Gone are the days when a person could say that he would make a journalist out of anyone.

Journalism is not only a craftsmanship ; it is a creative ability. It is not a journalist's job to print news only, but to print what is ' fit to be printed.' For that he has to combine in him the role of, among others, an educationist, sociologist and an economist. He will not only be well versed in subjects he is to deal with, but he has to understand their implications in the present context.

To be creative, he must develop the capacity to react to the events he is going to print or count on, he will have to be knowledgeable enough to interpret these properly. Above all, he must have the ability to communicate things. The subjects selected are to have universal appeal ; the words picked should be well chosen, clear and understandable. Though the press has been compared to an industry, it differs from an ordinary one in many respects. It is the character of the paper, the role of the journalist, the social importance of the written sheet, which makes it different from industries. To quote Mr. C. P. Scott : " Whatever its position or character, at least it should have a soul of its own."

Because of the role assigned to papers, journalists have a greater duty, than others in the society. Press has enjoyed particular privilege. It has constitutional guarantee for its liberty. The publishing industry, to take an example, has not any such. For that reason people expect much from newspaper. It has been assigned a particular role. This role of leadership it has to preserve, pursue and foster in years to come.

In the end, let us remember the words of the First Royal Commission on Press :

"There is still widespread among pressmen a sense of vocation ; they feel a call somewhat as sailors feel the call of the sea."

All work in whatsoever sphere was a means primarily of service in Gandhiji's eyes. Newspapers and journals can build up a fitting memorial to him in this matter by conforming or trying to conform to the unimpeachable standards of journalism practised by our revered and beloved leader.

The *Harijan*, March 29, 1948

Bibliography

AGARWAL, S. N. : *Constructive Programme for Congressmen*, New Delhi A.I.C.C., 1953.

——————— *Gandhian Plan of Economic Development for India*, Bombay, Padma Publications, 1944.

——————— *Gandhian Plan Re-affirmed*, Bombay, Padma Publications, 1948.

AGARWALA, A. N. : *Gandhism : A Socialistic Approach*, Allahabad, Kitab Mahal, 1944.

AKKAD, B. J. : *Mahatma Gandhi : A Short Life of Gandhiji*, Bombay, Vora & Co., 1948.

ALEXANDER, HORACE : *Consider India, An Essay in Values*, Bombay, Asia Publishing House, 1961.

——————— *Resisting Evil Without Arms*, London, Friends Peace Committee, 1959.

——————— *Social and Political Ideas of Mahatma Gandhi*, New Delhi, Indian Council of World Affairs, 1949.

ANDLEY, CHATUR BIHARILAL : *Gandhi, the Saviour*, Delhi, Andley Bros., 1933.

ANDREWS, C. F. : *Mahatma Gandhi's Ideas, including selections from his writings*, London, Allen & Unwin, 1949.

——————— *Non-Cooperation*, Madras, Ganesh & Co., 1922.

ARGUS : *Gandhism-Cum-Non-Cooperation Exposed*, Assam, Author, 1922.

ARYANAYAKAM, E. W. : *Crisis in Education*, Sevagram, Hindustani Talimi Sangh, 1952.

ASAF ALI : *Constructive Non-Cooperation*, Madras, Ganesh & Co., 1924.

ATHALYE, D. V. : *The Life of Mahatma Gandhi*, Poona, Swadeshi Publishing Co., 1923.

AUROBINDO : *Doctrine of Passive Resistance*, Calcutta, Arya Publishing House, 1948.

AVINASHILINGAM, T. S. : *Gandhiji's Experiments in Education*, Delhi, Publications Division, 1960.

——————— *Educational Reconstruction*, Wardha, Hindustani Talimi Sangh, 1939.

BALWANT SINGH : *Under the Shelter of Bapu*, Ahmedabad, Navajivan, 1962.

Bibliography

BANDYOPADHYAYA, NRIPENDRA CHANDRA : *Gandhism in Theory and Practice*, Madras, Ganesh & Co., 1923.

BANNERJEE, S. : *Nation in the Making*, London, Oxford University Press, 1931.

BARNES, A. M. : *My dear Child : Letters from M. K. Gandhi to Esther Faering*, Ahmedabad, Navajivan, 1956.

BARNES, M. : *India Today and Tomorrow*, London, Allen & Unwin, 1937.

BARNS, MARGARITA : *The Indian Press*, London, Allen & Unwin, 1940.

BAROS, JAN. : *Mahatma Gandhi : Pictorial History of a Great Life*, Calcutta, Jan Baros, 1949.

BARR, F. MARY : *Bapu : Conversations and Correspondence*, Bombay, International Book House, 1949.

————— *Mahatma Gandhi : His Life and Teachings*, Allahabad, Radha Krishanlal, 1934.

BEDELL, CLYDE : *How to Write for Advertising that Sells*, New York, McGraw-Hill, 1952.

BEDI, B. P. L. (Ed.) : *Gandhi's Non-Violent Weapon*, Delhi, Unity Book Club of India.

————— *Saint of Human Rights : Gandhi*, Delhi, Unity Book Club of India, 1948.

BELL, R. G. : *Alternative to War*, London, James Clarke, 1959.

BERNAYS, ROBERT : *The Naked Fakir*, London, Victor Gollancz, 1931.

BHATNAGAR, R. R. : *Rise and Growth of Hindi Journalism*, Allahabad, Kitab Mahal, 1940.

BIRLA, G. D. : *In the Shadow of the Mahatma : a Personal Memoir*, Madras, Orient Longmans, 1953.

BOLTON, GLORNEY : *The Tragedy of Gandhi*, London, Allen & Unwin, 1934.

BONDURANT, JOAN V. : *Conquest of Violence*, Princeton, Princeton University Press, 1958.

BOSE, NIRMAL KUMAR : *My Days with Gandhi*, Calcutta, Nishana, 1953.

————— *Selections from Gandhi*, Ahmedabad, Navajivan Publishing House, 1948.

————— *Studies in Gandhism*, 2nd Edn., Calcutta, Indian Associated Publishing Co., 1947.

BOSE, R. N. : *Gandhian Technique and Tradition in Industrial Relations*, All India Institute of Social Welfare, Etc., 1956.

BOSE, S. C. : *Indian Struggle*, London, Wishort & Co., Ltd., 1935.

BRIGHT, J. S. : *Gandhi in India*, Lahore, Indian Printing Works, 1947.

BRYANT, J. F. : *Gandhi and the Indianization of Empire*, Cambridge, J. Hall and Son, 1924.

CARNEGIE, G. : *Little Known Facts about Well-known People*, Bombay, Vora & Co., 1947.

CATLIN, GEORGE : *In the Path of Mahatma Gandhi*, London, Macdonald & Co., 1948.

CHAKRAVARTY, AMIYA : *Mahatma Gandhi and Modern World*, Calcutta, Book House, 1945.

CHANDRA, JAG PARVESH (ED.) : *Gandhi Against Fascism*, Lahore, Indian Printing Works, 1944.

172

————— *Gandhi and Tagore Argue*, Lahore, Indian Printing Works, 1945.

————— *Teachings of Mahatma Gandhi*, Lahore, Indian Printing Works, 1947.

CHANDIWALA, BRIJKRISHNA : *At the Feet of Bapu*, Ahmedabad, Navajivan, 1954.

CHATTERJEE, B. C., *Gandhi or Aurobindo* ? *And an Appeal to Mr. Gandhi*, Calcutta, Saraswati Library, 1921.

CHATTERJEE, B. L. : *Gandhi : Champion of the Proletariat*, Calcutta, Prakashani, 1944.

CHATTERJEE, LALITMOHAN : *Gandhiji*, Calcutta, The Popular Agency, 1931.

CHAUDHARY, RAMNARAYAN : *Bapu as I Saw Him*, Ahmedabad, Navajivan, 1959.

CHIROL, VALENTINE : *The Emergence of Mr. Gandhi*, London, Macmillan & Co., 1921.

DANGE, S. A. : *Gandhi vs. Lenin*, Bombay, Liberty Literature, 1926.

DANTWALA, M. L. : *Gandhism Reconsidered*, 2nd Rev. Edn., Bombay, Padma Publications, 1945.

DAS, FRIEDA MATHILDA (Hauswirth) : *Gandhi : A Portrait from Life*, New York, The Vanguard Press, 1931.

DASGUPTA, ARUN CHANDRA : *Non-violence the Invincible Power*, 2nd Edn., Calcutta, Khadi Pratisthan, 1946.

DATTA, K. K. : *Writings and Speeches of Gandhiji Relating to Bihar*, 1917–1947, Patna, Government of Bihar, 1960.

DESAI, CHITRA : *Sage of Sevagram*, Bombay, Bharat Prakashan, 1952.

DESAI, KANTILAL, S.: *Gandhi & Gandhism : Future Voice for India*, Ahmedabad, Sakarlal Bulakidas & Co., 1931.

DESAI, MAHADEV: *Diary Vol.* 1 (1932), Ahmedabad, Navajivan, 1953.

————— *Gandhiji in Indian Villages*, Madras, S. Ganesan, 1927.

————— *Gospel of Selfless Action or the Gita according to Gandhi*, Ahmedabad, Navajivan, 1956.

————— *Righteous Struggle*, Ahmedabad, Navajivan, 1951.

————— *Story of Bardoli*, Ahmedabad, Navajivan, 1929.

————— *The Epic of Travancore*, Ahmedabad, Navajivan, 1937.

————— *Wardha Interview*, 1942.

————— *With Gandhi in Ceylon: A Journal of the Tour*, Madras, S. Ganesan, 1928.

DESAI, VALJI, G. (Comp.) : *Gandhian Anthology*, Ahmedabad, Navajivan, 1952.

DESHMUKH, C. D. : *Selected sayings of Mahatma Gandhi in Sanskrit verses with the original*, 1957.

DESHPANDE, M. S. : *Light of India: Message of the Mahatma*, Bombay, Wilco Publishing House, 1958.

DESHPANDE, P. G. (Comp.) : *Gandhiana, A Bibliography of Gandhian Literature*, Ahmedabad, Navajivan, 1948.

DEVAS, S. : *Gandhiji & Some of his Thoughts*, Madras, Good Pastor Press, 1949.

Bibliography

DHADDA, SIDDHARAJ : *Gramdan : The Latest Phase of Bhoodan*, Kashi, Sarva Seva Sangh, 1957.

DHAWAN, G. N. : *Political Philosophy of Mahatma Gandhi*, Bombay, Popular Book Depot, 1946.

DATTA, DHIRENDRA MOHAN : *The Philosophy of Mahatma Gandhi*, Madison, University of Wisconsin, 1953.

DIWAKAR, R. R. : *Glimpses of Gandhiji*, Bombay, Hind Kitabs, 1949.

————— *Satyagraha*, Bombay, Hind Kitabs, 1946.

————— *Satyagraha in Action*, Calcutta, Signet Press, 1949.

————— *Satyagraha : The Pathway to Peace*, Patna, Pustak Bhandar, 1950.

DOKE, J. J. : *M. K. Gandhi : An Indian Portrait in South Africa*, Varanasi, Akhil Bharat Sarva Seva Sangh Prakashan, Rajghat, 1959.

DUNCAN, RONALD : *Selected Writings of Mahatma Gandhi*, London, Faber & Faber, 1951.

DURANT, WILL : *Gandhi*, New York, Simon & Schuster, 1930.

DWARKADAS, KANJI : *Gandhiji : Through My Diary Leaves*, 1915–48, Bombay, Author, 1950.

DEVOE, MERRILL : *Effective Advertising Copy*, New York, Macmillan, 1956.

EATON, JEANETTER : *Gandhi : Fighter Without a Sword*, New York, William Morrow, 1954.

ELWIN, VERRIER : *Gandhiji—Bapu of his People*, Shillong, Assam Government Press, 1956.

————— *Religious and Cultural Aspects of Khadi*, Madras, Seshan, 1932.

FIELDON, L. : *Beggar my Neighbour*, London, Secker and Warburg, 1943.

FINN, DAVID : *Public Relations & Management*, New York, Reinhold, 1960.

FISCHER, F. B. : *The Strange Little Brown Man Gandhi*, New York, R. Lond and R. R. Smith, 1932.

FISCHER, LOUIS : *A Week with Gandhi*, Bombay, International Book House, 1943.

————— *Gandhi : His Life and Message for the World*, A Signet Key Book, 1954.

————— *Gandhi & Stalin*, Delhi, Rajkamal Publication, 1947.

————— *Life of Mahatma Gandhi*, New York, Harper & Brothers, 1950.

————— *Life of Mahatma Gandhi*, London, Jonathan Cape, 1951.

————— *Life of Mahatma Gandhi*, 2 Vols., Bombay, Bharatiya Vidya Bhavan, 1953.

FULOP-MILLER, RENE : *Gandhi : The Holy Man*, London, G. P. Putnam & Sons, 1931.

————— *Lenin and Gandhi*, London, Labour Publishing Co., 1927.

GANDHI, M. K. : *All Men are Brothers : Life and Thought*, United States, UNESCO, Orient Longmans, 1959.

————— *An Autobiography or the Story of My Experiments with Truth*, Ahmedabad, Navajivan, 1948.

————— *Autobiography* (Abridged), Ahmedabad, Navajivan, 1952.

————— *Birth Control*, Bombay, Bharatiya Vidya Bhavan, 1962.

174

———————— *Cent Per Cent Swadeshi or the Economics of Village Industries,* Ahmedabad, Navajivan, 1938.

———————— *Character and Nation Building,* Ahmedabad, Navajivan, 1959.

———————— *Communal Unity,* Ahmedabad, Navajivan, 1949.

———————— *Constructive Programme, Its Meaning and Place,* Ahmedabad, Navajivan, 1948.

———————— *Cooperative Farming,* Ahmedabad, Navajivan, 1959.

———————— *Correspondence with the Government,* 1942–44, Ahmedabad, Navajivan, 1945.

———————— *Correspondence with the Government,* 1944–47, Ahmedabad, Navajivan, 1959.

———————— *Delhi Diary : Prayer Speeches from* 10–9–1947 to 30–1–1948, Ahmedabad, Navajivan, 1948.

———————— *Educational Philosophy of Mahatma Gandhi,* Ahmedabad, Navajivan, 1953.

———————— *Famous Letters of Mahatma Gandhi,* (Comp. & Ed. by R. K. Khipple), Lahore, Indian Printing Works, 1947.

———————— *Food Shortage and Agriculture,* Ahmedabad, Navajivan, 1949.

———————— *Freedom's Battle,* Madras, S. Ganesan & Co., 1922.

———————— *Gandhi at Work : His Work Story Continued,* New York, Macmillan, 1931.

———————— *Gokhale : My Political Guru,* Ahmedabad, Navajivan, 1958.

———————— *Hind Swaraj or Indian Home Rule,* Ahmedabad, Navajivan, 1956.

———————— *Hindu Muslim Tension, Its Cause and Cure,* Allahabad, Young India Office, 1924.

———————— *India's Case for Swaraj, Writings and Speeches,* 1931–32, Bombay, Waman P. Kabadi, 1932.

———————— *India's Food Problem,* Ahmedabad, Navajivan, 1960.

———————— *Jail Experience,* Madras, Tagore & Co., 1922. .

———————— *Jawaharlal Nehru : The Jewel of India,* Bombay, A. T. Hingorani, 1960.

———————— *Letters to Rajkumari Amrit Kaur,* Ahmedabad, Navajivan, 1961.

———————— *My Dear Child : Letters from M. K. Gandhi to Esther Faering,* Ahmedabad, Navajivan, 1956.

———————— *My Philosophy of Life,* Bombay, Pearl Publications, 1961.

———————— *My Religion,* Ahmedabad, Navajivan, 1955.

———————— *My Socialism,* Ahmedabad, Navajivan, 1959.

———————— *My Soul Agony : Statements from Yervada Prison,* Bombay, Provincial Board, Servants of Untouchable Society, 1932.

———————— *Non-Cooperation : Recent Speeches and Writings,* Madras, S. Ganesan & Co.

———————— *Panchayat Raj,* Ahmedabad, Navajivan, 1959.

———————— *Quit India,* Bombay, Padma Publications, 1942.

———————— *Rebuilding our Villages,* Ahmedabad, Navajivan, 1952.

———————— *Ruskin's Unto this Last : A Paraphrase,* Ahmedabad, Navajivan, 1951.

———————— *Sarvodaya,* Ahmedabad, Navajivan, 1951.

175

Bibliography

——————— *Sarvodaya—The Welfare of all*, Ahmedabad, Navajivan, 1954.

——————— *Satyagraha* : 1910–35, Allahabad, A.I.C.C., 1935.

——————— *Satyagraha* : *Non-Violent Resistance*, Ahmedabad, Navajivan, 1951.

——————— *Satyagraha in South Africa*, Ahmedabad, Navajivan, 1950.

——————— *Selected Letters*, Ahmedabad, Navajivan, 1949.

——————— *Self-restraint* vs. *Self-Indulgence*, Ahmedabad, Navajivan, 1933.

——————— *Socialism of My Conception*, Bombay, Bharatiya Vidya Bhavan, 1957.

——————— *Speeches and Writings*, Madras, G. A. Natesan & Co., 1918.

——————— *Thoughts on National Language*, Ahmedabad, Navajivan, 1956.

——————— *The Art of Living*, Bombay, Pearl Publications, 1961.

——————— *The Good Life*, New Delhi, Indian Printing Works, 1950.

——————— *The Idea of a Rural University*, Wardha, Hindustani Talimi Sangh, 1954.

——————— *The Mind of Mahatma Gandhi*, (Comp. R. K. Prabhu and U. R. Rao), Madras, Oxford University Press, 1946.

——————— *The Nation's Voice : Speeches, Sept. to Dec.* 1931, (Ed. C. Rajagopalachari and J. C. Kumarappa), Ahmedabad, Navajivan Publishing House, 1947.

——————— *The Story of my Life*, Ahmedabad, Navajivan, 1955.

——————— *The Wisdom of Gandhi : in his own words*, (Ed. by Roy Walker), Calcutta, Book Company, Ltd., 1943.

——————— *The Wit and Wisdom of Gandhi*, (Ed. by Homer A. Jack), Boston, Beacon Press, 1951.

——————— *To the Princes and their People*, Karachi, Anand T. Hingorani, 1942.

——————— *To the Protagonists of Pakistan*, Karachi, Anand T. Hingorani, 1943.

——————— *To the Students*, Ahmedabad, Navajivan, 1949.

——————— *To the Women*, Karachi, Anand T. Hingorani, 1943.

——————— *Towards Lasting Peace*, Bombay, Bharatiya Vidya Bhavan, 1956.

——————— *Towards New Education*, Ahmedabad, Navajivan, 1953.

——————— *Towards Non-violent Socialism*, Ahmedabad, Navajivan, 1951.

——————— *Views on Untouchability*, Ed. & Published by M. Bihari Lal, 1932.

——————— *Village Industries*, Ahmedabad, Navajivan, 1960.

——————— *Woman's Role in Society*, Ahmedabad, Navajivan, 1959.

——————— *Young India*, 1919–1922, Madras, S. Ganesan, 1922.

——————— *Young India*, 1924–1926, Madras, S. Ganesan, 1927.

——————— *Young India*, 1927–1928, Madras, S. Ganesan, 1935.

GANDHI, MANUBEHN : *Bapu—My Mother*, Ahmedabad, Navajivan, 1949.

——————— *Last Glimpses of Bapu*, Agra, Shivlal Agarwala & Co., 1962.

——————— *My Memorable Moments with Bapu*, Ahmedabad, Navajivan, 1960.

——————— *The End of an Epoch*, Ahmedabad, Navajivan, 1962.

GANDHI, PRABHUDAS : *My Childhood with Gandhiji*, Ahmedabad, Navajivan, 1957.

GENERAL COUNCIL OF THE PRESS : *The Press and the People*, London, Author, 1960.

GHOSH, S. L. (Ed.) : *Gandhiji's Do or Die Mission*, Calcutta, Book Corporation, 1947.

GUNTHER, JOHN : *Inside Asia*, London, Harper Brothers, 1942.

GUPTA, NAGENDRANATH : *Gandhi and Gandhism*, Bombay, Hind Kitabs, 1948.

HART, E. G. (Lt. Col.) : *Gandhi and the Indian Problem*, London, Hutchinson & Co., 1931.

HEATH, CARL : *Gandhi*, London, Allen & Unwin, 1948.

HENDERSON, ARCHIBALD : *Mahatma Gandhi*, London, D. Appleton & Co., 1930.

HOCKIN, JOHN : *First Step in Free-Lance Journalism*, London, Pitman, 1947.

HOCKING, W. E. : *Freedom of the Press*, Illinois, Chicago University Press, 1948.

HOGG, DOROTHY : *The Moral Challenge of Gandhi*, Allahabad, Kitab Mahal, 1946.

HOLMES, J. H. (Rev.) : *Gandhi the Modern Christ*, Triplicane, M. Ramaswamy & Co.

HOLMES, JOHN HAYNES : *My Gandhi*, London, Allen & Unwin, 1954.

———— *World's Greatest Man*, Bombay, National Literature Publishing Co., 1922.

———— *What Gandhi is Teaching the World*, New York, The Community Church, 1942.

HOLMES, W. H. C. : *Twofold Gandhi : Hindu Monk and Revolutionary Politician*, London, A. R. Mowbray & Co., 1952.

HOSSAIN, SYED : *Gandhi : the saint as statesman*, Los Angeles, Suttorhouse, 1937.

HOYLAND, JOHN S. : *Cross Moves East : A Study in the Significance of Gandhi's Satyagrahas*, London, George Allen & Unwin, 1931.

———— *They saw Gandhi*, New York, Fellowship Publications, 1947.

HUSSAIN, S. ABID : *The Way of Gandhi and Nehru*, Bombay, Asia Publishing House, 1959.

HUTHEESING, KRISHNA : *The Story of Gandhiji*, Bombay, Kutub Publishers, 1949.

INDIA GOVERNMENT : *Gandhian Outlook & Techniques*, New Delhi, Education Ministry, 1953.

———— M/o I. & B., (PUBLICATIONS DIVISION) : *The Collected Works of Mahatma Gandhi*, Vols. I-XIV, Delhi, Publications Division, 1958–1962.

———— M/o I. & B : *Annual Reports of the Registrar of Newspapers for India for* 1956, '57, '58, '60, '61, '62, New Delhi, Author.

IYENGAR, A. S. : *All through the Gandhian Era*, Bombay, Hind Kitabs, 1950.

JACK, HOMER A. (Ed.) : *The Gandhi Reader : A Source Book of His Life and Writings*, London, Dennis Doboon, 1958.

———— *Wit and Wisdom of Gandhi*, London, Beacon Press, 1951.

177

G 12

Bibliography

JAIN, JAGDISH CHANDRA : *I could not save Bapu*, Banaras, Jagram Sahitya Mandir, 1949.

JAISINGHANI, A. H. : *Mahatma Gandhi : A Study*, Karachi, Akbar Ashram, 1931.

JAJU, SHRIKRISHNADAS : *Ideology of the Charkha*, Kashi, Sarva Seva Sangh, 1957.

JAPHETH, M. D. : *Pursuit of Truth : A Short Story of M. Gandhi*, Bombay, Blaze Publications, 1948.

———— *The Truth about Gandhi*, Bombay, Modys Diamond P. Works, 1949.

JAYAPRAKASH NARAYAN : *A Picture of Sarvodaya Social Order*, Tanjore, Sarvodaya Prachuralayam, 1961.

———— *From Socialism to Sarvodaya*, Kashi, Sarva Seva Sangh, 1958.

———— *Jeevan Dan*, Tanjore, Sarvodaya Prachuralayam, 1954.

———— *Socialism to Sarvodaya*, Madras, Socialist Book Centre, 1956.

———— *Swaraj for the People*, Varanasi, Sarva Seva Sangh, 1961.

———— *Towards a New Society*, New Delhi, Congress for Cultural Freedom, 1958.

JHA, SHIVANAND : *A Critical Study of Gandhian Economic Thought*, Agra, Lakshminarayan Agarwala, 1961.

JONES, E. STANLEY : *Mahatma Gandhi : An Interpretation*, London, Hodder & Sloughton, 1948.

JONES, MARE EDMUND : *Gandhi Lives*, Philadelphia, Daird Mekay & Co., 1948.

JHA, S. C. : *A Concept of Planned free Press*, Calcutta, Bookland, 1958.

KALA, SATISH CHANDRA : *After Buddha Gandhiji*, Author, 1948.

KALARATHI, MUKULBHAI : *Anecdotes from Bapu's Life*, Ahmedabad, Navajivan, 1960.

———— (Comp.). *Ba and Bapu*, Ahmedabad, Navajivan, 1962.

KALELKAR, KAKA (Ed.) : *Bapu's Letters to Ashram Sisters*, Ahmedabad, Navajivan, 1952.

———— *Stray Glimpses of Bapu*, Ahmedabad, Navajivan, 1950.

KANETKAR, M. J. : *Tilak & Gandhi : A Comparative Character Sketch*, Nagpur, Author, 1935.

KARAKA, D. F. : *I Have Shed My Tears*, London, D. Appleton-Century Co., 1947.

———— *Out of Dust*, Bombay, Thacker & Co., Ltd., 1940.

KAUSHALA, RAM SWARUP (Comp.) : *Gandhian Gems : Teachings on 500 topics*, Ambala, Standard Publishing Co., 1954.

———— (Comp.) : *Precious Pearls : Teachings of Mahatma Gandhi*, New Delhi, Clifton & Co., 1948.

KHANNA, R. N. (Comp.) : *Gandhi : Saint or Sinner through Western Eyes*, Lahore, Allied Indian Publishers, 1941.

KHILAFAT COMMITTEE : *Letters from the Central Khilafat Committee of India and Mahatma Gandhi to His Excellency the Viceroy, Governor-General of India.*

KING, MARTIN L. : *Stride towards Freedom, the Montgomery Story*, London, Gollancz, 1959.

KOBE, W. : *Mohandas Karamchand Gandhi*, 1962.

KOHLI, M. S. : *Mahatma Gandhi's Confessions*, Lahore, Associated Publications, 1943.

KRIPALANI, J. B. : *Gandhi, The Statesman*, Delhi, Ranjit Printers and Publishers, 1951.

————— *Gandhian Thought*, New Delhi, Gandhi Smarak Nidhi, 1961.

————— *Gandhian Way*, Bombay, Vora & Co., 1945.

————— *Latest Fad : Basic Education*, Wardha, H. T. Sangh, 1948.

————— *Planning and Sarvodaya*, Wardha, Sarva Seva Sangh, 1957.

————— *Gandhi, Tagore & Nehru*, Bombay, Hind Kitabs, 1947.

KRISHNADAS : *Seven Months with Mahatma Gandhi*, Vol. I, Madras, S. Ganesan, 1928.

KRISHNAMURTI, Y. G. : *Gandhism for Millions*, Patna, Pustak Bhandar, 1949.

————— *Gandhism in the Atomic Age*, Madras, Shakti Karyalayam, 1946.

————— *Gandhism Will Survive*, Patna, Pustak Bhandar, 1949.

————— *Neo-Gandhism*, Bombay, Nalanda Publications, 1954.

————— *Reflections on the Gandhian Revolution*, Bombay, Vora & Co., 1945.

KUMARAPPA, BHARATAN : *Capitalism, Socialism or Villagism ?* Madras, Shakti Karyalayam, 1946.

————— *On Tour with Gandhiji*, Audh, Audh Publishing Trust, 1947.

KUMARAPPA, J. C. : *Economy of Permanence : A Quest for a social order*, Wardha, A.I.V.I.A., 1948.

————— *Gandhian Economic Thought*, Bombay, Vora & Co., 1951.

————— *Gandhian Way of Life*, Wardha, A.I.V.I.A., 1952.

————— *Non-violent Economy & World Peace*, Wardha, Sarva Seva Sangh, 1955.

————— *Overall Plan for Rural Development*, Wardha, A.I.V.I.A., 1948.

————— *Planning for the People by the People*, Bombay, Vora & Co., 1954.

————— *Why the Village Movement ?* Wardha, A.I.V.I.A., 1949.

KUMARAPPA, J. C. & V. L. MEHTA, : *Economics of Non-violence*, 2nd Edn., Bombay, Hamara Hindustan Publications, 1955.

————— *Planning for Sarvodaya*, Sarva Seva Sangh.

————— *Principles of Sarvodaya Plan*, New Delhi, Sarvodaya Planning Committee, 1950.

KUPER, LEO : *Passive Resistance in South Africa*, London, Jonathan Cape, 1956.

KURUP, T. C. K. : *Gandhi and Indian regeneration*, Madras, New Herald Office, 1922.

LEAGUE OF NATIONS : *The Educational Role of the Press*, Paris, League of Nations, 1934.

LEGER, J. A. : *Mahatma Gandhi*, National Literature Publishing Co., 1922.

LESLY, PHILIP, *Public Relations Handbook*, N.J., Prentice-Hall, 1962.

LESTER, MURIEL : *Entertaining Gandhi*, London, Ivor Nicholson & Watson, 1932.

Bibliography

————— *Gandhi : World Citizen*, Allahabad, Kitab Mahal, 1945.
————— *My Host the Hindu*, London, William and Norgate, 1931.
MAHADEV PRASAD : *Social Philosophy of Mahatma Gandhi*, Gorakhpur, Vishwa-vidyalaya Prakashan, 1958.
MALLIK, B. K. : *Gandhi : A Prophecy*, Bombay, Hind Kitabs, 1948.
MALLIK, GURDIAL : *Gandhi and Tagore*, Ahmedabad, Navajivan, 1961.
MANGALVEDKAR, V. : *Mahatma Gandhi*, Madras, Indian Literature Publishers, 1921.
MANI, R. S. : *Educational Ideas and Ideals of Gandhi and Tagore*, New Delhi, New Book Society, 1961.
MANSFIELD, F. J. : *The Complete Journalist*, London, Pitman, 1953.
MARTIN, KINGSLEY : *The Press the Public Wants*, London, Hogarth, 1947.
MASANI, R. P. : *The Five Gifts*, London, Collins, 1957.
MASANI, SHAKUNTALA : *Gandhi's Story*, New York, Oxford University Press, 1950.
————— *Story of Bapu*, London, Oxford University Press, 1952.
MASHRUWALA, K. G. : *Gandhi and Marx*, Ahmedabad, Navajivan, 1956.
————— *Practical Non-Violence : An Ideology of Non-Violence*, Ahmedabad, Navajivan, 1941.
————— *Vision of Future India*, Ahmedabad, Navajivan, 1953.
MATHUR, J. S. (Ed.) : *Economic Thought of Mahatma Gandhi*, Allahabad, Chaitanya Publishing House, 1962.
————— *Essays on Gandhian Economics*, Allahabad, Chaitanya Publishing House, 1959.
MATHUR, VISHWANATHA SAHAI : *Gandhiji, as an Educationist*, Delhi, Metropolitan Book Co., 1951.
MAURER, HERRYMEN : *Great Soul : The Growth of Gandhi*, New York, Country Life Press, 1948.
MAURICE, M. S. : *Ethics of Passive Resistance*, 1931.
MAZUMDAR, BUNAN BIHARI : *Gandhian Concept of State*, Calcutta, M. C. Sarkar & Sons, 1957.
MAZUMDAR, H. T. : *Gandhi : The Apostle*, Chicago, Universal Publishing House, 1923.
————— *Mahatma Gandhi—Peaceful Revolutionary*, New York, Scribner, 1952.
MENON, K. N. : *Passive Resistance in South Africa*, New Delhi, Roxy Press, 1952.
MIRABEHN : *Gleanings Gathered at Bapu's Feet*, Ahmedabad, Navajivan, 1949.
————— *The Thought of Mahatma Gandhi*, Ahmedabad, Navajivan, 1962.
MISRA, B. R. : *V for Vinoba*, Madras, Orient Longmans, 1956.
MORAES, F. : *The Story of India*, Bombay, N. V. Publishing House, 1944.
MUKERJEE, HIREN : *Gandhiji—A Study*, Calcutta, National Book Agency, 1958.
MUNSHI, K. M. : *Gandhi, the Master*, Delhi, Rajkamal Publications, 1948.
————— *I follow the Mahatma*, Bombay, Allied, 1940.
————— *Reconstruction of Society through Trusteeship*, Bombay, Bharatiya Vidya Bhavan, 1960.
MURRAY, GERTRUDE : *Child Life of Gandhiji*, Madras, Orient Longmans, 1949.

MURTHY, N. K. : *Mahatma Gandhi and Other Martyrs of India*, Mussoorie Journal Press, 1948.

NAG, KALIDAS : *Tolstoy and Gandhi*, Patna, Pustak Bhandar, 1950.

NAIR, C. SANKARAN : *Gandhi and Anarchy*, Madras, Tagore & Co., 1923.

NAMBOODIRIPAD, E. M. S. : *The Mahatma and the Ism*, New Delhi, People's Publishing House, 1958.

NANDA, B. R. : *Mahatma Gandhi : A Biography*, London, Allen & Unwin, 1958.

NARASIMHACHAR, K. T. (Ed.) : *Day Book of Thoughts from Mahatma Gandhi*, London, Macmillan, 1951.

NAVAJIVAN PUBLISHING HOUSE : *Bapu's Letters to Mira* (1924–48), Ahmedabad, Navajivan, 1949.

————— *Gandhiji's Correspondence with the Government*, 1944–47, Ahmedabad, Navajivan, 1959.

NEHRU, JAWAHARLAL : *Autobiography*, London, Bodley Head, 1949.

————— *Discovery of India*, London, Meridian Books Ltd., 1951.

————— *Glimpses of World History*, London, Lindsey Drummond Ltd., 1949.

————— *Mahatma Gandhi*, Calcutta, Signet Press, 1949.

————— *Nehru on Gandhi*, New York, John Day, 1948.

NEHRU, KRISHNA : *Gandhi*, New York, Didier Publishers, 1950.

PAGE, KIRBY : *Is Mahatma Gandhi the Greatest Man of the Age?* New York, 1922.

PAL, BEPIN CHANDER : *Indian Nationalism : its Principles and Personalities*, Madras, S. R. Murthy & Co., 1918.

————— *Non-Cooperation*, 4 *Lectures*, Calcutta, Indian Book Club, 1920.

PATEL, M. S. : *Educational Philosophy of Mahatma Gandhi*, Ahmedabad, Navajivan, 1953.

PEARE, CATHERINE OWENS : *Mahatma Gandhi : A Bibliography for Young People*, New York, Henry Holt & Co., 1950.

PIDDINGTON, A. B. : *Bapu Gandhi*, London, Williams & Norgate, 1930.

POLAK, H. S. L. & Others : *Mahatma Gandhi*, London, Odhams Press, 1949.

POLAK, MILLIE GRAHAM : *Mr. Gandhi : The Man* (2nd Edn.), Bombay, Vora & Co., 1950.

POWER, PAUL F. : *Gandhian World Affairs*, London, Allen & Unwin, 1961.

PRABHU, R. K. (Ed.) : *Bapu and Children*, Ahmedabad, Navajivan, 1962.

————— (Comp.) *Mohanmala*, Bombay, Hind Kitabs, 1949.

————— *This was Bapu*, Ahmedabad, Navajivan, 1954.

————— (Ed.) : *Truth Called Them Differently* (*Tagore-Gandhi controversy*), Ahmedabad, Navajivan, 1961.

————— (Comp.) : *Truth is God*, Ahmedabad, Navajivan, 1955.

PRABHU, R. K. & U. R. RAO, (Comp.) : *Mind of Mahatma Gandhi*, London, Oxford University, 1946.

PRITAM SINGH : *Gandhi's Constructive Programme*, Lahore, Paramount Publications, 1944.

PYARELAL : *A Nation Builder at Work*, Ahmedabad, Navajivan, 1952.

————— *A Pilgrimage for Peace—Gandhi and Frontier Gandhi among N.W.F. Pathans*, Ahmedabad, Navajivan, 1950.

G 13

———————— *Epic Fast*, Ahmedabad, Navajivan, 1932.

———————— *Gandhian Techniques in the Modern World*, Ahmedabad, Navajivan, 1953.

———————— *Mahatma Gandhi—The Last Phase*, Vols. I & II, Ahmedabad, Navajivan Publishing House, 1956–58.

———————— *Mahatma Gandhi—The Early Phase*, Vol. I, Ahmedabad, Navajivan Publishing House, 1965.

———————— *Santiniketan Pilgrimage*, Ahmedabad, Navajivan, 1958.

———————— *Thoreau, Tolstoy and Gandhiji*, Calcutta, Bensons, 1958.

———————— *Towards New Horizons*, Ahmedabad, Navajivan, 1959, (Reprint from *Mahatma Gandhi—The Last Phase*).

RADHAKRISHNAN, S. : *Mahatma Gandhi : Essays & Reflections*, Bombay, Jaico Publishing House, 1956.

———————— (Ed.) *Mahatma Gandhi : Essays & Reflections on His Life and Works*, London, Allen & Unwin, 1949.

RAJENDRA PRASAD : *At the feet of Mahatma Gandhi*, Bombay, Hind Kitabs, 1955.

———————— *Constructive Programme : Some Suggestions*, Ahmedabad, Navajivan, 1944.

———————— *Legacy of Gandhiji*, Agra, Shivalal Agarwala, 1962.

———————— *Mahatma Gandhi & Bihar*, Bombay, Hind Kitabs, 1949.

———————— *Satyagraha in Champaran*, Ahmedabad, Navajivan, 1949.

RAJKRISHNA : *Human Values & Technological Changes*, Kashi, Sarva Seva Sangh, 1957.

RAJU, J. B. : *Critical Study of Non-Cooperation in India*, Nagpur, Author, 1920.

RAM PRAKASH (Ed.) : *Gandhi's Birth Control*, Lahore, Diwan Publications, 1935.

RAMACHANDRAN, G. : *Sheaf of Gandhi Anecdotes*, Bombay, Hind Kitabs, 1945.

———————— *Whither Constructive Work ?* Wardha, Sarva Seva Sangh, 1957.

———————— *The Man Gandhi*, Madras, Gandhi Era Publications, 1947.

RAMAN MURTHI, V. V. : *Non-Violence in Politics : A Study of Gandhian Technique & Thinking*, Delhi, Frank Bros. & Co., 1958.

RAY, BINOY GOPAL : *Gandhian Ethics*, Ahmedabad, Navajivan, 1950.

RAY, N. R. : *Freedom of the Press in India*, Calcutta, General Pub., 1950.

RAY CHAUDHURY, P. C. : *Gandhiji's First Struggle in India*, Ahmedabad, Navajivan, 1955.

REYNOLDS, REGINALD, A. : *India, Gandhi & World Peace*, London, Friends of India, 1930.

———————— *Quest for Gandhi*, New York, Doubleday, 1952.

———————— *The True Book About Mahatma Gandhi*, London, Muller, 1959.

———————— *To Live in Mankind : A Quest for Gandhi*, London, Andre Deutsch, 1951.

RIVETT, KENNETH : *Economic Thought of Mahatma Gandhi*, New Delhi, Allied Publishers, 1959.

ROLLAND, ROMAIN : *Mahatma Gandhi : A Study of Indian Nationalism,* Madras, Ganesan, 1923.

———— *Mahatma Gandhi : The man who became one with the universal being,* New York, Century Co., 1924.

ROWE, J. G. : *Gandhi the Mahatma,* London, Epsworth Press, 1931.

ROY, KSHITIS : *Gandhi Memorial : Peace Number,* Shantiniketan, Visva Bharati, 1949.

RUTHERFORD, V. H. : *Mahatma Gandhi,* London, Labour Publishing Co., 1927.

SACHIDANANDA : *Sarvodaya in a Communist State,* Bombay, Popular Book Depot, 1961.

SANTHANAM, K. : *Satyagraha and the State,* Bombay, Asia Publishing House, 1960.

SARMA, D. A. : *Father of the Nation or the Life and Teachings of Mahatma Gandhi,* Madras, B. G. Paul & Co., 1956.

SARMA, V. SWAMINATH : *Essentials of Gandhism,* Madras, Shakti Karyalayam, 1943.

SAUNDERS, K. J. : " Mahatma Gandhi," Chapter in *The Heritage of Asia,* London, Students' Christian Movement Press, 1932.

SCHLIEPHACKA, B. P. : *Mahatma Gandhi.*

SEN, ELA : *Gandhi : A Biographical Study,* Calcutta, Susil Gupta, 1945.

SEN, N. B. : *Wit and Wisdom of Mahatma Gandhi,* New Delhi, New Book Society of India, 1960.

SEN, P. K. : *The Press, Publication and Copyright Laws of India,* Calcutta, Sarkar, 1958.

SENGUPTA, B. & R. CHOWDHURY, : *Mahatma Gandhi and India's Struggle for Swaraj,* Calcutta, Modern Book Agency, 1932.

SETH, HIRALAL : *Gandhi in Arms,* Lahore, Associated Publications, 1943.

SHAHANI, RANJEE : *Mr. Gandhi,* New York, Macmillan, 1961.

SHARGE, P. BRIJNATH : *Gandhi, His Life and Teachings* (2nd Edn.), Lucknow, Upper India Publishing House, 1958.

SHARMA, BISHAN SWARUP : *Gandhi as a Political Thinker,* Allahabad, Indian Press, 1956.

SHARMA, JAGDISH SARAN : *Gandhi : A Descriptive Bibliography,* Delhi, S. Chand & Co., 1955.

SHARP, GENE : *Gandhi Faces the Storm,* Ahmedabad, Navajivan, 1961.

———— *Gandhi Wields the Weapon of Moral Power,* Ahmedabad, Navajivan, 1960.

———— *The Meaning of Non-Violence,* London, Houseman's, 1957.

SHEEAN, VINCENT : *Lead Kindly Light,* London, Cassell & Co., Ltd., 1950.

———— *Mahatma Gandhi,* New York, Alfred A. Knopf, Inc., 1955.

SHRIDHARANI, K. : *Mahatma Gandhi and the World,* New York, Duell, Sloan & Pearce, 1946.

———— *My India, My America,* New York, Duell Sloan & Pearce, 1941.

———— *The Journalist in India,* Calcutta, Patrika Syndicate, 1956.

———— *War Without Violence : Sociology of Gandhi's Satyagraha,* New York, Harcourt, Bruce & Co., 1939.

Bibliography

SHRIMALI, K. : *Wardha Scheme*, Udaipur, Vidya Bhavan Society, 1949.

SHRIMAN NARAIN : *One Week with Vinoba*, New Delhi, A.I.C.C., 1956.

SHUKLA, CHANDRASHANKER (Ed.) : *Conversations of Gandhiji*, Bombay, Vora & Co., 1949.

———— (Ed.) *Gandhiji, as We Know Him*, Bombay, Vora, 1945.

———— (Ed.) *Incidents of Gandhiji's Life*, Bombay, Vora, 1949.

———— (Ed.) *Reminiscences of Gandhiji*, Bombay, Vora & Co., 1951.

SITARAMAYYA, PATTABHI : *On Khaddar*, Madras, Ganeshan & Co., 1931.

———— *History of Indian National Congress*, 2 Volumes, Bombay, Padma Publications, 1946.

SKINNER, J. ALLEN : *Towards a Non-Violent Society*, London, Peace News, 1959.

SNOW, E. : *Glory and Bondage*, London, Victor Gallancz, 1945.

SOMAN, R. J. : *Peaceful Industrial Relations—Their Science & Technique*.

STERN, ELIZABETH-GERTRUDE (LEVIN) : *Women in Gandhi's Life*, New York, Dodd, Mead, 1953.

SUMNER, G. L. : *How I Learned the Secrets of Success in Advertising*, Surrey, The World's Work, 1953.

SUNDAY TIMES OFFICE : *Mahatma Gandhi : The Superman of Age*, Madras.

SURESH RAMBHAI : *Progress of a Pilgrimage*, Banaras, Sarva Seva Sangh, 1956.

———— *Vinoba & His Mission*, Banaras, Sarva Seva Sangh, 1954.

SYKES, MARJORIE : *Earth is the Lord's : Shri Vinoba & the Land*, Oxford, Church Army Press.

TALEYARKHAN, H. J. H. : *I have it from Gandhiji*, Bombay, Jam-e-Jamshed, 1944.

TENDULKAR, D. G. : *Gandhi in Champaran*, Delhi, Publications Division, 1957.

———— *Mahatma—Life of Mohandas Karamchand Gandhi*, Vols. 1–8, Bombay, V. K. Jhaveri and D. G. Tendulkar, 64, Walkeshwar Road, 1951–53.

THAPAR, (MRS.) RAJESH KAUR : *Weaponless Warrior*, Lahore, Civil & Military Gazette, 1946.

TIKEKAR, S. R. : *Gandhigrams*, Bombay, Hind Kitabs, 1947.

TENNYSON, HALLAM : *Saint on the March*, London, Victor Gollancz, 1955.

UNESCO : *All Men Are Brothers : Life and thoughts of Mahatma Gandhi as told in his own words*, Orient Longmans, 1959.

UNESCO : *The Training of Journalists*, Paris, Author, 1958.

UNNITHAN, T. K. N. : *Gandhi and Free India : (A socio-economic study)*, The Netherlands, Wolters-Gronningen, 1956.

VAIRANPILLAI, MRS. AND M. S. VAIRANPILLAI, : *Mahatma Gandhi for the Millions : a Basic Biography*, Tallakulam, Madura Book House, 1949.

VARMA, V. P. : *The Political Philosophy of Mahatma Gandhi and Sarvodaya*, Agra, L. N. Agarwal, 1959.

VASTO, LANZA DEL : *Gandhi to Vinoba : The New Pilgrimage*, London, Rider & Co., 1956.

VEILLIER, JULLIETTE : *Mahatma Gandhi*, Madras, Ganesh & Co., 1928.

VINOBA BHAVE : *Bhoodan Yajna : Land Gift Mission*, Ahmedabad, Navajivan, 1953.

———— *Talks on Gita :* Kashi, Sarva Seva Sangh, 1958.

VISHWANATH IYER : *The Indian Press*, Bombay, Padma Publishers, 1945.

WADIA, A. S. N. : *Mahatma Gandhi : A Dialogue in Understanding*, Bombay, New Book Co., 1939.

WALKER, ROY : *Sword of Gold : A Life of Mahatma Gandhi*, London, Indian Independence Union, 1945.

———————— *Wisdom of Gandhi in His Own Words*, London, Andrew Daktrs, 1943.

WATSON, BLANCHE (Comp.) : *Gandhi & Non-Violent Resistance*, Madras, Ganesh & Co., 1923.

WATSON, FRANCIS & MAURICE BROWN, : *Talking of Gandhiji*, Madras, Orient Longmans, 1957.

WEBER, T. A. : *Gandhi*, London, Pallas Publishing Co., 1939.

WELLOCK, WILFRED : *Gandhi as a Social Revolutionary*, Varanasi, Akhil Bharat Sarva Seva Sangh Prakashan, 1953.

———————— *India's Social Revolution led by Mahatma Gandhi and Now Vinoba Bhave*, Tanjore, Sarvodaya Prachuralayam, 1959.

WESTERN THINKERS : *Reflections on Gandhiji's* "Hind Swaraj," Bombay, Theosophy Coy., 1948.

WINSLOW, JOHN COPLEY & VERRIER ELWIN : *Gandhi : The dawn of Indian Freedom*, London, Fleming H. Revell Co., 1931.

WOLSELEY, R. E.: *Journalism in Modern India*, Bombay, Asia Publishing House, 1953.

YAJNIK, INDULAL, K. : *Gandhi as I Know Him*, Delhi, Danish Mahal, 1943.

ZACHER, R. V. : *Advertising Techniques and Management*, Illinois, Irwin, 1961.

Institutions founded or guided by Gandhiji

Akhil Bharat Goseva Sangh (1928), Sabarmati.

All India Harijan Sevak Sangh (1933), Rajpath, New Delhi.

All India Nature Cure Foundation (1946), Poona.

All India Spinners' Association (1925), Sevagram. Khadi Vidyalaya, Sevagram, was also started under its auspices.

All India Village Industries Association (1934), Maganwadi, Wardha. Under its auspices, Gramsevak Vidyalaya and Magan Sanghrahalaya, Wardha, also started functioning in 1938.

Dakshina Bharat Hindi (Hindustani) Prachar Sabha (1918), Thyagaraya Nagar, Madras-17.

Gandhi Seva Sangh (1923), Wardha.

Gujarat Vidyapeeth (1920), Ahmedabad.

Harijan Ashram (1918), Godhra.

Hindustani Prachar Sabha (1942), Wardha.

Hindustani Talimi Sangh (1938), Sevagram, Wardha.

Kasturba Gandhi National Memorial Trust (1944), Bajajwadi, Wardha.

Majur Mahajan (the Labour Union) (1920), Mirzapur Road, Ahmedabad.

Navajivan Press (1919), Ahmedabad.

Nisargopachar Ashram (1946), Uruli-Kanchan, Poona.

Rashtriya Gujarati Shala (National Gujarati School) Satyagraha Ashram (1915), Sabarmati.

Satyagraha Ashram (1915), Sabarmati.

Satyagraha Ashram (1920), Wardha. Under its auspices, the following institutions at Wardha and near-abouts also started functioning at some time or the other : (a) Kanya Ashram, (b) Mahila Ashram, (c) Gram-Seva Mandal, (d) Goseva Charmalaya, (e) Maharogi (Leper) Ashram, (f) Goseva Sangh, Gopuri, (g) Gram Seva Mandal, (h) Swaraj Bhandar, (i) Paramadhan, Panvar.

Sevagram Ashram (1936), Segaon.

Swaraj Ashram (1922), Bardoli, Surat.

INDEX

Index